MW01014246

Ways of the Heart

Robert D. Romanyshyn

Ways of the Heart

Essays Toward an
Imaginal Psychology

Preface by Robert Sardello

Trivium Publications, Pittsburgh, PA

Copyright © 2002 by Trivium Publications, Pittsburgh, PA
All rights reserved.
Printed in the United States of America

Requests for permission to reproduce material from this work
should be sent to Permissions, Trivium Publications, P. O. Box 7914
Pittsburgh, PA 15216

Cover photo by Victor Barbetti

ISBN 0-971367I-I-6

0 0 I 2 3 4 5 6 7 8 9 0 0

Contents

To Veronica, who knows the ways of the heart.

Acknowledgments

Many friends and colleagues have over the years contributed to this work. Certainly, I need to thank those with whom I spent many fruitful years at the University of Dallas, where with Robert Sardello, James Hillman, Louise and Don Cowan, Gail Thomas, and Ray Di Lorenzo so much of this work began. In addition, I want to express my thanks to my colleagues and friends at The Institute for Humanities and Culture. Thanks is also due to my friends and colleagues at Pacifica Graduate Institute. I am particularly grateful to Charles Asher who, as Provost, has the uncanny gift of seeing the virtue of each member of the faculty and providing a sheltering place for its talent to blossom. In this respect, he is like a wise old abbot in a secular monastery. Steve Aiszenstadt, the founder and President of Pacifica, is also to be thanked. Through his vision and effort he has made a unique place in the world for this work to be done.

Special thanks is also offered to J.H. van den Berg. Not only has his work been foundational to all my studies, his friendship has been indispensable. In the same vein, I want to offer my gratitude to Kathleen Raine. Her generosity and support have kept me true to my vocation to the imaginal, and have encouraged me in my love of the poets.

I would also like to thank my publishers, Victor Barbetti and Brent Dean Robbins for giving me the opportunity to bring this collection together. And a special thank you to my editor, Claire Cowan-Barbetti, for her hard work and diligence. Through their combined efforts, they have provided a place for the incarnation of this work.

Finally, I want to express my deep and loving gratitude to my wife, Veronica Goodchild. She is a fierce lioness, and in her loyalty to the imaginal realm she has witnessed with love and without judgment my many mistakes. Beyond that she has also taught me many things about the landscapes of soul. I cherish in memory those many early morning coffee discussions in our garden, and the beach walks when she listened to my ramblings with heart and soul. Without her wisdom, patience, integrity and guidance, I am sure I would have lost my way. Without her, this work would surely not have been attempted.

R. D. R.
November, 2001

Preface

There is much to praise in this book, this truly extraordinary writing. Psychology is able to breathe again because Robert Romanyshyn restores the cosmological soul dimension. That dimension can be situated within a tradition of soul best exemplified by Dante's *Divine Comedy*. There, in that greatest of all comedies, we find ourselves interpreted by the cosmos. Rather than trying to interpret our lives and actions and motives, we best understand human reality when it is placed within the harmonies and tensions and dramas of the cosmos; we find ourselves by discovering our place within these large dimensions. We find out who we are, learn what it is to be human, enter into the soul's path of desire, take our proper place within the dramatic action of the whole of the universe, from the depths of hell where egotism reigns supreme, to the mid-realm of purgatory where the imagination gains ascendancy, to the heights of heaven-bound consciousness, where soul lives in inspiration. While I want to be careful not to embarrass my friend by comparing him to Dante, the inspiration of these essays lies in that direction. For example, in Dante's *La Vita Nuova* there are numerous images of *tears of the heart*. The deep and abiding loss of Beatrice motivated Dante to relinquish a long excursion into philosophy and politics to return to the poetry of desire. Robert Romanyshyn belongs to this long, honored, and mostly forgotten tradition of the weeping soul. He gives us a psychology of desire, and wisely remembers the full range of desire, from longing to loss, from joy to sorrow and mourning, locating these experiences always in connection with a desiring cosmos.

Each of the essays of this book explores the intricacies of the currents of the heart, developing the vocabulary for soul's own voice rather than the speaking for soul that characterizes most psychology. Psychology always fares better and approaches its true destiny of perpetual subtlety and elusiveness, when its adherents do not approach soul head on, but rather work in the interstices of several disciplines. The life of the soul in this book shines through the intersecting labyrinths of phenomenology, depth psychology, and poetry. Perhaps the most important of disciplines for this work is phenomenology because it assures that our author never falls into theorizing about the soul but is committed to letting the inner qualities of the things of the world speak for themselves. The fundamental tenant of this book is that we are here to learn to listen.

The discipline of adhering to being present to what is present also guarantees that the speaking of the heart never falls into sentimentality or poetic flourish. Like Dante, Romanyshyn is constantly concerned that the speaking of the heart never obscures the search for the truth of soul. Such adherence to the truth of soul becomes particularly important in the development of a depth psychology emphasizing embodiment. The most creative aspects of this book center in locating soul at the meeting point of body and world. Situating psychology here requires a capacity to shape language from the substance of desire, an ability to freely feel desire without it turning into imaginative fantasy. It requires a perfect balance between the will of making, working in conjunction with a completely receptive waiting.

Romanyshyn reluctantly describes himself as a psychologist. The title of this book utilizes the term "imaginal psychology." He likes the term 'metaphorician' better, and the term 'failed poet' perhaps the best. These terms indicate that this writing is stretching toward a new discipline for which there is still no name. While, on the one hand, it may be unsettling for a reader who comes to this book expecting direct answers to questions concerning soul life to find that immediate answers blunt the capacity to receive what one is looking for— once the intellectual dimension of the searching settles down, great internal joy awakens as we are privileged to participate as readers with someone who has developed the capacity to be a witness to soul life. We experience a quieting of the kind of speculative knowing through distance that our author characterizes as the way of knowing that belongs to the critic.

These essays take a form conforming to the metaphoric nature of soul life. One essay nests within another and that one within yet another, each resonating the rest. Because we are taken into the domain of desire, longing, reverie, and dream, what is being conveyed cannot be understood in the way we understand the language of abstract thought and information. You will find repetition from one essay to another, a spiral-like movement from one essay to the next. Soul loves repetition. It perceives little, subtle differences from one way of saying something to the next. Where the mind can only construe that the same thing has been said again, the soul enjoys the little difference in nuance, the different way that something is said. For example, when you have a dream that moves you, you feel a desire to tell and re-tell it. Part of the delight of soul consists in the re-telling. Notice in the essays how there are subtle but distinctive differences when a description shows up more than once, a story told again, a point reiterated. This going over things more than once is essential to the language of desire. Repetition invites daydreaming, a way for the night-dreaming soul to enter into the day world; if you find yourself drawn more toward daydreaming as a result of this book, it is indeed a successful writing.

Now that a plethora of books concerned with soul are available, it has become necessary for readers to become much more discriminating concerning what belongs and does not belong to the terrain of the soul. There are but a handful, maybe less, of writers who have developed the capacity to witness soul from within and do so consciously. Robert Romanyshyn ranks high on that short list. Mostly, books about soul are actually speculative thoughts that stand outside what is being spoken about. Very few writers are able to navigate that in-between language that speaks of the ever-present domain between spirit and matter. Most works that claim to be about soul approach the subtle without subtlety — head-on, directly, ascending to the heights with a project to get better, have more hope, more faith, do better, be better. The imaginal realms project no such goals. Their aims, as shown so well herein, have more to do with maintaining and deepening the erotic field and pushing us toward individuating within the arduous process of desire.

While Freud rightly called the dream the royal road to the soul, Robert Romanyshyn proposes reverie as the royal road to the soul of the world. Of that small handful of soul psychologists now writing, there exists a common intention to get soul out of the consulting room and into the world. Many times, even within this group, the actual doing of a world-oriented soul psychology is more of a hope, a possibility, rather than an actuality. It takes a radical departure from the soul psychology of Jung and the post-Jungians to engage the soul of the world because the methodologies were not yet worked out in that tradition. Reverie is one of the key methods that can be truly fruitful in this endeavor. It is a way of being with the actual presence of the things of the world while letting soul shine through them. The standard methods of depth psychology— dream interpretation, myth, amplification, interpretation, tend to leave what is present and seek for the soul 'behind' what is present rather than within it. Reverie is a dual mode of consciousness— it is a way of being phenomenologically present to whatever reality is of interest — art, buildings, mountains, the glance between people, the endless variety of the world — while also being present to the autonomous image-character that speaks through that reality. No interpretation is involved; only the capacity to let the language of soul speak through what is at hand by developing the capacity of the witness, that ability to be present without seeking after answers, an ability also characteristic of the poet.

Reverie is completely different from fantasy. The ego is always the center of fantasy images, seeking to get some personal pleasure out of what it concocts or seeking to transcend the arduous reality of the present. Reverie dwells in the interior of the moment; it lies on the border of the subjective and the objective, letting each complete the other in order to have a glimpse of the whole and of the context of the whole as nothing short of the universe itself. Romanyshyn demonstrates over and over how in reverie we are in communion with the depth of our own existence, the existence of the world, and in communion with the dead, the angels, the spirits, and with the gods — all at once. Such multiple experiences that are nonetheless unified are possible because he has discovered that the imaginal grounds the whole of our being and that of the world and shows us how to practice the kind of inner hospitality needed to receive such a large gift.

The capacities to be developed for becoming adept at reverie are given in detail. We have to find our way into stillness and silence as objective qualities. We are asked to find and value the melancholic side of ourselves, a necessary quality needed for the humility characterizing this way of the soul. We are taught how to seek the truth at a slant, and how to encounter the radical otherness of angels, angels who are far more than messengers, friends, or companions, angels who bring us into the fearful void and darkness where we can be quiet enough to hear the quiet speaking of the soul. We are shown how some streams of poetry — Rilke, certainly, but also T. S. Eliot, E.E. Cummings, Keats, Yates, Kathleen Raine, to name but a few, have known and quietly promoted these ways of the soul in their poetry and thus are our best instructors.

The methods we use in investigating soul determine what we are able to find as belonging to the essence of soul. Because the method of reverie, brought by Gaston Bachelard into a legitimate mode of philosophic investigation, had not been applied to psychology, an essential element of soul life remained unspoken. Grief, mourning, loss, longing, are ways of speaking of this element. We, according to standard psychology, are supposed to get through our sorrows and return to productive life as soon as possible. For Romanyshyn these are the most valuable experiences of life because they can take us into deep memory, reverie, and hope. Do not think this is a psychology for depressives! It is a psychology that recognizes hope as the capacity to live in possibility without rushing to seek its fulfillment.

The soul, when felt through the kinds of experiences developed in this book, is like the slight undulation of air left in the wake of the movement of the wings of a bird. It takes an attunement to what can almost but not quite be seen to enter soul's domain consciously. Romanyshyn quotes Jung as saying that such a realm is like "a subtle perceptible smoke." Such stuff is imaginal psychology made of. And because it is so light — I do not mean the opposite of heavy, but rather so innerly brilliant — the tendency is to claim this domain as the non-utterable. Maybe soul is to be experienced in silence, in ever-deepening silence.

Ah, but there is only one kind of courage that dares step from this silence and speak it into the world, and that is the therapeutic courage shown everywhere in this book. It is not a book about psychotherapy but a therapeutic way of life that allows silence to dwell in the word and thus a soul-speech. It turns out that there is not a specialized language of psychology, and when it pretends to have one the soul thankfully escapes it. The soul rests in the *how* of language, not in the *what*. This writing demonstrates that *how*. It is not essentially a book of information. It is one of those rarest of writings that lives as a gestural field that invites the reader to come in and rest, and in that rest find the solace of soul, fleeting though it may be.

Unfortunately, soul is a noun while its reality has no such substantiality. This psychological fact — that soul is not an entity of any kind or sort — accounts for why Romanyshyn concentrates so much on poetry as a better language model for psychology than science. Not only does poetry have the power to speak the beauty of soul, it is nearly the only way available to speak the act of making rather than the already made. Soul can be better understood as a making in its inception, in which soul is the maker, the making, and the made all at once and inseparable. Imagine the kind of discipline, then, needed to speak such an ephemeral reality. If you read this work slowly, savoring each word, not trying to read it as you would read other books, something of the wonder of this creative psychologist will begin to dawn on you. It is discipline backed by years of study, surely. And then, it is a discipline able to completely let go of those years and instead of flaunting knowledge, holds it all back. That is the discipline — one of having a lot — given through study, experience, sorrow, wanting — and then holding it all back and waiting and listening and speaking out of that inner silence.

Is imaginal psychology transferable? Can it be studied, learned, placed into text books and applied in the world? Yes, of course. Robert Romanyshyn has been doing exactly this, in varied forms, for the past thirty years. To be a student of such psychology requires, however, that one be more like an apprentice than a consumer of information. In order to get the meaning of this book, to really get it, the reader also has to approach it realizing that all the knowledge and prior learning one brings to this book also has to be held back and one has to apprentice oneself, not to the author, but to the reality that finds voice through this author. The reader is asked to feel the words, sentences, paragraphs, chapters, in a bodily way, as if you are engaged in a beautifully choreographed dance. Let yourself dance with this book and then you will get it.

There are two essays in this collection that at first reading may not seem to fit into the themes I have thus far mentioned. These essays, one on media and one on virtual reality, are, I think, the gems of this book. We get a glimpse of another side of Romanyshyn. He is able to see through the technological world and what it does to soul life without reacting against it. For someone so engaged with the imaginal realms, with poetry and reverie, it might seem odd that technology is seen as helping re-discover soul in the modern world. Television is presented as image-consciousness that, through bypassing literacy, invokes the sensuous, embodied, non-rational, dream-making capacities characteristic of soul. That is, television is presented as an ally to the kind of soul psychology presented here.

Virtual reality is seen as disembodying us. This technology, Romanyshyn argues, certainly takes us into an imaginal world, but a disincarnate one. At the same time, this disincarnate imaginal world is analogous to a dream world in which one is not quite sure who is in control — the dreamer or the dream. Thus, in spite of its disembodying potential, virtual reality is seen as holding the power to teach us how to be awake while dreaming.

These two essays can be seen as depicting a frame within which imaginal psychology takes place. Imaginal psychology as presented by Romanyshyn is not a nostalgic attempt to go back to what soul used to be. It is a postmodern psychology, made possible by the technological world. If television and virtual reality teach us to inhabit dream consciousness in the waking world, we do so unconsciously. That is, we now live in a dream world but do not know that is so. It is, however, only in such a world that it now becomes possible to develop the discipline of waking dream consciousness that knows imaginally what it is doing. Imaginal psychology was not possible at the time of Freud or Jung because television and virtual reality had not yet taken hold in the culture. This realization is, I think, an amazing insight. It prevents a lurking opposition between soul and technology. In addition, Romanyshyn shows us that psychology is always historical and contextual. When true to soul, this strangest of all disciplines does not make any claims to permanent knowledge. We cannot say "this is what soul is all about, forever." We can only say that this is the kind of psychology needed to reflect how soul can live and thrive in this present world.

Robert Sardello
Director, The School of Spiritual Psychology
Author of *Freeing the Soul from Fear,*
Love and the World, and
Facing the World with Soul.

Introduction

The dozen essays in this collection have all been written in the last decade. They present a ten year effort, which reflects a twenty year history, of working in the space between the two traditions of phenomenology, especially the work of J.H.van den Berg, and depth psycholgy, especially the work of Carl Jung.

To practice phenomenology is always to be surprised by the epiphanies of experience, by the extraordinary that bewitches the ordinary, by the invisible world that haunts the visible. A key consequence of this surprise is the revelation of the metaphoric character of psychological life, and indeed this theme of metaphor has been central in the dialogue between phenomenology and Jung's psychology.

On the side of phenomenology, metaphor describes an autonomous domain of reality, which is neither about things nor thoughts. It is the domain of the image, especially as it reveals itself in a phenomenology of the mirror. My first book, *Psychological Life: From Science to Metaphor*, explored in detail this phenomenology of the mirror image and showed how the reality of the image, which is neither an empirical fact nor a mental idea, is metaphoric in its structure, texture, and function. Recently this book has been re-published under the title *Mirror and Metaphor: Images and Stories of Psychological Life*. The essays in this collection have their seed in this book in its original and re-published form.

On the side of Jung's psychology, the metaphoric character of psychological life links up with his studies of alchemy. As metaphor articulates a reality that is neither about facts nor ideas, neither about things nor thoughts, the images of alchemy articulate a domain of soul that is neither about matter nor mind. The images of alchemy, like the salamander roasting in the flames or the green lion devouring the sun, are epiphanies for a consciouness attuned to the soul of nature. These images, like the mirror image, are neither facts to be verified or falsified, nor ideas projected onto the world. They have, as Jung says, a neither/

nor character, which is the structure of metaphor.

The fruit of this dialogue between a phenomenology of the mirror experience and Jung's psychology, especially his studies of alchemy, is imaginal psycholgy. The field of this psycholgy is the autonomous domain of soul, which is neither body nor mind, even though it partakes of them and reveals and conceals itself symbolically and symptomatically through them. Imaginal psychology is about an-other world, the world of soul, which is neither the public, exterior material world to which we are accustomed, nor the private, interior world of ideas, which is equally familiar. The imaginal world is a subtle world, known to us in our dreams and fantasies, in our symptoms and our symbols, in our reveries and emotions. Caught, however, between the dualisms of matter and mind, public and private, interior and exterior, things and thoughts, facts and ideas, we learn to dismiss these subtle realities as unreal, or we reduce them to the material or the mental realms. While these subtle realms are different from the realms of matter and mind, imaginal psychology insists they are real. Indeed, imaginal psychology insists that the imaginal world is the invisble that subtends the visible world. The imaginal world is the real world, and the real is fundamentally imaginal.

For imaginal psychology every event is enscorceled by a dream, every fact nourished by a fanatsy. To be in the world in this way requires, however, a radical shift in attitude. The ontological surprise of the imaginal, the collapse of the dreams of soul into this or that event, into this or that moment of experience, induces an epistemological crisis. Neither an empirical consciousness nor a rational one is appropriate. Imaginal psychology requires an aesthetic-ethical way of knowing the world and being in it.

Each essay in this volume articulates some aspect of the imaginal world and our experience of it. Some of the essays are concerned with defending the imaginal world as the autonomous domain of the soul, as a reality in its own right and on its own terms, equal to but different from the realms of matter and mind. These essays, like "On Being a Fool: In Defense of the Pathetic Heart," "Alchemy and the Subtle Body of Metaphor," "On Angels and Other Anomalies of the Imaginal Life," and "The Backward Glance: Rilke and the Ways of the Heart," deal with the issue of what the imaginal world is, which in more formal terms would be called ontology. They are concerned with the nature of the imaginal world, with the geography of its landscapes, particularly its meatphoric as compared with its factual or logical structure. Although each essay in this collection in one way or another contains this issue, these four more or less focus on it as a theme.

While the above essays deal with the geography of the imaginal world, another group deals more or less with the question of how we get to it. In other words, these essays are concerned with how we know the imaginal world, which in more formal terms would be called epistemology. For the empirical or logical mind, the imaginal world is an ontological shock, which forces an epistemological revolution, and these essays explore some of the features of that revolution. They deal with issues like reverie, hospitality, the difference between being a witness and a critic, the metaphoric mind, the heart and its ways of knowing, the role of grief in awakening the heart to this world, and the relation between an imaginal psychology and a poetic sensibility. "On Not Being Useful: The Pleasures of Reverie," "The Orphan and the Angel: In Defense of Melancholy," "For the Moment That's Enough: Reveries on Therapy and the Poetry of Language," and "Psychology Is Useless; Or It Should Be," contain many of these themes. The rest of them, however, appear in some of the essays cited above, like "On Angels and Other Anomalies of the Imaginal Life," "On Being a Fool: In Defense of the Pathetic Heart," and The Backward Glance: Rilke and the Ways of the Heart."

The intertwining between the essays that deal with the nature of the imaginal world and how we know it indicates a reflexivity between what is and what we know, between the being of nature and the knowing of it by mind, between ontology and epistemology. But within this reflexivity, an imaginal psychology gives a priority to the ontological realm. For imaginal psychology, ontology preceeds epistemology, the being of nature preceeds the mind's knowing of it

For imaginal psycholgy the being of nature is the "anima mundi," the soul of the world. Imaginal psycholgy emphasizes that mind is part of this nature, that it flows out of it. In this respect, mind is always suited to what it explores. But, while mind informs us of nature, it does so only insofar as it is formed by its roots in the soul of the world. When it forgets these origins, the rational mind loses heart, and when it loses heart it loses its acces to its ways of knowing the world via passion, love, feeling, and emotion. Jung has often said that we can not know the being of nature, but we can experience it, especially through the feeling function. When the rational mind walls itself off from the experience of nature with the fantasy of objectivity, which declares our passions and feelings to be a contamination of knowledge, it loses its connection with the soul of the world. Soul falls into the abyss between an inanimate nature, which mind identifies with its empirical knowledge, and consciousness, which it identifies with thinking purified of the feeling heart

A metaphoric mind bridges the abyss between nature and consciousness, and in this regard it re-animates the world. In addition to restoring the reflexivity between what is and our knowing of it, the metaphoric mind, which is rooted in an intuition of things that preceeds our thinking about them, recovers the priority of ontology over epistemology, of soul and its cloudy intuitions over mind and its clear intentions. The metaphoric mind is, therefore, particularly informative of and formed by the imaginal realm, in the same fashion that the empirical mind is suited to the realm of matter and its exploration, and the rational mind to the world of ideas.

A consequence of this reflexivity between what is and how we know it is that action is transformed. Action that is mindful of its embeddeness within a context, within a particular perspective or point of view, is essentailly responsive rather than initiative. Action, including language, is drawn out of us in response to what has addressed us, and in this respect it gives presence and voice to what is otherwise silent or forgotten. The symptom in the event, the symbol in the idea, the fantasy in the fact, the dream in the institutional structure, are brought from darkness into visibility. In this regard, the one who acts, including the one who speaks, is a witness for the un-spoken, one who, in being responsive to being addressed, is response-able. Action, including langauge, in-formed by the imaginal perpspective is, therefore, essentially ethical.

A third group of essays focuses on this theme of action. They include "Yes,Indeed! Do Call the World the Vale of Soul Making," "Psychotherapy as Grief Work," "The Despotic Eye and its Shadow: Media Image in the Age of Literacy," and "The Dream Body in Cyberspace." As with the first two groupings, however, some of the issues regarding action also appear in the other essays cited above.

The grouping of these essays around these themes of the nature of the imaginal world, how we know it, and the kind of action that arises within this landscape, are the result of a backward glance that I have taken in assembling this collection. And, although this backward glance brings a form to these essays which is accurate, I would be remiss were I not to admit that I had no such form in mind when these essays were being written. These essays do not articulate a straight line from conception to goal. Rather they articulate a meandering path along which this form was present, like a seed waiting to sprout, or like an invisible crystal that collapses out of a supersaturated solution. Indeed, I would say that these essays and their form are as much the product of the soul and its wishes as they are of the mind and its intentions.

Because these essays have been working me over as I have worked on them, and because they do intertwine with each other, I have chosen to arrange them chronologically rather than in terms of the form described in this introduction.

The reader can use this form as a guide, but I do not wish to impose it as a rigid frame. Indeed, in the final analysis the essays can be read in any order, because each is a working and re-working of the material in varied contexts.

In conclusion, I would like to add that in addition to the traditions of phenomenology and depth psycholgy, these essays toward the imaginal have been steadily and increasingly influenced by the poets. I would also say that as I look back over this ten year effort, I realize that the term psychology might be too small to encompass the range of the imaginal realm, because psychology as it generally exists today is too small for the reality of soul. Be that as it is, however, I am a psychologist, and these essays are in service to psychology. My hope, then, is that they can in some small measure expand the boundaries of psychology to embrace the chthonic depths of the earth and the ceslestial radiance of the cosmos. Because soul is nature, perhaps, in the end, any psychology must become a cosmology.

R. D. R.

Ways of the Heart

1

The Despotic Eye and its Shadow: Media Image in the Age of Literacy

Introduction

> Postmodernism . . . assumes the task of reinvestigating the crisis and trauma at the very heart of modernity; the postmodern [is] a testament to the fact that the end of modernity is . . . a symptom as it were of its own unconscious infancy which needs to be retrieved and reworked if we are not to be condemned to an obsessional fixation upon, and compulsive repetition of, the sense of its ending. In this respect, the task of a postmodern imagination might be to envision the end of modernity as a possibility of rebeginning.[1]

This quotation strongly suggests that the task of postmodernism is to attempt a therapeutics of culture. Such is the intention of this essay. It is an experiment in cultural therapeutics which begins not with the past but with how the past is present in the present as symptom. To say symptom in this manner, however, requires caution. At the outset we must eschew the primarily modern and mostly negative idea of the symptom, an idea which would invite us to evaluate the symptom in order to "cure" it, that is, dismiss it. In place of that idea we need to embrace the more difficult notion that the symptom is a vocation, a call to listen and give voice to what would otherwise remain silenced.

The experiment in this essay is to demonstrate media image consciousness, illustrated here via TV consciousness, as the symptomatic ending of modernity. Such an experiment, however, initially needs some justification, because the media image industry in general, and television in particular, seems so much to be an expression of modernity, and even the epitome of its values. I confess that I have no argument with this position. Television is the intensification of many of the values of modernity; indeed it is the incarnation of these values in the extreme. But that is precisely the sense of television as symptom. As exaggeration and caricature of the values of modernity, it brings those values to our attention, inviting us not to call them into question but to wonder about them, perhaps in some instances for the first time. As symptom, then, television asks for a hearing, not a judgment.

The hypothesis of this experiment is that television is the cultural unconscious of the book. It is the other side, the shadow side, of a book consciousness whose origins coincide with modernity. Through a double anamnesis of these origins, one through the *Meditations* of Descartes and the other through the fifteenth-century invention of linear perspective vision, we return to those generative sites of modernity in order to rework, to remember, these sites as also sites of initial forgettings. And in this work what we recover is the way in which the ocularcentrism of modernity, the hegemony of vision, the installation of the reign of the despotic eye, is also a verbocentrism, the consciousness of the book, and an egocentrism, the consciousness of a separated, detached atom of individuality.

Through this double anamnesis, the sense of modernity is presented in this essay as ego-ocular-verbocentrism. It is this gestalt out of which many of the unquestioned values of modernity arise. Television as the shadow of the book makes visible the pathology of verbo-ocular-ego consciousness by challenging its values of linear rationality, contextual coherence, narrative continuity, focused concentration, infinite progress, individual privacy, productive efficiency, detached comprehensiveness, and neutral objectivity. The challenge, of course, is not for the sake of negating these values. On the contrary, the challenge is for the sake of pointing up their symptomatic character, of remembering their genesis at those cultural-historical moments when things could have been otherwise. That these values have not been otherwise attests to the fact that these moments of genesis were also moments of forgetfulness, in which these values were transformed from perspectives into unquestioned cultural conventions, sedimented habits of mind. Moreover, the importance of this challenge should not be missed. It is important to take up this experiment, important to allow ourselves to be addressed by television as a symptom in place of simply castigating and dismissing it, because the recognition that things could have been otherwise reminds us of our responsibility for our creations. That television seems intent upon the destruction of the verbo-ocular-ego values of modernity invites from us not an unthinking, even self-righteous defense of those values, but an attentive response to our participation in the creation of those values. It is not safe simply to defend the book against television. On the contrary, we need to attend to how television, as the shadow of the book, as its symptomatic expression, calls us to become responsible by remembering what we have made.

In this essay, television as symbolic of the ending of modernity is presented as the symptomatic breakdown of modernity. Whether or not this breakdown is also a breakthrough to another kind of cultural consciousness, postmodern, remains for the reader to decide. In the closing words of this introduction, I will offer my own assessment of this experiment. For the moment, however, I want to summarize a few ways in which television consciousness, or media image consciousness in general, can be a breakthrough to a postmodern style.

The television experience can be a breakthrough to a postmodern style insofar as it breaks the gestalt of verbo-ocular-egocentrism, and in so doing redefines the ocularcentrism of modernity. If television is ocularcentric—and in many ways it is—it nevertheless revisions the eye. The eye of ego consciousness, the eye of the reader of the book, arises within a cultural-historical moment in which the ego as disembodied spectator is invited to keep his or her eye, singular, fixed, and distant, upon the world. The double anamnesis of this spectator eye makes these features quite clear. The television eye, the ocularcentrism of the television experience, is of a quite different sort. As the essay suggests, beginning with its opening image, the eye of television consciousness is *re-minded* of the body. Seduced by images, a seduction which to be sure is not without its problems, the eye of the television body is an emotional vision, a vision that is moved at a bodily level.

As emotional-rationality, the television body is not verbocentric. In place of a literate consciousness, the television body is an image consciousness. Drawing upon psychoanalysis, the television body is said to be more like the dream body than the waking body. Drawing also upon the preliterate body of poetic performance in Homeric Greece, the television body is said to be more akin to this body of orality, where knowing is emotional, participatory, and sensuous, rather than rational, detached, and logical, and where waking and dreaming are less clearly distinguished and are more confused. In these respects, the postmodernism of the television body is presented as a postliterate orality, a surreal reality in which the values of literacy are confused with a new, technologically produced orality.

Finally, television body consciousness can be postmodern insofar as it is the decentering of the ego. Jut as the dream in psychoanalysis decentered the ego, television can move the ego out of its privacy and isolation into a kind of group—even tribal—consciousness, where the tension between fusion with the other and distance from the other is refigured. The figure of the borderline patient is offered as an illustration of this decentering of ego consciousness that the television experience brings. It is suggested that working with the borderline is more like watching television than it is like reading a book. The symptomatic value of television, then, might very well lie in its invitation toward another kind of consciousness now visible in our culture only as the pathology of the borderline.

Does this experiment in attending to the symptomatic character of television consciousness in particular, and media image consciousness in general, succeed? Does this effort to *re-member* out of forgetfulness the generative sites of modernity allow us to value the differences between modernity and postmodernity, especially with respect to its ocularcentric character, in place of evaluating them? The reader is the judge. For myself, I need to say that in praxis the experiment has not yet even begun. What I offer here is a possibility, a work to be done. To achieve it, however, would first require acknowledgment of this historical fact. Television and the media image industry have been and continue to be held captive by the force of economic capitalism, in much the same way that psychoanalysis was taken captive. These forces have an inertial mass that makes them resistant to change. The dream in psychoanalysis, and of psychoanalysis, became profitable and so lost its symptomatic edge. So too have television and the media image industry. Revolutions in consciousness, shifts from a modern style to a postmodern one, have little if any chance of succeeding so long as there is money to be made in their exploitation. So far that seems to be the case, making television a mid-twentieth-century version of the therapy room, the place where the dream and the symptom are not only matters of profit but of amusement as well.

The Television and the Book

Neil Postman's 1986 paperback edition of *Amusing Ourselves to Death* has a provocative and illuminating cover.[2] Framed within a square, which gives the potential reader of this book the impression that he or she is looking through a window, is what appears to be a nuclear family gathered together around a television set whose back faces us, the potential readers looking at this family looking at television. Besides this visual double play, one is also struck by the fact that each family member is headless! But there is no sense of shock or horror at their condition. They have not been decapitated. On the contrary, the scene is amusing, and inspires a question: Who are these people who, fully clothed and sitting upright, confront us watching them watching television? And here for the first time some sense of shock does enter. They are us, mindless zombies whose heads, who capacities for critical discourse and discursive thinking, have atrophied into nothingness, perhaps for lack of use in the age of the entertaining image. Entranced and amused, they (we) sit passively and expectantly, waiting to be fed and to be filled with the glut of images dispensed by the tube. Information addicts, we might say, enslaved by the hypnotic power of the image!

Postman's book poses a serious question about the possibility of reasonable public discourse in what he calls the "Age of Show Business," and his analysis of how electronic media have refashioned matters of knowledge into matters of entertainment is difficult to fault. When he states, for example, that the nineteenth-century invention of the telegraph cut the connection between communication and transportation, between the message and the messenger, making it possible not only to transmit messages more quickly but also to transmit more messages, producing a flood of information which without local context has become increasingly irrelevant, trivial, and even incoherent, and which in its sheer volume has put us on overload and made us powerless in the face of it all, our daily experience with newspaper headlines, radio broadcasts, and television news from around the globe strongly supports him. When he describes how television in its "Now this" syndrome breaks the continuity of experience, fragmenting it into bits of information by presenting segments of news not only interrupted by commercials but also, like newspaper headlines, presented with no internal connection among them, offering as it were a collage of news events, our daily experience again confirms him. Or, when he argues that TV takes away any sense of reality by inviting us to attend to a news story about war followed by a commercial for fast food, presenting sequence without consequence, a pattern that is more like a dream or a fantasy than perceptual contact with the world, we are ready to agree. And finally, when he proposes that TV should, therefore, aspire to do nothing more than what it does best, which is amuse, we are convinced by his proposal. After all, when coverage of the Persian Gulf War produces images of allied bombing missions spoken of in terms of video games, the line between matters of serious import and games, between fact and fiction, has been more than broken; it has been erased.

My intention is not to challenge Postman's diagnosis of our state of mind in the age of the media image. I applaud the diagnosis for its accuracy in portraying our current condition. I do wish, however, to differ with him about the prescription which follows his diagnosis, and about the anamnesis through which the diagnosis is made and from which the prescription follows.

That television should simply amuse, that it should abandon its pretense that it is or can be anything other than entertainment, is a prescription resulting from the way in which Postman uses the perspective of the book as a standard against which television is measured. The values of book literacy—linearity, coherence shaped by context, continuity, focused concentration, and privacy, to name only a few—are the presumed natural frame within which television consciousness, that is, consciousness shaped by the immediate image rather than the discursive world, is placed and judged in an essentially negative way. But is such a judgment a defensive reaction of typographical consciousness, of that kind of consciousness shaped these last four hundred years by the book, a consciousness for which loss of coherence, continuity, and context can only be experienced as a form of schizophrenia?

Postman, I believe, is guilty of this defensive reading in spite of the fact that he is aware of the historical and cultural character of the relationship between instruments of technology and styles of consciousness. Postman knows that cultural instruments are metaphors as well as mediums for experience, epistemologies incarnate, tools that not only inform us but formulate how we are in-formed. He knows this, yet the differences between book and television become for him matters of evaluation. I suppose, then, that unlike Plato he would not have banned the poets from the polis at that time when a shift occurred, from myth to logos, a shift engineered in large measure by the invention of the phonetic alphabet.[3] But defending the Homeric poets and mythic consciousness against the philosophers and rational consciousness then would have had, I suspect, as little impact as Postman's defense of typographic consciousness against media consciousness will have now.

In saying this, however, I do not mean to imply that we surrender ourselves to television consciousness as a matter of historical necessity or inevitability. That is not the point. The point is to appreciate whatever positive transformations in consciousness are being brought about by changes in our technological ways of knowing the world, and to appreciate that the instruments through which we encounter the world are made by us, even if for motives which are largely unknown. Television, like the book, incarnates a collective psychological condition. I want to propose, then, that before evaluating the differences, we value the difference in order to understand something of ourselves. I want to propose that the challenges which media culture pose today are symptoms. As such, "television" asks not for a diagnosis which would emphasize only what is wrong with it (and us), but for a hearing that would challenge the "book" to remember what *it* has (and we have) otherwise forgotten. The symptom, then, not as a sign of disease but as a vocation, as a call to remember.[4]

Interlude

A reader, when starting a book, intends to make sense of it. Recently I attempted an experiment in what I called "complex reading," which invited graduate students in a class that was reading Freud's case histories to suspend this intention. Throughout the semester we tried to remain with the question of how the texts make sense of us even as we were trying to make sense of them. Five themes guided this experiment. For example, bracketing the effort to make sense of the text raised *anxiety* over the following issues: Where is one's reading going? Is the reading producing nonsense? How does the interplay of text, memory, fantasy, and feeling fit together? Is the text a repository of information being correctly interpreted? Is one doing a good job of reading, doing it efficiently, and finishing the task? In all these concerns, we learned how our trying to make sense of the text is "a means of mastery and control, the perspective of an ego consciousness in the stance of detached observer of the world." We also learned how the bracketing of this intention to make sense of the text, allowing the text to make sense of us as readers, challenged "the position of ego consciousness by undercutting its fantasies of power and progress, of virtue and purity, of efficiency and comprehensiveness," and revealed that these fantasies lie "behind the ideals of objective reading, of a finished text, of a correct interpretation."[5]

Television on a daily and hourly basis, already does to ego consciousness— to that consciousness which, as we shall see, historically has developed in relation to the book—what this experiment at complex reading did. It challenges the values and assumptions of ego consciousness, and in this respect it seems proper to say that *television is the shadow of the book*. As such, television (and the electronic media of the image in general, from television and film to neon advertising signs) makes visible the pathology of ego, literate, book consciousness, by bringing into question the values of linear rationality, contextual coherence, narrative continuity, infinite progress, individual privacy, productive efficiency, detached comprehensiveness, and neutral objectivity.

To attend to television as shadow is to approach it as a cultural symptom, and this approach is no more a celebration of the new in praise of progress than it is a defensive protection of the old. Rather it is a work of remembering, an anamnesis of the hidden in the given, an attending to how already in the givenness of the book the television is hidden, a witnessing to how book consciousness, the consciousness of the word, forgets and yet still remembers television consciousness, the consciousness of the image. J. F. Lyotard makes the point in this fashion:

> The modern is all too easily snapped up by the future, by all its values of pro-motion, pro-gram, pro-gress . . . dominated by a very strong emphasis on willful activism. Whereas the post-modern implies, in its very movement . . . a capacity to listen openly to what is hidden within the happenings of today. Post-modernism is deeply reflexive, in the sense of anamnesis or reminescence, and that itself evinces what is best in modernity.[6]

Postman's question, therefore, of how rational public discourse is possible in the age of the media is best served not by dismissing image media or confining them to amusement, but by recovering through the image media the cultural unconsciousness of the book. I would only add that it is important to be about this work of cultural anamnesis at this time. "In an age and at a time overtaken by linear and programmed thinking, by obsessions with the bottom line and the straight path, by a passion for straightening things out and straightening them up,"[7] we need to remember the complex character of psychological life and the way in which it twists, weaves, and blends together fact and fiction, sense and nonsense, continuity and discontinuity, order and chaos, reason and dream. It is important today because we have already missed an opportunity to do this work of re-membering. The dream of psychoanalysis, meant in both senses of its vision of the unconscious as the shadow of the ego and its appreciation of the dream as a royal road to this unconscious, has been appropriated and tamed insofar as psychoanalysis has become less a cultural critique and more an established profession in the service of this ego. We make sense today of the dream as much as we make sense of the text. Ignoring the shadow, however, it has returned with greater intensity and insistence. The TV, I am suggesting, is dream consciousness made public and visible. Can we afford the attempt to situate television consciousness within the confines of the ego, literate, book consciousness as we have situated dream consciousness within the service of the ego? Can we dismiss TV consciousness's challenge to book consciousness by confining it to the task of amusement, as we have done with dream consciousness by confining it to the therapy room?

The First Re-Membering: The Cogito Project

Our anamnesis of book consciousness begins with that headless nuclear family in front of its television set. It begins with the claim that members of this family are the descendants of Descartes. To appreciate this claim, we need to remember that moment in time when we, the children of his meditations, were being conceived. Specifically, we need to remember Descartes' *Meditations on First Philosophy* and especially that moment in the work when he sets his conditions for who and what the reader must be in order to read his book.

"I would not recommend it to any except to those who would want to meditate seriously along with me."[8] Those who are invited to read the text, those who are serious, are defined by what they are not. The instruction is a negative requirement, a requirement that asks the reader to purify himself or herself of something in order to read the text. Susan Bordo, in a provocative reading of Descartes' work, has also noted this theme of purification, and she places it within a psycho-historical framework which illuminates the *cogito* project in insightful fashion.[9] Along with her, we need to ask of what should the reader be purified so as not to contaminate the text? The answer is found in the figure from whom the serious reader is distinguished. It is found in the figure of the "vulgar." The serious reader is the one who is *not* vulgar, that is, the one who in an act of negation which purifies becomes "capable of freeing the mind from attachment to the senses."[10] The reader of Descartes' text turns out to be a disincarnate mind, a head minus the body, a bodyless reader.

It would seem at this point a false claim that the nuclear family looking at television are children of Descartes. They are headless bodies, while the reader of Descartes' text is a bodyless head. But the claim is not false, nor are the children faithless or rebellious. On the contrary, they are exactly what this kind of thinking had to produce, "bastards," in the sense of unwanted and unintended offspring. "Monstrosities" might be better, except that it has too negative a connotation. Let us say they are Descartes' neurotic offspring, shadows that continuously remind practitioners of the *cogito* project of their vulgar heritage.

The *cogito* project establishes a way of thinking that takes leave of its senses. To take leave of one's senses is, however, a way of thinking shadowed by madness, and the headless bodies in front of their TV screen are one form of this madness: life as continuous, repetitive entertainment and amusement. Purifying itself of the body, the serious practitioner of the *cogito* project abandons the body which becomes, as I described elsewhere,[11] not only the corpse, the body as anatomical object, but also the consumer, the body as object of pleasure and profit. This corpse and the body addicted to pleasure are twins, the former the legitimated offspring of Cartesian vision and the latter the black sheep.

I am suggesting that the entertainment industry, incarnated in the electronic media of the image, is the shadow of that thinking which has taken leave of the senses. The technology of media culture as entertainment haunts a Cartesian consciousness which, in creating a thinking that is disincarnate, has also created a body fit only for amusement, a body of endless appetites addicted to its need for continuous stimulations and distractions. Postman, in his critique of the media image, says as much and adds the features of triviality and passivity to his description of media consciousness. Possessing an unlimited capacity for distraction from our boredom, we are also overwhelmed by the amount of information that is produced and made available. In the face of this information glut the capacity for distinguishing the true from the false is lost. Pieces of disconnected information without a surrounding context generate a mountain of trivial details, reducing us to passive consumers of advertised items and reported information, and rendering us powerless to frame any of it within a perspective. Reflecting on this state of affairs, Postman adds that the last refuge of the powerless individual in a culture of the image is pleasure. Pleased and entertained, we are narcotized against our condition of helplessness. Amused to death, we are distracted from our condition of indifference. Pleasure becomes the anodyne of the powerless. "Big Brother," Postman says, "turns out to be Howdy Doody."[12]

It is difficult to resist the rhetoric of Postman's critique, but we must recall here that his diagnosis rests upon a preference for the book which becomes the evaluating measure of television. Television, for Postman, is not the shadow of the book, a view that would lead to an equally critical questioning and diagnosis of book consciousness. On the contrary, he considers television the antithesis of the book, and its threatened elimination.

Distraction, triviality, and passivity are the judgments then of a book consciousness watching television. They are the diagnosed symptoms of the serious reader who has distanced herself or himself from the vulgar. The headless nuclear family watching television is the nightmare of the bodyless reader, the terrible image of what we become when we lose the book. We need to remember, however, the kinship between the two, the connection between that kind of thinking which, in splitting off the serious from the vulgar, the mind from flesh, reason from emotion, first created a mindless body and its needs for distraction, and produced the means to do it. Indeed, we are called to this task of re-membrance in order not to take the easy path which would lead us to conclude that the fault and the danger are with the media of the image, and which would make us forget that the danger and the fault are with that way of thinking which in taking leave of its senses has fashioned a body capable only of being stimulated and entertained. To do any less would leave that way of thinking safely in place. We need to remember that the fault is not with television itself. The fault is with that historically created situation within which Descartes' shadow children watching television were originally conceived.

Second Re-Membering: Alberti's Window

If Descartes is the father of the body of amusement, the reluctant, unintentional author of the television body, of the body left behind by the flight of the *cogito* from the flesh, then Leon Battista Alberti, fifteenth-century artist, architect, and author is the father of that father, the grandfather of our nuclear family ensconced in front of its television. Our second re-membrance starts, therefore, with the claim that Alberti's codification of the laws of linear perspective vision inaugurates a psychology of distance between the eye of mind and the flesh of the world, upon which the *cogito* project of Descartes rests and of which it is an elaboration.

Linear perspective vision was a fifteenth-century artistic invention for representing three-dimensional depth on the two-dimensional canvas. It was a geometrization of vision that began as an invention and became a convention, a cultural habit of mind. We will not trace out here the full story of this shift from a technique or method to a world-view or metaphysics. Rather, we will concentrate on one aspect of Alberti's technique that prepared the ground for Descartes.[13]

Imagine that you are looking at the world through the lens of a camera. The scene which you see stretches out before you in such a fashion that objects nearer to you are bigger while those farther away appear smaller. This is as it should be, for we have become used to the convention that size represents the distance from the perceiver. Indeed, this connection between size and distance seems a natural fact. Medieval, prelinear perspective paintings appear to us, therefore, as strange, as messengers of another world. And in fact they are of another world. Medieval men and women did not look at the world through a camera eye. We do habitually, even without the presence of the instrument. With Alberti the eye was beginning its education in a new way.

A camera is a little room, and the lens is a special kind of window which lets in the world as a matter of light. When Alberti described his procedures for making a perspective drawing, that is, a drawing in which things become smaller as they recede from the viewer, he invited his readers to imagine the canvas on which one would paint to be a window. In other words, Alberti began his perspective drawing by becoming a spectator on one side of a window looking at the world on the other side. A window, however, does not stand by itself. It is a frame within a wall attached to other walls. It is part of a room, and precisely that part which admits the world as a matter of light.

Linear perspective vision is an invitation to enter into a room and to become on this side of its window a spectator looking at a world transformed into a spectacle, that is, into a matter of light. It is an invitation to become a subject with his or her eye upon a world which now has become an object of vision. We have become quite accustomed to being in this little room, living in it as our outpost or outlook upon the world. We call it ego consciousness, and we locate it, uncritically, inside our heads that, like cameras themselves, have film inside them, have impressionable material called a brain.

Ego consciousness, consciousness as private, interior subjectivity, was initially invented and imagined by the artist as a way of envisioning the world as a matter of vision. The *cogito* of Descartes, the 'I think therefore I am,' begins as the eye of mind. And I say "eye of mind" because in looking at the world through a window, we are destined to lose touch with the world, except in those ways which matter for the eye alone. The eye, which of all the senses favors contact at a distance, already defines that contact in terms of its limits and its preferences. What is visible, observable, measurable, and quantifiable will increasingly become, therefore, the index of the real, while what is invisible and not observable, qualitative, and nonmeasurable (like the beauty and awe of the rainbow which Newton will later in another closed room quantify as the spectrum) will become at best subjective, secondary qualities projected onto the world now cleansed and purified of those qualities. In addition, this eye will exercise its preference for surfaces, transforming the invisible, imaginal depths of the world into a visible display of surface images, probing each and every surface and exposing beneath it only another surface ready and capable of being made into another piece of visibility. For the eye of mind behind the window, the world as a tension or play between visible surface and invisible depth will be eclipsed to become a project of progressively unveiling potential surfaces hidden beneath manifest surfaces. The instruments through which the eye of mind will enforce its project already demonstrate its vision. The telescope and the microscope, for example, will open surfaces only to reveal other surfaces, surfaces moreover from which the human body will become alien and distant. The world transformed into a matter of light will become the counterpart of a subject increasingly distant and withdrawn into its room of private subjectivity, a solitary, isolated atom of disincarnate individuality incapable of sensing and hence making sense of a world which has become measurably insensible. This subject with its eye upon the world is the start of the modern reign of the despotic eye, that eye of mind that in draining the world of its qualities purifies it of its substance, making it into a matter of light.

It is no accident of history that the subject spectator looking at the world through a window will also within his or her room begin to engage in another activity. At approximately the same time that Alberti's procedures are mapping the world as a geometric grid, laying it out in linear fashion, the book will be introduced and mass-produced. The linearity of the geometric world will find its counterpart in the linear literacy of the book, where line by line, sentence by sentence, the chronological structure of the book will mirror the sequential, ordered, linear structure of time in the sciences. In addition, the interiorization of individual subjectivity within the room of consciousness will find apt expression in the private act of reading and in silence, unlike the manuscript consciousness of the Middle Ages, where reading was done aloud.[14] The increasing standardization of grammar will also mirror the increasing homogenization of a world quantifiably defined. In these and in other respects too, linear vision will create an ego consciousness not only separate from the world and distant from the body, but also literate, private, and silent, an ego paradoxically standardized in its individuality.

The *cogito* project invites, as we saw, the serious reader to part company with the vulgar by taking leave of his or her senses. And this bodyless head, we also saw, leaves behind a body capable only of amusement. Alberti's window anticipates this project, creating a spectator for whom the world has become a matter for the eye alone. It is only a small step, I would suggest, from envisioning the world as a matter of light to the world becoming a *light matter*, which it is, in both senses, for our nuclear family looking at television.

Media as Shadow and Symptom

Television is a *light matter* and the parentage which we have traced of our nuclear family looking at television confirms it. It is a matter of light and a matter fit only to amuse. My claim, however, is that the first sense, which is descriptive, becomes in the second sense an evaluation, a judgment passed by the despotic eye. Against that judgment, I will attempt an experiment. I will suggest that television as a medium, along with film, is an evolution of human consciousness, a new style of consciousness that is imprisoned in the heady eye of mind. The problem with television is that we treat it like a book, that we measure it by the book, by those patterns of consciousness appropriate to the isolated atom of individuality ensconced within the room of ego subjectivity. TV, however, is a challenge to ego consciousness, as much as it is a challenge to the political counterpart of ego consciousness, the individual nation-state. Indeed, I will go further and say that TV as a medium brings out such strong criticisms because it is the *breakdown* of literate, linear, ego consciousness, the consciousness of the book. The evolution is a revolution, akin in its implications to that earlier transformation in Platonic times from mythic to literate consciousness. Whether this breakdown can also be a *breakthrough* is what I will explore.

Near the very end of his *Meditations*, in the sixth and final one, Descartes returns to the issue of the difference between waking and dreaming, a difference which in the beginning of his work was central in securing the ego *cogito* from the shadows of doubt. Proclaiming his earlier efforts less than satisfactory, he says that now he has found a very notable and secure difference between them. Memory, he says, "can never bind and join our dreams together [one with another and all] with the course of our lives, as it habitually joins together what happens to us when we are awake."[15]

On the surface that is a key difference, and one that is phenomenologically astute, at least for that ego consciousness that has defined the project of modernity. Whether such a distinction, however, is as true for a nonliterate ego, or in preliterate cultures, is a debatable question, and certainly the Homeric epic poems, which historically precede literate consciousness, suggest otherwise. Eric Havelock and Julian Jaynes have both suggested that in oral culture the separation between dreaming and waking is less fixed. Indeed in his discussion of the psychology of poetic performance, Havelock describes a state of waking consciousness characterized by a sense of possession. Poetic performance, like the dream, envelops, and the listener, like the dreamer who is fused with the dream, is fused with the singer. If this was "a life without self-examination," a critique which Plato made and which the literate ego of modernity presumes, it was, as Havelock acknowledges, nevertheless "a manipulation of the resources of the unconscious in harmony with the conscious [that is] unsurpassed."[16]

But we need not speculate on this matter of the preliterate mind, since the media image poses also for the postliterate mind a challenge to Descartes' difference between waking and dreaming. To appreciate this challenge we need to know what Descartes does with his idea about memory's function in waking and sleeping. Immediately after citing the failure of memory to weave our dreams together and to weave them into life, he says: "And so, in effect, if someone suddenly appeared to me when I was awake and (afterward) disappeared in the same way, as (do images that I see) in my sleep, so that I could not determine where he came from or where he went, it would not be without reason that I could consider it a ghost."[17]

But what after all is this experience—which if it happened to Descartes would convince him that he had seen a ghost and that he was therefore either mad or dreaming—but a description of the nuclear family in front of its television set switching channels with a remote control? What haunted Descartes, and necessitated for him a strict line between waking and sleeping, has become for us our daily fare. What the ego *cogito* of Descartes dreamed has become a reality which now threatens ego literate consciousness with the dream consciousness of television. TV consciousness, as Postman remarks, is discontinuous. But it is so for an ego that, educated in the model of the linear rationality of the book, separates itself from the episodic pattern of the dream. The television image, appearing and disappearing before me, is the ghost banished by Descartes. Television does on a daily basis exactly what Descartes feared, and in this respect it is a continuous witness to the fact that the *cogito* project contains in its origins its own undoing.

The nuclear family in front of its television set is neither sleeping nor insane. It is awake and it is dreaming. Television consciousness today haunts book consciousness because it eclipses those boundaries between waking and sleeping (reason and madness; fact and fiction) which ego literate consciousness so firmly established at the foundation of modernity. In doing so, it exposes the modern ego to a new sense of time, disrupting the familiar pattern of narrative and replacing it with the episodic pattern of the dream. Perhaps the term *replace* is not the best to describe the experience, because the medium of television does not so much eclipse the boundaries between waking and sleeping as confuse them. Television consciousness, as Donald Lowe remarks, is "a surreality," that is, an electronic media mentality superimposed on the older typographic mentality of the book.[18] The episodic pattern of time, more peculiar to the discontinuous medium of television, rests upon the still more familiar habits of narrative time, with its patterns of linear and even causal sequence. Watching television, then, exposes the ego to the bizarre experience of being awake in one's dreams. Or, watching television is akin to interpreting dreams, making sense of them, while dreaming. TV's coverage of the San Francisco earthquake in 1989 is a good example. The episodic and even random character of the events were plotted as a story line. We were watching chaos being ordered and order being dissolved again into chaos. Recent coverage of the Persian Gulf War is an even better example, since the illusion of being informed was continually broken. Coverage of that event did demonstrate that the accounts of the war were allusions to what remained frustratingly elusive. To be sure, some of this frustration can be attributed to the way in which the U.S. military restricted television coverage. But not all of it is explained in this fashion. Indeed, the frustration in this experience is built into the relation between the medium, with its multi-perspectival, collage type of consciousness, and the viewer, with his or her still relatively intact linear perspectival consciousness. The frustration belongs to the surreal quality of this relation which con-fuses or blends together episodic and story line time. And it is generated by the effort to dismiss this play of levels between a collage of images and the story line by forcing the former into the latter.

Before television, we had another instance of this frustrating effort. Freud's psychoanalysis also challenged the ego with the dream, discovering the multiple ways in which the ego's efforts to make sense of life and to bring order to it were illusions. Before dream consciousness had to become a cultural insistence, incarnating itself in the medium of television, it attempted to break through its separation from the ego by incarnating itself as a symptom of the body of the hysteric. In her symptoms she was suffering from reminiscences, Freud said with Breuer. She was suffering from memory, from time, becoming in a bodily way a collage of symptoms overdetermined in their meanings, threaded with events, wishes, dreams, and other symptoms, a constant interplay of allusions superimposed upon an ego consciousness unable to make sense of it all, a living, breathing, surreal figure lost in the linear landscapes of the modern world. But Freud, the intrepid explorer of as-yet unmapped domains, did make the effort to make sense of it all. He interpreted the dream, transforming it as it were into a book, placing over it the narrative story line of a case history, and in so doing he got memory back on line, securing the hysteric's symptomatic sexuality in the past, erasing memory as presence of the past in the present.

In retrospect, Freud's effort was a mistake, generated by a literate ego consciousness too threateningly challenged by the dream. The hysteric's symptomatic sexuality was not a repressed past. It was, on the contrary, a fullness in the present. The hysteric suffered from memory, from time, and in that suffering she was an appeal addressed to the ego. She was the shadow of that ego reminding it that time and memory can become a disease when in an attempt to plot time as a line one lives outside of time, above it, detached from it. She was a shadow which, through her symptoms and dreams, was flooding the present with the full presence of past and future, presenting everything—event, memory, dream, wish, symptom—at once, recalling the ego out of its spectator detachment from life, re-minding its bookish distance with immediate sensual presence, re-membering that the past is not and never can be only a cause, and that the future is not and never can be a plot line of infinite progress subjected to one's will.

Diagnosing or treating the hysteric has in effect silenced the effort of the dream in psychoanalysis to breach the isolation of ego consciousness. Moreover, insofar as the media image has been co-opted by the capitalist mentality of consumption and profit, the television body, with its infinite appetite for distraction and amusement, has become first cousin to the hysteric body, with its symptomatic confusion of memory and event, fantasy and dream. In its resistance to dream consciousness, ego, literate, book consciousness has not, however, treated this symptom away. On the contrary, it has simply elevated it into a form of mass entertainment. Television has become the therapy room of the hysteric transformed into a public spectacle. Talk shows, as public confessionals for the secrets of the soul, have become a form of mass hysteria made palatable as amusement.

If, however, we have become insensitive to the mass hysteria disguised as entertainment which television consciousness induces, inculcating within us that same *belle indifference* so characteristic of the early hysteric, the media image persists as shadow of ego, literate, book consciousness at another level. In another symptomatic form, very much akin to the borderline, media image consciousness might very well be serving as a reminder of the unconscious legacy of literate consciousness.

The television experience is a radical separation of body and mind. On one hand, the headless *body* of the *cogito* seems fused with the emotional appeals of the media image, moved by these images without either judgment or reflection. On the other hand, the very absence of these capacities, so visible in the iconographic display of the *headless* body in front of its TV, betrays a distance between the person watching television and his or her emotionally infected body already fused with the television. Of the many complexities and difficulties which the borderline patient presents in psychotherapy, it is this tension of fusion and distance which often stands out. At one moment the therapist can be overwhelmed by the intense affects of his or her patient, engulfed either in a sea of abuse which often seems to threaten the therapist's own well-defended ego structures, or in a whirlpool of fascination at the patient's courage, spirit, insight, and secret knowledge. Commenting on the latter, Nathan Schwartz-Salant says in fact that the borderline often can envelop the therapist within an atmosphere which is experienced as "a link to the *numinosum*, the power of the gods and especially gods that the normal collective awareness has long since displaced."[19]

However, at another moment, the next moment in fact, which shifts with the same rapidity as channels on a television, the therapist can feel herself to be in the presence of an absence so remarkable as to give the impression that the borderline individual is somehow less than human, a chillingly cold, aloof being from another world. At such moments the remark of the American psychiatrist Harry Stack Sullivan about schizophrenics, that we are all much more human than otherwise, seems off the mark. The therapist can, I believe, more easily recognize the absurd humanity of the schizophrenic than the borderline, for the schizophrenic, despite his or her bizarreness, escorts ego, literate consciousness only to the borders of order and chaos, whereas the borderline seems to be introducing another kind of order, an order that first erases the borderline and then confuses order and chaos in unexpected and unfamiliar ways. To be with a borderline is to be in a moment that is simultaneously "too full and too empty." It is to be in "a fairy tale world of abstract characters that then, quickly, turn back to flesh and blood reality."[20] No fairy tale that is merely being read evokes this experience. We are, on the contrary, describing here an experience more akin to the magic of television and movies, where the distance from the characters portrayed is eclipsed as these very same characters, like some ghosts haunting the world, emotionally impregnate one's body. The borderline individual radically challenges the comfortable distance and secure detachment of ego, literate consciousness. Being with a borderline is more like watching TV than it is like reading a book.

What the borderline challenges on the *idiographic* symptomatic level, the media image challenges on the *cultural* symptomatic level. On both levels we are being called to reimagine the separation and opposition of mind and body through this intense con-fusion of fusion and distance. On both levels we are being asked to attend to the shadow of ego, literate, spectator consciousness with its detached, despotic eye upon the world. The danger, of course, is that we will miss the opportunity, as happened with the hysteric. The borderline, then, will remain a negative diagnosis, and television an irritating distraction only to be dismissed by the more serious and sober-minded. The opportunity, however, is that on each level we might hear, as Schwartz-Salant does with the borderline, an appeal for union which this tension of fusion and distance dramatizes. We might hear an appeal for a sense of communion which the distance of ego, literate, book consciousness, ensconced behind the window, has shattered, and which the fusion of media image consciousness, seated as the headless nuclear family in front of its television set, dissolves.

Conclusion: Toward a Postliterate Orality

The kind of consciousness which characterizes the media image, television consciousness for example, is a breakdown of the kind of consciousness which characterizes ego, literate consciousness, book consciousness for example. The remarks about the borderline propose, however, that breakdown can also be breakthrough. That the latter is resisted, however, is evidenced by the fate of psychoanalysis. Although Freud described the relation of transference between patient and therapist as a playground, the dream never quite made it into the arena of play. The dream in psychoanalysis remained for the ego a humiliation, a threat to its mastery and control, a matter of disguise, deception, illusion. That it was a way of playing with the ego, that it was a matter not of illusion but allusion to what remains elusive, was lost. The psychoanalyst as detective intended to uncover what the dream was hiding, making the ego of analysis a discoverer of buried secrets, forbidden wishes, arcane and illicit desires. As detective and discoverer, the ego of analysis made use of the dream in its search for origins and causes.

The dream, however, is an invitation which asks to be played with by a wakeful consciousness aware of its continuous and reciprocal relation of making the dream while being made by it. In doing so, the dream infects the seriousness of *cogito* consciousness with play, even as it undermines the idea of an origin outside that process which in searching for origins simultaneously creates the origins that are discovered. The dream, then, breaks through to a consciousness which in its playfulness is participatory, and which in its sense of participation accepts its oxymoronic character of created-discoveries, of serious-play, of constructed-origins. It breaks through to a consciousness which in its acceptance of paradox is radically metaphorical.[21]

Television consciousness certainly partakes of these features of the dream. It is no less participatory, especially at the level of the emotional body, working upon it in much the same fashion that the dream works upon the body. It is also oxymoronic insofar as it continuously presents us with those juxtapositions of experience—the news story followed by the commercial, for example—which to the serious eye of ego, literate consciousness seem only like an opposition. And it is finally radically metaphorical insofar as its images, like Magritte's pipe, are not what they appear to be and yet are. Or at least television consciousness might break through to these features which characterizes much of postmodern consciousness, if its symptomatic character is attended as a vocation.

To call media image consciousness postmodern is not, however, sufficiently descriptive, for its postmodernism is a postliterate orality. The television body, like the dreaming body, is in many respects a re-presentation of the preliterate body of orality, of that body of speaking and listening which is always prior to the body of the text. The television body is this oracular body, the body which Havelock presents in his descriptions of poetic performance. It is a body which culturally and historically spirals out of the body of the book, out of the literate ego, a body which is not a repetition of preliterate orality but a re-membrance of that body, a re-play of it after the reign of the despotic eye. Like the body of poetic performance, the television body is emotional-rationality, drawn out of itself and into the world aesthetically, sensibly, as a matter of sense. It is also a body of group consciousness, a body already wedded via the sensuous and even erotic experience of the image to other bodies—a tribal body, then, immersed in a landscape that is more mythical than it is logical, and invited into action that is more ritual in texture than moral in outlook. That this kind of bodily presence to reality is open to exploitation and manipulation is obvious. Television has been manipulated, primarily by submitting to the industry of capitalism the potential of the medium to be a breakthrough to another kind of experience. But it need not do so. The use of television during the Vietnam War demonstrated its power to de-isolate the ego of literate consciousness and to create a coherent tribal identity, held together with a powerful myth of its place in history and prepared to act in such fashion that its emotional thought, contained within the space of dramatic ritual, was an important catalyst to stop that war.

As a psychotherapist with a perspective of psychopathology, and who attends to the symptomatic and shadow character of the symbols of culture, I believe we stand at a crossroads. The very same features of television consciousness described above were sufficient for Plato to ban the poet-singer from the polis. The danger was that in becoming enmeshed in the poet's song one would be diffused, distracted, unfocused, and without fixed moral direction. The danger was that one would become plural in place of the unified, self-contained, self-organized, and autonomous individual. For Plato there was a "direct connection . . . between rejection of the poets on the one hand and the affirmation of the psychology of the autonomous individual on the other."[22]

The history of the Western psyche shows the results of the exclusion of the poets from the polis. We have sketched it here in terms of Descartes' *cogito* project, Alberti's window, and the book. It is a history of a radical shift from ear to eye, and particularly to that eye of detached, spectator distance, a history of the despotic eye. Media image consciousness, especially the television, seems to be the shadow and the symptom of that eye, and in this respect a retuning of it.

The images of television are not mere spectacles. They are spoken images, oracular insights, emotional visions. Perhaps with the television the poetic returns, or at least might do so.

Notwithstanding Postman's criticism that today political discourse is not possible on television, television might be the means by which the poet is restored to the polis. Such a restoration would bring in its wake a re-membrance of the body's participation in vision, a re-minder which would restore a sense of limits to a vision which, detached from the body, developed a singular, fixed devotion to the infinite, pursued in a linear, active, willful fashion. Postman's criticisms of television as fostering distraction, passivity, and the trivial might then be reimagined. Distraction might be revalued as an appreciation for what lies off to the side, an attention to the oblique, an openness to allusion. Passivity might be restored as a balance to the hyperactivity of willful consciousness, an antidote to the ego as will to power, the development of an attitude of receptivity. And the trivial might be recovered as a sensitivity for the detail, a refound sense of the local so easily lost sight of in the big picture achieved with distance. Each and all might be rescued from the current negative condition assigned to them by an ego consciousness in its head-long pursuit of separating its vision of life from living.

2

The Dream Body in Cyberspace

Virtual reality is a technological medium which already, even in its youth, challenges our ordinary sense of reality and re-defines the meaning of our physical existence. Between the flight simulators used to train pilots during the Second World War and the "holodeck" on the Enterprise in the *Star Trek* series lies the territory that is the fact and the dream of virtual reality. While the technology of virtual reality today far exceeds those rude simulators of World War II, it nevertheless still lags far behind the technology that the crew of the Enterprise had at its disposal. And yet . . . ?

Virtual reality is the product of an interactive technology that envelops its users in a three-dimensional world generated by a computer. Immersed within this environment, the user is able to see, her, and touch the virtual objects which comprise that world. To enter virtual space, you don a headset that looks like a pair of goggles but which, in fact, contains a miniature television set for each eye. With this headset the computer-generated images fill your entire visual field. At the present state of development, the images are still rather grainy and somewhat cartoon-like, but phenomenologically you see the virtual world as you do the ordinary perceptual environment. The use of stereophonic headphones adds panoramic sound to the virtual world, while "datagloves" allow you to sense the position of your virtual hand and arm in virtual space and to manipulate the virtual objects in that space. Commercial availability of full body suits, which allow you to sense the movement of your entire virtual body in virtual space, are only a short time away.

In exploring some of the psychological implications of virtual reality, the historical irony can be noted at the heart of this new technology. While virtual reality is a celebration of the Cartesian separation of mind and body and reason and dream, it is a technology that is reintroducing the body of the dream.

Galileo and the Moon

In 1609 Galileo's telescopic eye danced on the moon. Aided by this newly invented instrument of the telescope, Galileo took another step in the development of a kind of consciousness that required him to organize his experience and make sense of the world by leaving his body behind. That instrument not only extended the range of human vision, it also detached the eye from the context of human embodiment and gave it a privileged place in knowing the world. In so doing, the telescope opened another chapter in the development of modern science. In addition, it also incarnated a new style of psychological existence.

Between that event and the first American moon landing in 1969, we have traveled a path that has repeatedly invited us to take leave of our senses. Virtual reality both continues along that path and challenges it. It continues a psychology of dis-incarnation insofar as it nourishes the fantasy of a "new subculture [that is] busy mutating— downloading its consciousness into the computer, leaving its obsolete body behind, and inhabiting the datascape as new age cyborgs." And it challenges that psychology insofar as this consciousness, which would take leave of its senses, is haunted in cyberspace by the body of the dream.

The Astronaut in Cyberspace

Cyberspace, a term coined by science-fiction writer William Gibson, describes the simulated landscapes of virtual reality—landscapes that are the product of a marriage between the technologies of television and the computer. Unlike the television viewer, however, the user in cyberspace is transformed from being a spectator of, to being an active participant in, an imaginal, virtual world. Cyberspace, according to John Walker, ". . . provides users with a three-dimensional interaction experience that includes the illusion they are inside a world rather than observing an image." In cyberspace, the screen—the boundary—between us and the virtual world dissolves; we go *through* the screen, if not down the tube. In noting the difference between virtual reality and televison, Michael Heim says "[In virtual reality] you can interact with the animated creatures. You shoot them down and hide from them or dodge their ray guns. And they interact with you. They hunt you in three-dimensional space, just as you hunt them." In this respect, virtual reality is like a video game without the machine. The user melts or falls into the digital landscape, much like the character Flynn does in the 1982 film *TRON*.

Scott Bukatman notes that "virtual reality has become the very embodiment of postmodern *disembodiment*." In this respect, virtual reality is the *telos* of a flight from the body, the origins of which go back to the fifteenth-century invention of linear perspective vision. That artistic technique of representing the illusion of three-dimensional space on the flat, two-dimensional plane of a canvas requires the viewer to act as if he or she is looking at the world through a window. In becoming a conventional habit of mind, this artistic invention set the stage for the development of the scientific-technological attitude that has characterized the Western psyche for the last five hundred years. In commenting on the impact of linear perspective vision, art historian Samuel Y. Edgerton has noted: "Space capsules built for zero gravity, astronomical equipment for demarcating so-called black holes, atom smashers which prove the existence of anti-matter— these are the end-products of the discovered vanishing point."

Ensconced behind the window of linear perspective vision, the subject is invited to keep an eye upon the world, as vision becomes the measure of reality and the method by which the world is to be known. Within this context, a psychological shift in human existence occurs. The self behind the window is born as an ego consciousness, a spectator-observer distant and detached in its privacy from a world which, on the other side of the window, recedes toward an infinite horizon and becomes a spectacle for observation and measurement, a matter for the eye and the eye alone, a light matter. In addition, the body, as an impediment to the infinite vision of this spectator consciousness withdrawn from the world, becomes dispensable. The body becomes a specimen, an object for dissection, a corpse. Indeed, spectator, spectacle, and specimen become the codes of a cultural psychology that have progressively developed within the fractures between person-world, subject-object, body-mind, emotion-reason, dream-perception, sanity-madness, and a host of other so-called dichotomies.

The history of the specimen body and its shadows shows how technological consciousness is not only an abandonment of the body, but also a re-making of the body under the gaze of distant vision. First re-fashioned as corpse, as the anatomical body, this abandoned body from which we take flight is resurrected and re-energized in a series of stages culminating in the body of the astronaut. From origins to this culmination, the dream of technological consciousness is to distance itself from the world and from the flesh that ties us to the world. The astronaut, as a body fashioned for departure from the earth, is the transformation of this dream of distance into the event of departure. "Poised on the launch pad, prepared to leave the earth, the figure of the astronaut sums up the dreams of reincarnation and departure which have animated the discovery-invention of the abandoned body." These dreams have been and continue to be our dreams. In the cultural unconscious of the technological soul, "we are . . . all astronauts."

Virtual reality amplifies this dream of dis-incarnation, and it is no accident of language that the body in cyberspace has been called an "electronic cadaver." *Cadaver* preserves the origins of technology's flight from the body, while *electronic* indicates that the corpse has been transformed in cyberspace into the digital body. But even as the technology of virtual reality continues the dream of dis-incarnation, it also reverses its direction. With virtual reality, outerspace has become cyberspace and within that space, each of us becomes, as it were, an astronaut of inner space, a *cybernaut* floating in the wide expanse of the digital, electronic ocean. This reversal is a significant transformation. The body of the astronaut who floats in outerspace is made in the image of the corpse. The body of the cybernaut who floats in cyberspace is made in the image of the dream. We can well ask if virtual reality might be a path of re-animation by remembering that the human body made in the image of the corpse nevertheless still has its dreams. We can wonder if virtual reality will lead us back to the animated, *ensouled* body. But we can also wonder if, and perhaps even worry that, this technology might simply implant the dream into the corpse resurrected as machine, producing a nightmarish caricature of our human existence: a dead body programmed with electronic dreams. One cannot help but wonder here if the androids in Ridley Scott's 1982 film *Blade Runner* are an image of that future where the electronic cadaver, programmed with dreams, has escaped the digital webs of cyberspace to invade the world in which we live.

The Ghost in the New Machine

A phenomenology of perceptual experience reveals the human body to be a "point of view on the world." Merleau-Ponty's phenomenological description of perceptual experience shows how the mobility of the human body shapes space into place by arranging "round the subject a world which speaks to him of himself, and gives his own thoughts their place in the world." In our lived bodily experience of the world, the world wears the face of our intentions, and our gestures carve into the environment the trace and shape of their meanings. The physiognomy of the world is the mirror of our actions.

In one respect virtual reality faithfully mimics the phenomenology of our embodied lives in the world. Bukatman even calls action in cyberspace "an ecstatic exaggeration of Merleau-Ponty's phenomenological model." In cyberspace and in perceptual space "world and body comprise a continually modifying feedback loop . . ." A *gestural metaphysics*, we might say, operates in both cyberspace and the space of daily life.

There is, however, a fundamental difference between the *cyberbody* in the space of virtual reality and the *perceptual* body in the space of the physical world. The moving body in the world of daily life has no tangible counterpart in the world of cyberspace. While the cyberbody, like the perceptual body, arranges around itself a world, it does not dwell amidst the things that surround it. On the contrary, it is closer to the phenomenology of cyberspace experience to say that the cyberbody *haunts* the things of its virtual world. Indeed, it is closer to the experience to say that the cyberbody is a *ghostly* presence, and to note that its interactions with its virtual environment leave no tangible marks upon its digital flesh. In perceptual life, our carnal bodies of flesh, bone, muscle, and blood wear the marks and show the scars of our interactions with the world. The face is lined and furrowed and character is stamped into the body.

Michael Heim notes that "with its virtual environments and simulated worlds, cyberspace is a metaphysical laboratory, a tool for examining our very sense of reality." That ghostly body that haunts cyberspace forces a critical re-examination of the nature of the human self. Replacing the tactile with the digital, virtual reality *simulates* embodied presence. The technology of virtual reality, therefore, raises concerns about how far the felt sense of selfhood is co-extensive with one's lived body. Indeed, in very specific and concrete ways, the technology of virtual reality raises anew the Cartesian dualism of mind and body, the place of *Cogito* in relation to animate flesh, the relation of the "I think" to the "I am."

The technology of virtual reality opens up the real possibility, already anticipated with the computer, of "a mind independent of the biology of bodies, a mind released from the mortal limitations of the flesh." Bukatman notes that "cyberspace is a celebration of spirit, as the disembodied consciousness leaps and dances with unparalleled freedom," much like Galileo's disembodied telescopic eye danced on the moon. Cyberspace, Bukatman adds, is "a place for the return of *the omnipotence of thoughts*." But if virtual reality offers such a return, it is a return with a vengeance. The technology of virtual reality can realize a kind of hyper-*cogito*, the range of which appears to be virtually unlimited. As the datascapes of cyberspace spread, the *Cogito* can become a planetary consciousness. And while we are busy interacting with each other through the web or net of electronic impulses, the body can increasingly be imagined as archaic and dispensable. At a certain point we might reach the stage of "terminal identity," a phrase Bukatman takes from novelist William Burroughs. On one hand, such an identity, in fulfilling the Cartesian dream, would terminate any sense of selfhood imbricated with the body. On the other hand, terminal identity would provide a sense of self "constructed at the computer station or television screen"— that is, a self in flux, continuously made and re-made as a flow of information, a digitally generated electronic self not unlike the digital character Max Headroom. In fact, such a fluid self might already exist in the form of the borderline personality. This pathology might very well portray the symptomatic side of this technology, the cultural unconscious shadow of the terminal subject.

The Dream Body in Cyberspace

At the computer station or television screen, we might truly become a ghost in the machine. But terminal identity is only one possibility of virtual reality technology. Another possibility takes us in the direction of the dream.

The cyberbody in the space of virtual reality is closer to the dream body than it is to the perceptual body. It haunts its virtual landscapes but does not inhabit them in the same way the perceptual body of waking life inhabits its world. In cyberspace a subject can "hear a sound behind her, turn to see its source, walk toward it, and even (with the aid of a dataglove) pick it up, while to an outside observer, of course, nothing is there."

This description of cyber-experience parallels the phenomenology of dream experience. The relation of the subject in cyberspace to the outside observer mimics the relation between the dreamer while dreaming and the ego consciousness of the dreamer when he or she awakens. Nothing of the dream landscape remains for our waking consciousness. When we awaken, the airy stuff of which dreams seem to be made floats away. Dream space is a u-topic landscape— a no-place where no-things are— when seen in the light of waking consciousness. Cyberspace, too, is a no-place. It, too, is a u-topic place where no-things are, when seen from the place of the observer.

William Gibson calls cyberspace a "consensual hallucination." It is an apt and accurate metaphor, for it suggests that, in cyberspace, the user is immersed within the experience just as the one who hallucinates is enveloped within the hallucination. Moreover, it recalls John Walker's description of a cyberspace system, quoted earlier, as one which gives the impression that you are inside a world rather than observing an image. For Gibson and Walker, therefore, the cyberbody does not *have* an experience. On the contrary, the cyberbody *is* the experience.

The comments of Gibson and Walker suggest a second parallel between cyber experience and dream experience. A key difference between the dreaming and waking state occurs in the relation of the dreamer to the dream. Awake I say, "I *had* a dream" and, in doing so, I invert the relation between myself and the dream. Dreaming, I am *had by* the dream. Dreaming I *am* the dream. To put this difference another way, we can say that while dreaming, *we are in the dream*; the dream is not in us. Upon awakening, however, ego consciousness reverses this relation and distances itself from the dream. The dream is now *in* the dreamer; the dreamer is no longer in the dream. Ego consciousness becomes the observer of its dreams, thereby allowing the possibility of subjecting them to interpretation. A fantasy of control and mastery of the dream arises, and one can even begin to program one's life based upon one's dreams. The nightly humiliation of ego consciousness, humbled by the dream, is forgotten and the ego imagines itself as the author rather than the agent of its dreamings. Indeed, this very attitude of inflation infects the *Cogito*, the "I think, therefore, I am" metaphysics of Descartes. In his *Meditations*, Descartes separates himself rather forcefully from the dream, which he equates with madness, and believes he has secured the safety of reason. At the beginnings of modernity, Descartes purifies reason of the dream and thereby sets the stage for the dream to haunt ego consciousness until it reappears again in the consulting rooms of Freud and Jung in relation to patients' symptoms.

The technology of virtual reality is a late twentieth-century version of the Grail, and to it the same question, "Whom does it serve?" applies. Will virtual reality be another way of mastering the dream, amplifying the hegemony of the *Cogito* that would purify itself of the dream? Will it lend technical assistance to the ego's dominion over the dream? Or will it serve to remind waking consciousness that dreaming belongs to reason and that, in having a dream, we are also always *had* by it? Will its technology serve the same function that the dream served in relation to the symptom— as the "royal road to the unconscious"? Whatever the answer, the technology of virtual reality brings the dream and the dreaming body before ego consciousness at the end of this century, just as it did at the beginning. The repetition should give us pause to wonder. From the viewpoint of the dreaming soul, have we failed to hear the message the first time around? Freud's psychoanalysis "challenged the ego with the dream, discovered the multiple ways in which the ego's efforts to make sense of life and to bring order to it were illusions." But the first major publication inaugurating psychoanalysis was *The Interpretation of Dreams*. In the art and the act of interpretation, Freud restored the ego's illusion of power over the dream. Was it a mistake, a refusal to hear the dream on its terms, inspired by an "ego consciousness too threateningly challenged by the dream?" *The Interpretation of Dreams* dates from 1900. Where will ego consciousness be in relation to the dream in the year 2000? Where will the technology of virtual reality lead us, or where will we lead it?

In cyberspace the virtual body is not marked by its interactions with the no-things of its virtual world, and it is this difference that suggested the parallel between the cyberbody and the dream body rather than between the cyberbody and the perceptual body of waking life. But while the cyberbody, which is digitally programmed and projected into virtual space, remains untouched, the fleshy body of the person who is wearing the goggles, the helmet, and the datagloves *is* affected.

This differentiation between two bodies in cyberspace, this co-existing on two levels simultaneously, is also true of the dream state. In dream space, the fleshy body and the dreaming body are co-present, and while the dreaming body is untouched by the no-things in the virtual landscapes of the dream, the fleshy body of the dreamer *is* affected. It is as if, in cyberspace and in dream space, the fleshy body sends an emissary into another time-space dimension and, by virtue of telepresence, experiences what that emissary experiences. Between the dream body both in dream space and cyberspace and the fleshy body, there is an experience by indirection, a communication by proxy, and yet a bond that is so intimate that finally the relation between the two can be understood only as a paradox. The dream body in dream space and cyberspace is identical with the flesh of the dreamer and the user, and also different from it.

The nightmare offers an example of this way in which the dream body in cyberspace parallels the dreaming body. Phenomenologically, a nightmare is the experience of being trapped within a terrifying story, a frightening world. The landscape of the nightmare is filled with danger and, within the virtual world of the dream, the dreaming body is hyper-alert, ever watchful, and in continuous flight. Pursued, the dreaming body attempts to escape, but the faster one runs, the more one feels overtaken by a relentless dread.

The physiology of nightmare faithfully mirrors this experience. The heart beats faster, the eyes move continuously and quite rapidly, and brain activity increases. It is the fleshy body that feels and registers the events which the dream body of the nightmare is experiencing. Folk wisdom acknowledges this sympathetic relationship between the dream body and the fleshy body in its belief that, if the dream body dies, then so, too, does the dreamer—and science fiction plays upon this belief. In the film *Dreamscape*, a technology is developed for the purpose of controlling dreams and the abuse of this power leads to murder. The murder, however, takes place in the virtual world of the dream. One dreamer enters the dream world of another dreamer, and when the former kills the dream body of the latter in the dream, the fleshy body of this murdered dreamer, the dreamer himself, dies.

Although the technology portrayed in the film seems farfetched, it is not too far removed from the possibilities that cyberspace already allows. In cyberspace one can enter into the virtual landscape of another user and actually participate in a shared activity. One of those activities is virtual sex, and it is quite obvious in this instance that the sexual interaction between two cyberbodies in virtual space affects the fleshy bodies of the two participants. If death has not yet entered the arena of cyberspace, orgasm certainly has. Indeed, according to Michael Heim, for science-fiction writer William Gibson, "cyber entities appear under the sign of Eros." Commenting on Gibson's work, Heim notes that the "fictional characters of *Neuromancer* experience the computer matrix— cyberspace— as a place of rapture and erotic intensity . . ." It is an intensity, he adds, that "inevitably conjures up the reference to orgasm . . ." Cyberspace is already the stuff of which erotic dreams are being made.

Dream and Reality

> Now she straddled him again, took his hand, and closed it over her, his thumb along the cleft of her buttocks, his fingers spread across the labia. As she began to lower herself, the images came pulsing back, the faces, fragments of neon arriving and receding. She slid down around him and his back arched convulsively. She rode him that way, impaling herself, slipping down on him again and again, until they both had come, his orgasm flaring blue in a timeless space, a vastness like the matrix, where the faces were shredded and blown away down hurricane corridors, and her inner thighs were strong and wet against his hips.

The passage above is from William Gibson's *Neuromancer*. Does it describe an event in real space or cyberspace? Is it real or cybersex? The technology of virtual reality collapses the difference. It erases the question, in fact, it collapses the boundaries between the real and the imaginal, fact and fiction, waking and dream. In cyberspace we are on the borderline of these categories, prompting again the suggestion made earlier that the pathology of borderline consciousness is the cultural symptomatic expression of an evolution and revolution in human psychological life engineered through the technology of virtual reality. The borderline, I suspect, lives in cyberspace, and when we enter cyberspace, I suspect we enter into borderline experience. To be in cyberspace is, in effect, to be on the borderline between waking and dreaming. Or perhaps it is better to say that, to be in cyberspace is to live a confused blending of waking and dreaming. But, however one might say it, it is apparent that in cyberspace one is, in effect, awake in one's dreams.

The collapse of the boundary between waking and dreaming indicates that the technology of virtual reality is not only mimicking the dream but is also remaking reality as dream. Indeed, virtual reality is dream consciousness now made visible, public, and programmable. Cyberspace is the u-topic place where the dream maker, once called the unconscious, has become conscious. It is the u-topic place where what was formerly unconscious has become a matter of technological wizardry. In a dramatic reversal of the origins of technological consciousness, outerspace has become dream space, and what began as a flight from the body and a departure from earth has become a flight into the depths of the dreaming soul. In cyberspace, technological consciousness has become dream consciousness.

Consequences of Virtual Reality

The technological culture within which we live incarnates the soul of our age, and if we are to understand ourselves psychologically, we need to understand not only the landscapes within which we dwell, but also *how* we dwell within them. Virtual reality is a landscape that we haunt with the body of the dream, and its oneiric character has political, ethical, and social consequences. Politically, we need to acknowledge that a potential for addiction to the pleasure of dreaming in cyberspace can leave the issue of who programs and controls the dreams unexamined. Indeed, something of this possibility already exists with the medium of television, where "talk shows, as public confessionals for the secrets of the soul, have become a form of mass hysteria made palatable as amusement." In such a situation, we run the risk of isolating those who have power from those who are simply to be amused.

Ethically, we need to recognize that no matter how intense the encounter between dream bodies in cyberspace, the fleshy body is erased from such encounters or, at best, participates only indirectly and privately. Reflecting on this situation, Michael Heim wonders, "How long and how deep are the personal relationships that develop outside embodied presence?" "Without the direct experience of the human face," he adds, "ethical awareness shrinks and rudeness enters." But it is not simply a matter of rudeness, of the loss of manners. It is also a matter of violence, of which examples abound in our culture. Without the medium of the other's fleshy presence, he or she is in danger of becoming only a telepresence, a presence without substance and hence without humanity.

Socially, the increasing expansion of the digital network has diminished the sense of neighborhood and of community. Cyberspace is an electronic community and the geographical distances which it spans make the intimacies of an organic community difficult, if not impossible. What creates and binds an organic community together are not only shared beliefs, but *enacted* shared beliefs communicated through the fleshy bodies of neighbors in a communal space of odors, textures, tastes, and gestures. Without such communal spaces, we run the risk of living in a reality without any sense of a center. In the electronic sprawl of cyberspace, we run the risk, finally, of losing our sense of home.

My thanks to Mr. Mark Kelly at Pacifica Graduate Institute. Our conversations are a continuing inspiration for this work, and his fund of knowledge, an apparently inexhaustible source, is an indispensable aid.

3

The Orphan and the Angel:
In Defense of Melancholy

And we, spectators always, everywhere,
looking at, never out of, everything!
It fills us, We arrange it. It decays.
We re-arrange it, and decay ourselves.

Who's turned us round like this, so that we always,
do what we may, retain the attitude
of someone who's departing? Just as he,
on the last hill, that shows him all his valley
for the last time, will turn and stop and linger,
we live our lives, for ever taking leave.

--Rainer Maria Rilke

I am sitting in my office, looking out the window toward the mountains.
How long have they endured! A mood of melancholy attends my vision. These
mountains, to which I feel so drawn, are so close and yet they are so far away.
Rilke's poetic image of the man on the hill, who for the last time surveys his
valley, who for a moment, for one final moment, stops and turns and lingers,
stirs the depths of my soul before it touches the surface of my life. Forever
taking leave, always on the verge of departing, we wander the world and always
along the way, at one time or another, we meet others and, together for a brief
moment, arrange things. We fall in love and care deeply, marry, raise a family,

start a work, become knitted into the fabric of a community. Yet all the while we always see with a deeper, third eye, the subtle erosion of all that was so patiently and lovingly built.

One by one the things we make slip away. One by one those whom we love pass on. Always in the dark silence of the night we know. Always in that deep hour of solitude we understand that, in spite of love, success, achievement, we are restless, beckoned beyond ourselves, called to another place. Before each morning's sun banishes these shadows of night, we feel in the deepest chambers of our hearts that we are still so far from *home*.

We live in a time when the things of the material world—the songs of the birds, the smell of the flowers, the endurance of the mountains, and yes, even the sound of the cool wind as it moves through the trees—bear continual witness to a melancholy. It is as if we have arrived at a moment in time when, having traveled so far from home, we are being addressed by those simple, daily things from which we have taken leave. Is it our melancholy that they address? Or is it theirs, the sadness of the things themselves? Or is it, truly, a melancholy which we share, which is now, at this moment in history, the bond that yokes us together?

I do not know the answer to these questions. But I do know that an abiding melancholy is the pervasive mood flowing beneath the surface of our lives as we approach, not only the end of a century, but also the end of a millennium. And I know, too, that this mood of melancholy betokens the presence of the Orphan, and as such, heralds a spiritual awakening. St. Augustine said that to be an orphan relates one to God. Rilke's poetic image, which stirs the depths before it touches the surface, taps the archetypal figure of the Orphan. It is the figure of the Orphan, with its mood and melancholy, who beckons us home, into the spiritual depths of our existence, and toward the Angel.

The Angel

It was the stillness that was most impressive . . . a kind of stillness I had felt only once before, in Africa . . . the stillness of the early morning of the world, before *we* came. It was *not* that *I* was aware of the silence. Rather it was only that *there was the silence*, a silence wrapped within itself, complete, fulfilled, without need of sound. This silence was its own consciousness, aware of itself as a slow, rhythmic, vaporous liquidity, the mist of the early morning of the world, floating, condensing, dissolving, congealing in a sleepy kind of dumbness. And the light, soft yellow-white, spreading itself with the mist, textured, itself a palpable thing, diaphanous, the veil of the world's first morning, gathering itself, and in the next moment an appearance. Formed, out of nothing but this light, a being so composed within itself, so tranquil, unstirred by the mist, calm, serene, beatific. A being so beautiful, before distinctions, neither male nor female in form nor young nor old in face, neither conscious nor unconscious, neither awake nor asleep. Creation's first image, before time, eternal, unmoved, so peaceful in its splendid indifference. Creation itself, the whole of it. So fierce its streaming beauty, so terrible its averted gaze! The mirror of our failure, the measure of our loss?

I shall not tell you the occasion of this encounter, the second of three, except to say that the occasion, the setting, mattered, and to add that some work which I was doing at the time seems, in retrospect, a kind of preparation. But I begin in this way, with fumbling words, because it is the truest thing I can say about the Angel, and the best. Against its silence, all else that I have to say seems a rather feeble effort to evoke that moment, to keep it open. I had wondered and thought about the Angel before this encounter, but now I only wait for its appearance and watch for its signs. Words can serve that function, the work of keeping a place open, the task of continued preparation.

Who is the Angel? Blaise Pascal, 17th-century philosopher, mathematician, polymath, looking into the endless depths of the heavens, felt the acute loneliness of our human condition and the anxiety that accompanies the recognition of the vast spaces of emptiness that engulf our mortal lives. He knew, too, the deep recesses of the human heart and that in these chambered spaces this "heart had its reasons which reason does not know."

Matters of the human heart, like the question of the Angel, always lie on the far side of either factual or logical proof. For the things that I am about to say, therefore, I can offer no proof. Or perhaps it is better to say that I can offer only the proof of the heart, the proof, for example, of the poetic image. Such a proof is an emotional proof, the opening to a truth that, in stirring the depths, moves us. It is what happens in the best moments of psychotherapy, where the wounds of soul are not healed by what we come to know or to understand, but by the fact that, via words, we are moved.

I depend on the poets, therefore, when confronted by questions about such a phenomenon as the Angel. I depend upon poets, as I do upon painters and musicians, all of whom explore those regions where reason is embroidered with dream and where fact is touched by the fairy wings of fiction. Indeed, poetry is praised by John Keats precisely for this power to release us from the truth into fiction.

"Tell all the truth," Emily Dickinson enjoins us, "but tell it slant." When the Angel comes, it is only out of the corner of one's eye that it can be seen. Only an oblique vision, a way of experiencing that eschews the focused stare of definition, can meet the Angel, and only a sideways telling—which sidesteps not only our defenses but also our rational criticisms—can properly serve that gaze. I know, for example, that the Angel and the Orphan are somehow one, that they are yoked together by the same mood of melancholy . . . that the Orphan is the way in which we touch the Angelic, and that this melancholy of the soul is the dim reminder, the aftertaste, as it were, of our Angelic existence. But if you ask me to prove what I know, to illustrate it with some reasonable precision, I cannot. I can only fumble for those slanted words, those metaphors, those poetic images, which indirectly allude to a reality that remains forever elusive. As a witness I can offer only some testimony to those experiences of the invisible which, on occasion, part the curtains of reality—of the tangible, visible, sensible world—and open us to the awe of creation and to the terrible kind of beauty that attends that opening.

"Every angel is terrible," says Rilke, and in saying so, he acknowledges one of those moments of mystery when the veils of perception lift from our eyes and we stand, motionless, for a small, brief moment, between two worlds. The terrible Angel is an earthquake of the soul, a tear in the fabric of space and time, a miracle. Rilke addresses Angels as "almost deadly birds of the soul," "early successes, creation's pampered darlings." They are "dawn red ridges of all beginning,— pollen of blossoming godhead," emptying or exploding like seeds out of the center of creation, cascading and tumbling into the corridors of time to germinate in the recessed chambers of the human heart. "Hinges of light," he calls them, shining pivots of energy, shimmering, resonating, vibrating frequencies which we, with our own poor consciousness, can tune into with only just enough awareness to be filled with longing. "Shields of felicity, tumults of stormily-rapturous feeling, and suddenly, separate," the Angel is aloof, withdrawn, nearly beyond the boundaries of our gaze, and, yes, even indifferent to our presence. Imagine Angels as "mirrors, drawing up their own outstreamed beauty into their faces again." In such a moment one is struck dumb, as those of old were: "So fierce its streaming beauty, so terrible its averted gaze!"

Again I ask, "Who is the Angel?" An imaginal being? That seems too poor, almost a debasement, of its radical otherness. Indeed, that is the major sadness of much that is being said and written today about the Angel. So much of it brings the Angel into the human realm, reduces the Angel to a guardian, a friend, a companion, a messenger. So much of it is filled with advice about channeling or evoking one's Angel, including instructions. Certainly I recognize a genuine human hunger at the core of all this Angel talk today, but I believe we unwittingly reinforce our *spiritual starvation* to the degree that we appropriate the Angel so quickly, to the degree that we domesticate the Angel and rob it of its awe-ful splendor. When the Angel comes, it comes unbidden, and it is we who are addressed, challenged, called. The Angel is a moment of breakdown which, if we tend its vocation, might herald a break*through*. But even that is not a promise, because whatever else the Angel might be, it is not within our ken.

We cannot say the Angel is a symbol either, because the Angel lies beyond our understanding. To under-stand something or someone is to *stand under* it, ground it, to give it our support. If anything, it is the other way round with the Angel. To be sure, we do symbolize the Angel; the great Medieval paintings of the Angel, with its dominant size and powerful wings, are a treat for the eye. But the symbol only alludes to what remains elusive. It yokes together, *in a tension that must always remain unstable,* the visible and the invisible. Indeed, *at its best, the symbol allows, and even encourages, what it would momentarily grasp to fly away instead.* And perhaps that is the purpose of those majestic Angelic wings, to remind us that whatever and however Angels might be, they fly from our grasp, always escaping our comprehension. We who depend so much upon the visible are always in danger of yoking the invisible, to which the symbol alludes, too tightly to the visible, which it portrays.

We do better, therefore, to attend to the Angel through what Jung has called the feeling function. We best grasp, however lightly and briefly, the Angel's presence by attending to shifts in mood, to changes in the landscape's emotional tone. These "tumults of stormily-rapturous feeling" can still the air. These "almost deadly birds of the soul" can shake a tranquil heart. And at this feeling level, I am persuaded of the immense gap between the Angel and us. At the feeling level the Angel is the being who validates our highest but dimmest inspirations, and also the figure who reminds us of the distance between what we are and would become . . . or perhaps it is equally true to say of *what we are* and *what we (once) were.* In its presence nothing is certain except knowledge, born of feeling, that the Angel is not us; indeed, it displays what we are *not*: the *other*, which the human heart veers toward but never reaches, the shapers of our sense of the real.

It is the tone of sadness which has persuaded me most about the presence of the Angel, this mood of melancholy. I do not know if we suffer this mood today more than our ancestors did, nor do I know if melancholy has always tended the presence of the Angel. But I sense today that it does, that melancholy is the Angel's way of tapping us. *And I wonder if this melancholy is an aftertaste of an Angelic existence, or perhaps a foretaste, or perhaps a bit of both.* In *The*

Prophetic Imagination, Walter Brueggemann writes that grief is "radical criticism." Certainly grief is a pathway into melancholy. Could it be, then, that *melancholy is a way in which we are being opened to the Angel, so that we might begin that work of radical criticism* . . . that work of reflection, which asks us to reach deeply into the core of our lives, to open our hearts, in order to recover what we have lost, in order to remember what we have forgotten? Criticism is a pause, an invitation to listen. When the Angel enters *through* or *as* melancholy, to what are we being asked to listen? In *Technology as Symptom and Dream* I wrote the following:

> It is not enough only *to fear* the horrible destructiveness of an imagined holocaust. We also need *to mourn* now, in the present, the loss of *all* that faces us, that is near to us, that matters to us. We need to develop the capacity to feel the sorrow of the trees, the lament of the oceans, the sadness of the stars.

Is this what we are being called to hear? Is it the dying of creation to which the Angel now *awakens* us? And do we have to be called to this sorrow, which the things of the world are now bearing because we have grown so far away from the world, because we have gone so far from home? Have we become so distant, to remote, so removed from creation, that we are no longer able to respond to the simple appeal of things? And, thus, unable to respond, have we become irresponsible, careless, neglectful, and, yes, even destructive? Rilke knew this simplicity of things, this appeal they lay before us:

> These things that live on departure
> understand when you praise them: fleeting, they look for
> rescue through something in us, the most fleeting of all.

The Angel comes through our feeling function and, as a mood of melancholy, touches the Orphan in us, which is the beginning of spiritual transformation. Becoming awakened to the Orphan is the necessary precondition for hearing the lament of the world, for witnessing its dying, and perhaps, if we are lucky, assisting in its healing. Political action is necessary, but it is not enough. Today we desperately need a transformation of soul, a spiritual revolution. And we need to be awakened in this way *not* in order to save ourselves or to save the world. Too much of the old arrogance clings to such dreams, too much of our busyness, our hyperactivity, our stubborn refusal to listen. On the contrary, we need to be awakened in order *to be saved.* We have forfeited our birthright in the scheme of creation, and as such we have lost any right, if we ever really had one, to save the world. Only the world can save us. We need this humility. We need to learn again how to pray.

The words I have just written echo in my ears, and I wonder if they sound as strange to others as they do to me. How have I come to this place? How has the vocation of psychotherapy, the confines of the consulting room, led to Angels and to prayer? What labyrinths have I wandered with my patients, such that the sufferings of the individual soul have led to the sufferings of the world? But again I have no answer. The only thought that comes to mind is a line from John Milton: "They also serve who only stand and wait." Yes, for me, that seems right. Psychotherapy is, among other things, the act of waiting and the practice of taking a stand, as a witness, for what asks to be heard.

Touched by the Angel we wait, we listen, and we bear witness as orphans. Earlier I asked, "Who is the Angel?" Now I ask, "Who is the Orphan?"

The Orphan

The poet's image of the man on the hill, overlooking his valley for the last time, is where we first met the figure of the Orphan. Forever taking leave, always on the verge of departing, the Orphan is the one perpetually in search of *home.* The image conveys distances, separation, broken connections. It also conveys the longing and the tension of being *between* a home, which is a heritage, and one that beckons as a destiny.

We are not Angels, and yet, through our melancholy, we are awakened to a horizon that claims us. In such a moment we begin to understand that to move toward the Angelic, perhaps as our destiny, requires a leave-taking, and perhaps we also recognize that we have already taken leave. Somewhere in the early morning of the world, when the Angel and the Panther were one, we began a journey. Becoming conscious of being conscious, aware of being aware, we parted company with the Animal and took the first steps to distance ourselves from the order of creation.

A few years ago I took a drive with a colleague to see something of the rugged Oregon coastline. Quite unexpectedly we encountered an invitation, a sign on the side of the road, that said Sea Lion Cave, so many miles ahead. It was raining and cloudy, as it has been for the four or five days we had been in Oregon, so it seemed like a good idea to have a destination. Along

the way I noticed whales, dolphins, and sea lions swimming down the coast—
or at least that was my vision, perhaps colored by the anticipation of what
the caves would offer.

At the entrance to the cave is a series of long, windings stairs leading
to an elevator, which took us the last three hundred feet or so into its
depths. By the time we arrived, the day was already quite chilly and the
wind, needle-like in its sharpness, whipped our faces as we stood on the
outside platform awaiting our descent. Low angry clouds hung close to the
water, intensifying my growing feeling of quiet isolation, as if the world
was silencing the busy ways of human consciousness in the physiognomy
of this landscape.

Much of my life's concern for soul has been nurtured by these kinds of
moments, and the best that I have been—either as a therapist, teacher, or
writer—has been only the translation of such moments into word and
image. For this reason I have felt and known for a long time that at our best
moments we are always surprised, and that fundamentally we are never the
authors of meaning but its agents—agents of, or witness for, soul in its
desires for revelation. Still I was not prepared for this moment, when the
door of the elevator opened and we descended the final flights of stairs
into the cave. The journey I had been taking in the world found its reflection
as a journey of soul.

The sea lions are visible from a platform perhaps fifty feet above the
hollowed-out inlet—females actually, with their pups born from the last
mating. It is the largest rookery on the North American coastline, a deep,
wide scar cut into the rocks by the perpetual thrashing of the ocean tides.
How long this has gone on is difficult to say, but one cannot escape the
impression of a kind of patient force at work here, a force of wind and tide
marked with the index of eternity. Layer upon layer of rock has been sculpted
by these forces, and once our eyes became accustomed to the darkness in
which we stood, we saw that almost every inch of layered rock was pulsating
and quivering, animated by the sea lions that inhabit the place. Actually,
long before we saw these creatures, we heard their incessant, continuous
barking. Deep, throaty sounds already shaped the deep cave and, all around,
those sounds and their echoes filled the air with a sense of perpetual,
unending hunger. Here, in the descent into this cave, I could hear the
insatiable hungers of the animal soul, barking, pounding, rhythmical
crescendos of longing, crashing like the tides against the rocks in the darkness
of the everlasting night, blind appetites knowing nothing but hunger and

its urgencies. Animal flesh: appetitive, instinctual, voracious, and eternal—the terror of the dark and of blind, carnal hunger.

I stood there, mesmerized by the sound, lost within it. Indeed it was only in retrospect, only after noticing another feature of the landscape, that I realized the power of this event and why and how it had affected me as it did. What broke me away from the scene, what freed me, so to speak, from this eternal sea of instinctual hungers, was the dim ray of light that weakly, so very weakly, was struggling to enter the cave from the upper right. I was caught by the light when I saw it, especially by its feebleness, and in a strange way I knew that somehow I was that light in the midst of all that darkness, struggling with the darkness, and perhaps even against it. In that moment, with a feeling of awe, terror, and sadness, I also knew that it was that light that distanced me from those sea lions, that light which placed between me and them an unbridgeable gap . . . that light, which was—at that moment, and had been, once before in the dawn of human consciousness—the tremulous bridge we had crossed out of the blindness of those instinctual hungers, out of the darkness of the night.

It was time to leave. As I turned away from this scene which had given me this gift, I noticed that the sounds had grown farther away. When I rode the elevator up to the surface, Rilke's words came to mind: "and already the knowing brutes are aware/ that we don't feel very securely at home/ within our interpreted world . . ."

Rilke's words have a tone of melancholy about them. Looked at from the point of view of the Animal, those knowing brutes, our world often does seem a hollow home. Indeed, meditating on Angel and Animal, Rilke says:

And yet, within the wakefully-warm beast
there lies the weight and care of a great
sadness.
For that which often overwhelms us clings
to him as well, a kind of memory
that what we're pressing after now was once
nearer and truer and attached to us
with infinite tenderness. Here all is distance,
there is was breath. Compared with that first home
the second seems ambiguous and draughty.
Oh bliss of *tiny* creatures that *remain*

forever in the womb that brought them forth!
Joy of the gnat, that can still leap *within*,
even on its wedding day: for womb is all.

What I find astonishing in these words is the way in which Rilke invites us to become acquainted with our melancholy. "The weight and care of a great sadness" that lies within the "wakefully-warm beast" is the memory of a kinship we once seemed to share. For the poet, and thus too for the poetic dimension of our souls, it is as if the Animal dimly remembers for us our departure. It is as if the sadness of this knowing brute is for our folly, for the way in which we continually press after something which once, in the early morning of the world, was perhaps nearer and truer and already attached to us with that infinite tenderness about which the poet speaks. It is as if the Animal marks with its sadness our loss of home, longs for our return, bears witness for a kinship we once shared but then sacrificed when we followed the light. It is as if the Animal awaits and desires our homecoming.

It would be a grave mistake to anthropomorphize the poet's sensibility; it would be a cheap psychology to see within the poet's vision a projection onto nature of our own romantic yearnings. The poet works in the imaginal realm, in that space between the empiricism of facts and the rationalism of ideas. Such a space is always *prior to* the separation of us from the world, *prior to* the split of a subjective knower and an objective world. In the imaginal realm of the heart, the flesh of body and that of world are a *con-spiracy*, a breathing together, an intimacy as close as the ties of love. Indeed, this engagement of two bodies, ours and that of the world, this intercourse of the imaginal, is the very root of language. Before meaning there is desire. Every word ever uttered by the human voice was first and originally a way of giving breath and sound to the soul of the world. Inspired by the world, we take in with every breath in the moment of *in-spiration* that which surrounds us, and in the next moment, the one *ex-piration*, we breath out and transform air into word.

Perhaps the sadness which the Animal holds for us in the space between us is in faithful remembrance of the *sacrifice* we have made in crossing to the light. In becoming conscious of the world in a human way, we have participated in its continuous *real-ization*, in the continuous creation of this world. But to do so we had to take leave of the world's intimate embrace of us, and in doing so it seems we have forgotten our mission, forgotten that we have been ordained, as it were, to assist the evolution of creation. We speak but no longer hear the voice of the world. We speak and proclaim ourselves the authors of meaning, forgetting we are, at our best, the agents of a continual unfolding of creation. The Animal's melancholy recognizes that sacrifice, a mood of kin for kin, just as it is also a sad remembrance of how we seem to have lost our way.

It was a winter day during a visit I made to the Central Park Zoo in New York City. I have always been drawn to zoos in moments of melancholy, drawn to them by loneliness and a hunger which pulls me toward the Animal. Winter days, particularly in mid-week, have always been the best season and time for me to visit, because I have had in such moments some solitude, some private time with the Animal.

On this occasion I was going to see the gorillas, which the zoo still housed at that time. Standing in front of the cage of a large silver-back male, I felt the presence of the bars between us. The gorilla was sitting in the front corner of his cage, and I could see him only in profile. On occasion, however, as gorillas will do with zoo visitors, he would turn his head for a quick glance in my direction. His deeply set dark black eyes seemed like pools of time, and in those few brief moments of exchange I felt dizzy, as if I could swim through his eyes into another world. But the gorilla would just as quickly look away, and the spell would be broken.

The cage was so small, especially for so large an animal, and I wondered how he could bear it. His lethargy was inescapable, and I thought of the many hours of boredom he must daily endure, wondering, too, if I was reading my own sense of loneliness through him. But I had also been with animals in the wild, and the difference in behavior, in gesture, and in that imaginal space between us was pronounced. Caught up in these reveries, I had absent-mindedly withdrawn an orange from my pocket and was tossing it in the air. The gorilla turned and began to watch me. Without thinking I tossed the orange through the bars to him, momentarily oblivious to the prohibition about feeding the animals. The toss of the orange through the bars covered a distance of only a few feet in "real" space and took perhaps only a second in "real" time. But the gesture, and what unexpectedly followed, bridged an ocean of time and space.

One would have expected the gorilla to take the orange and retreat to a far corner of the cage to eat it. But the gorilla of this day did not do that. On the contrary, he tossed it through the bars back to me, I caught it, and in my astonishment, I tossed it to him again. We continued like this for perhaps three exchanges, until this rhythm between us, this embrace of a game, was broken by the sound of a voice from the far end of the corridor.

"Don't feed the animals!" When I turned toward the voice, the gorilla turned away. He moved to the far end of the cage. He kept the orange.

I left the zoo and walked out into the city. The cold, bright, winter afternoon did little to cheer the sadness I felt at having left the gorilla inside. I was different, changed by that encounter, even more lonely in the midst of a crowded city. The gorilla had suspended his appetite for a moment. For the sake of an encounter, he had bridged an immense gap between our worlds. In his gesture of tossing the orange back to me, he had reached out his hand across an emptiness so vast as to be beyond measure. Together we had built a tremulous bridge of gestures, and for a brief time we stood on opposite sides of that bridge, connected in a way that seemed to acknowledge in each other a lost kinship. Even to this day, nearly twenty years later, I know that I shall never forget the eyes of my winter companion on that day. He remembered me, and as strange as it may sound, I felt so grateful for that recognition. But I also felt how far I had come, and I knew with a deep feeling of sadness that we would remain forevermore on opposite sides of this bridge, and that at the best moments of my life, I would be able to stop and linger and turn round to see, once again, what was left behind. I knew that, and I knew, too, that what I saw in his eyes before the spell was broken was his sadness for me.

Living In-Between

Our second home, "our interpreted world" about which Rilke speaks, the city of that winter day of long ago, is an ambiguous, dubious achievement. Rilke calls it "draughty," and how true that can be, especially when the winds of some deep sorrow whistle through the cracks in the walls of meaning we build to deal with suffering, with pain, with absence, loss, grief. In such moments, in the depths of our bones, we feel the cold draftiness of our place *between* the sleepy dumbness of the Animal and the self-contained narcissism of the Angel. Like the man on the hill who views his valley for the last time, we have departed. And like that same man, or woman, we have not yet arrived at that place toward which we are going.

Tempted by the light, we truly are beings of the between, stretched between two longings—between, perhaps, what once was and, perhaps, what will be—far from the Animal and even farther still from the Angel, orphaned between the heritage of nature and the destiny of the stars. Yet in this place, on this earth, we make our way: between lightness and darkness, meaning and ignorance, knowing and not knowing, we live our lives; between sickness and health, life and death, body and mind, we fashion our characters; between evil and virtue, sin and salvation, heaven and earth, we dream our dreams; between love and hate, joy and sorrow, community and isolation, we wait for tomorrow.

The between *is* our place, and in the end, our condition of being an Orphan is our privilege. Indeed, to be awakened to it through the mood of melancholy is a blessing. Melancholy is the beginning of a spiritual transformation which allows us to begin to know that, as Orphans between the Animal and the Angel, we have the special work of continuing the world's *real-ization*. When Jungian psychology describes the process of individuation as an ongoing incarnation of God for the sake of divine transformation, it is underwriting what Augustine knew so long ago: that to be an Orphan—or a widow, Augustine also says— relates one to God. The Orphan is our god face. It is the moment when we are first made *able-to-respond* to the call of becoming truly who we are, who we are destined to be. It is the moment when we are first able to become *response-able* as creation's continuing witness for *its* real-ization.

Accepting the *responsibility* of our orphanhood, we become faithful sentinels for the passing and the flowering of the world. The Animal *perishes*, the Angel is *eternal,* but we *die*. In this difference, in this space between Angel and Animal lies our glory as an Orphan. Here, in the between, we become the spokespeople for the continuing miracle of creation. Here, in the between, we turn, we stop, we look, we linger, we behold, and we have drawn out of us the power of the word. We speak and proclaim.

"Earth, isn't this what you want: an invisible re-arising in us?" Rilke asks. Yes, is his reply! Yes, again and again:

> For the wanderer doesn't bring from the mountain slope
> a handful of earth to the valley, untellable earth, but only
> some word he has won, a pure word, the yellow and blue
> gentian.

We are called to speak, called out by the world, but to hear this call requires again that mood of melancholy, which opens us to the solitude and the silence within which we can discern our vocation:

> Are we, perhaps, here just for saying: House,
> Bridge, Fountain, Gate, Jug, Olive tree, Window,—
> possibly: Pillar, Tower? . . . but for saying, remember,
> oh, for such saying as never the things themselves

hoped so intensely to be.

Such an awesome responsibility the Orphan carries. *Possibly* we are called to say *pillar, tower,* Rilke says. *Possibly!* Something so simple as this act, this gesture, one word, and still it is weighted with caution, with care, with concern. But of our responsibility there is no doubt: "Here is the time for the tellable, here is its home/ Speak and proclaim."

Indeed, to speak is our privilege, and a gesture which we are to make even to the Angel.

> Praise the world to the Angel, not the untellable: you
> can't impress him with the splendor you've felt; in the cosmos
> where he more feelingly feels you're only a tyro. So show him
> some simple thing, remolded by age after age,
> till it lives in our hands and eyes as part of ourselves.
> Tell him *things*.

I have wondered at times if the Angel, in tapping into us through our melancholy, desires nothing more than a word. Neither Angel nor Animal speaks, but *we* do, and when we speak out of those depths of melancholy, when the Orphan in us speaks, are we perhaps the envy of Angels? Wim Wenders' *Wings of Desire* suggests as much. Perhaps, indeed, he is correct. Perhaps we truly are the envy of the Angel:

> Angels wish they had beards
> To enjoy the pleasure of the sound
> of scrapping the passage of time from faces
> worn with sorrows, lighted with joys.
> They wish too to sense the clarity of lemons
> and to smell the scent of someone in love.
> They want to hear a lover say,
> "I will always tease your flesh."
> In their airy kingdoms beyond this world,
> In their beautiful indifference,
> In their silent stillness,
> They dream, always, their own betrayals:
> To grow old and ill, even to die,
> And to hear a lover say,
> even once, if only once,

"I would rather lose you to another lover than to God."

At night, when the last patient has gone, when the lights have been dimmed, I wonder about this strange vocation of psychotherapy, which I have practiced for a quarter of a century. So many ways of being injured, so many sorrows, so many tears, so many losses! And all the patients I have seen, the dreams I have listened to, in this place, the therapy room, so small a container! I am tired, my eyes close, and the room dissolves. Patients' faces, their voices, begin to melt away, and long corridors of time open before me.

Somewhere in the midst of time there was a moment when a spark ignited between Animal and Angel, and the Orphan was born. We are the continuance of that moment, a small flame that lights the way toward creation's continuing evolution. Burden and privilege! We are the arc that connects matter and spirit, the pivot around which the Animal and Angel dance, beings with two faces, who remember the early morning of the world when Angel and Panther were one, and who are continually called to bring that first morning into tomorrow.

Between that first morning and tomorrow we are asked to endure, to live our lives, to bear our burdens, to love our families, to bury the dead. It is so difficult a place to be, yet it *is* the only place we have. Rilke says:

> Between the hammers lives on
> our heart, as between the teeth
> the tongue, which, nevertheless,
> remains the bestower of praise.

So fine an image: The tongue between the teeth continues to praise. In the spiritual transformation which melancholy initiates, the "orphanic" voice registers the instinctual cry of the Animal and the holy, holy, holy of the Angel. In the midst of our sorrows we are always so much less than we would be, so far from that holy, holy, holy, but also so much more than what we are. In the mirror of the world, the Orphan is the one who sees two faces, Animal and Angel, each turning round the other, *our* god face, the face of god.

4

Psychotherapy as Griefwork: Ghosts and the Gestures of Compassion

On Stage

I first met Michael when he was a student in one of my undergraduate psychology classes. He was a drama major at the university where I was a guest lecturer, and at that time one of the bright lights of its theater. He was one of several theater people, who, during the past year, were attending my classes, and I generally found them to be the most interesting of my students. It was not only their eccentricity that made them stand out. More to the point, it was their sense of dramatic presence that I noticed. In retrospect, I now recognize that this dramatic presence was inseparable from the ways in which they inhabited the space of the classroom. At that time, I did not have the language, but, looking back, I intuitively knew that they thought with the liveliness of their gestures, and as a psychologist and psychotherapist trained in phenomenology I was sensitive to these nuances: the tilt of a head in making a point, or the movement of a hand in sweeping out an arc in the space of a question or a comment. This was nearly twenty years ago, and little did I realize then that this was the beginning of a small revolution in my ways of knowing and being.

Of all those many students whom I taught and recall, the one who haunts me now, as I write these pages, is Michael. He was a tall, swarthy, handsome young man whose intensity was immediately evident in the fierce glow of dark, gypsy eyes, and the chiseled hardness of a firm jaw. Often, after class, he would sit with me over a cappuccino and he would talk, not about his studies or his acting but mainly about himself, and especially about his deep sense of loneliness. It was in these moments I saw how young he was and how at odds his intensity was with this vulnerability. It was also in these moments that I learned a remarkable fact. Michael suffered, often quite painfully, from intense bouts of nausea which frequently enough resulted in severe spells of vomiting, and he had already been diagnosed as having a gastric ulcer. One of his great fears, he said, was that such an attack would happen on stage, and indeed it was the case that some of his worst moments occurred when he was waiting in the wings for his cue to enter the performance. Remarkably, however, none of these fears were ever realized when he was on stage. Quite the contrary! Crossing that magic threshold which separated the wings from the stage, Michael was in a sense always re-created. He was, he said, no longer himself and he experienced this difference not as an idea but in a deeply felt embodied way.

Even now after twenty years, I remember my thought at that moment: the body on stage, unlike Michael's body, did not have an ulcer. The body of Michael the actor and the body of the characters Michael portrayed were different bodies. When I next saw him on stage, I could not help but notice how this difference revealed itself. On stage, Michael was bigger and his gestures more fluid and expansive than in lived life.

It was in watching Michael on stage that I first understood that the lived body of phenomenology is most radically a gestural body. It is not the lived body which makes gestures or out of which gestures flow, like water from a container. Rather, it is the gestures which create the lived body, the water in its flowing which creates the vessel.

Getting into Character

Over the intervening years, I have learned much from my work with actors, actresses and directors. Like Michael, Alex also was one of my teachers. A graduate student in performing arts, Alex was the one who helped me understand how the actor gets into character. Over the course of many conversations, I learned that for many actors and actresses the defining moment comes when the gestures of the character to be portrayed are captured and impregnate the body of the actor. Alex told me that the lines to be memorized came alive only in the movements and gestures that accompanied them, and until that moment the dialogue remained in the mind. From Alex I learned to speak about the muscular incarnation of memory, and I learned to appreciate how central it is for the memories of mind to become gestures of flesh. Years later I came upon an interview with the great English actor Anthony Hopkins. In this interview he said that he finally understood the character of Picasso (whom he was portraying in that film) one morning when he was descending the stairs on his way to breakfast. It was in the movement of walking in a certain way, of going down a staircase, and in the gestures of the arms and trunk and legs which accompany such a movement that Picasso was born in him. I recall how incredulous the interviewer seemed, for it was no grand theory that Hopkins was presenting to indicate how an actor gets into character. It was, rather, something quite simple and ordinary, and yet most profound. By waiting for the gestures, by making oneself a vehicle to be impregnated by the other, the character was/is born. When you watch an actor like Hopkins, or Robert Duvall, or Dustin Hoffman, you can see that transformation when the person of the actor fades and the figure of the character appears. The gesture creates the body.

It was through this relationship with Alex that my work with dreams was changed. Dream interpretation always seemed to me to be more in the service of the therapist and his or her theories than in the service of the patient. It was not that dream interpretation did not have value, for I frequently witnessed its effectiveness both in regard to my own dreams and those of my patients. What always seemed lacking, however, was that muscular, incarnational sense of validity which would make the interpretation vital, which would move its understanding closer to the dream as it was dreamed in all its felt bodily sense. Taking the clue of how the actor gets into character, I began to do dream enactment, inviting the dreamer to take on the gestures and character of the dream figures. Candace DuPuy, one of my graduate students at Pacifica Graduate Institute, wrote her doctoral dissertation on this topic.[1] In her study, she has shown how the multiple techniques an actor/actress uses for getting into character are applicable to dream work. All these techniques emphasize a phenomenology of the senses, an acute attunement of the body to the nuances of the situation. In my own work, gesture is the term I use to contain all the multiple ways of *making sense* of the world in its varied textures, moods, contours, seasons, shapes, directions, colors, and lighting. In the gesture, the body holds and unfolds, like a flower in the sun, these multiple, evanescent, ephemeral impressions. Watching the gesture you enter a world of experience. The gesture is the portal through which each of us enters into the mystery of the other. It is a magic mirror, a dynamic mirror, through which you and I meet and are transformed.[2]

The use of dream enactment requires a careful regard, because it effects a powerful release of memories and emotions. Indeed, it is not unlike the way in which we are affected and moved by a superlative dramatic performance. Only it is more so, because it is, so to speak, closer to the bone. The dream body enacted is and is not you, and indeed I suspect that this confusion of identify and difference is closer to the phenomenology of the actor on stage than is my earlier assertion in this essay regarding Michael. The body of the actor-actress is *and* is not the character's body, just as you and I are and are not ourselves in our moments of encounter. Your gestures decenter me, and mine you. A gesture is the power to dissolve and recreate in the moment who each of us. Each gesture is a potential *ec-stasy.*

Speaking in this way, I am moving toward the claim that the gesture is a field which precedes me and you. Depth psychology long ago recognized this fact in calling attention to the theme of transference, but it has sadly mis-placed it by linking it to the notion of projection, a term which still smacks of a Cartesian splitting between self and other, me and you, body and world. A phenomenology of the body revisions transference as a gestural field, and emphasizes that it is the field that is primary, the gestural field out of which you and I blossom and fade. You and I no more precede this gestural field, than the lived body precedes the gestures which create it. Or said in another way, it is you who give me "my" gestural body just as I give you yours, with you and I understood here not as elements within a field but as the precipatates or crystallizations out of the field. To do dream enactment, then, is to be given an-other gestural body by the figures of the dream.[3]

Considerations of space prohibit me from saying much more about dream enactment. I would like, however, simply to indicate those steps which I follow in the process, because they give an indication of the bodily complexity and the leveled nuances involved in this focus on the gesture. The sequence is not a fixed schedule. It is heuristic, attuned to the situation and its shifting moments:

1.   Breathe and pay attention only to your breathing. More and more allow yourself to become your breathing, to become the act of your breathing. As you let yourself surrender to the act of your breathing, you will feel more and more relaxed. Give yourself over to this deep feeling of peace and relaxation. Become your breathing, float on it as if you were a cloud, floating in the sky, drifting, carried by the wind. Surrender to that larger field of your breathing. Let yourself be held and contained by your breath.

2.   When you are in this deep sense of relaxation, allow yourself to recall

a dream. Wait on it, and wait for an image from it to appear. Allow a dream figure to approach you. Let it be there in front of you. Attend to it with a state of open curiosity.

3.   Carefully allow that dream figure to in-spire you. Breathe the dream figure in, take it in with every breath so that you can actually begin to see and to experience how it dissolves and becomes part of you, part of the very act of your breathing, part of the marrow of your bone, and the blood coursing through your veins.

4.   Once you have allowed yourself to be in-spired by the figure of the dream, wait. Wait until it moves you. Lend your body to the dream figure and wait for what it wants from you. If it helps, you might imagine a question: what gesture, what movement, what posture, what action does this figure want?

5.   Without judgment or criticism, without interpretation, allow that gesture to take place. Follow its movement. Stay with the gesture. Stay with the movement for as many enactments as it needs or wants. It might be helpful at this moment to do the movement slowly, to enact the gesture in a slow, rhythmical manner. Allow this to take place until this movement, this gesture, seems finished.

6.   Now it is important to let the dream figure go. Now it is important to pay attention to the out breathing. With each breath that you exhale, begin to see the figure forming again in front of you. Do so until the figure is as complete as it was in the moment just before you allowed it to in-spire you. Attend to that figure now as it stands there over in front of you.

7.   When that moment seems completed, offer a gesture or a word of thanksgiving.

8.   Attend now to what you need at the moment. Attend to your feelings. Attend to your felt bodily senses and do the gesture or the gestures that seem to express those feelings.

I have indicated in brief form the sequence which I use to do dream enactment. I have done so in order to emphasize not only the complexity involved in this focus on the gesture, but also to highlight the very important moment of thanksgiving. In doing this work, I have learned that this moment of differentiating oneself from the dream figure which has in-spired you is crucial. This moment of letting go is as important as the moment of in-spiration, the breathing out of the dream figure as important as the moment of taking it in.

Grief

While my work with actors and actresses taught me to appreciate the gesture and the gestural field, it was a shattering personal loss and its attendant grief which brought me to a deeper understanding of the relational character of the gesture.

Grief is a cellular matter. When the one who has been your spouse, your lover, your companion, and your friend has died, it is the body in its deepest levels and rhythms which measures the time of grief and mourning. No act of will, no decisions of the mind matter, because grief is the winter of the soul, and like the seasons it can only be endured. And in this time of endurance, there is only a waiting. One lives a kind of cocoon existence: the world fades and the body shrinks into the space of its grieving.

In *The Orphan and Angel: Grief and the Reveries of Love*, I presented a poetics of the mourning process, and here is neither the time nor place to present it again.[4] Let me say only that this poetics of mourning emphasizes how the grieving process is a dying of that gestural body formed in a relation with the one who has died. In this dying of the gestural body, conscious awareness of the loss is never enough. Slowly, ever so slowly, each gesture which tied you to the other is continually made and undone in the absence of that other. The right arm which unthinkingly one always draped over the shoulder of the other no longer finds its reciprocal in the world. Or the hand which grasped the hand of the other reaches out and encounters only a void.

At first there is a kind a haunting and the other who has gone lingers as an absent-presence, soliciting the gesture without confirming it. The haunting, like the seasons of the world, has its own rhythms, while the grieving you continues to exist in a world where your haunted body has no place. An awkwardness ensues, registering the disjunction and disharmony between the world which continues on its way and your failed gestures. At the same time a shrinkage begins, as the repeated gestures, made with their own volition, become more and more like a phantom limb, until the once familiar body you were begins the slow process of dying. The gestural body made in relation to the other who now lingers as a ghost fades, slowly, into a kind of invisibility, and you actually do feel that you have become a shade, pale, lifeless, thin, without the spark of any animation, so far away now that the world's appeals no longer solicit you. You live in limbo. You live suspended in a world between the living and the dead.

I learned in a deeply painful way that there is no way out of this moment, which I called a cocoon, and that there is no guarantee that one can or will emerge from it. And so in *The Orphan and the Angel* I gave only a poetics of the experience, a description of it, and not a psychology addressed either as an explanation or as advice. That for me the mourning blossomed into love is a miracle. I can say only that this blossoming began as and continues also at the cellular level as the crafting of a new gestural body in a field of love. And those who know me well register this change, for they mirror back to me what I, myself, feel in the deep marrow of my bones: that in saying I have changed, I am saying that I have been given a new body. Its gestures are looser, more fluid, and much amplified and it is no surprise to me, therefore, that my writing has also changed.

A Phenomenology of the Gesture

At the Doorway

He was about seventy, and maybe about seventy-five, an old man with thinning white hair, shoulders bent by age, a slight limp in his walk, accompanied by a woman, whom I assumed to be his wife, a woman about as old as he, also with white hair, but straighter in her posture and more supple in her walk. They approached the door of the coffee shop as I was about to leave. Opening the door for them, I stepped aside, but the old man took the door in his right hand, and, with a sweeping gesture of his left arm accompanied by a very slight bow and a very broad smile, he ushered me across the threshold and into my day. We exchanged only one word, the thanks which I spoke as I passed them. Beyond that one word something like a small miracle happened, and though I never saw them again I have remembered that moment, that brief moment, these long years.

At the threshold the old man outlined with his gesture a whole universe of manners, a landscape of civility, an old world of grace and charm, whose space and time echoed an earlier, slower, more quiet rhythm. Present to that gesture, I was offered a kind of citizenship in the world that it carved out, gifted with a sense of belonging to a common space, a community, a tradition of which somehow I was already a part but had forgotten. Beyond that man, his wife, and myself, the gesture brought with it an assembly of all those others who belonged to that old world of practiced etiquette, polite manners, genuine respect and measured patience. Later I found myself thinking of my father and remembering those long, monthly Saturdays, when we would sit in the kitchen of his aunt and uncle, old European immigrants, and I, as a young boy, would listen to their stories. The smell of strong coffee served in a glass, the taste of hot, freshly baked bread, the slow ticking of an ancient clock in the next room, the fading afternoon light filtered through yellow shades: all of that was enlivened again by this simple gesture, all of it made to live again as an assembly of ghosts brought to presence with a courteous bow and a sweep of an arm. That was the gift of this gesture, an appeal to enter into that world, an appeal addressed by the old man at the door to me, a stranger, and yet one who was made to feel that he now belonged.

The Gesture

The gesture, like the old man's sweep of his arm, is the outline of a world, the chiseling of what is otherwise a neutral space into a significant place. It is the seed from which a cosmos is born, a field of radiating lines and vectors which draws the participants into a mutual presence. As such, every gesture is an appeal, an invitation not only to enter into a world, but also to partake of its experience. The appeal of the gesture of the old man at the door was for me to inhabit again those Saturday afternoons of my boyhood, when in the ambiance of their fading light I felt something of the presence of my ancestral heritage.

The ancestors are a haunting presence and indeed every gesture is a haunting by significant others. The gestures which each of us make carry the signature of those significant others who have gone before us, those others who have *mattered* to us, who live again through us. Those ancestral ghosts who haunt our gestures are often those of whom we have heard only in story, but who, nevertheless, have captured our hearts and have lived in our dreams. Carl Jung attested to this when in *Memories, Dreams, Reflections* he confessed that in going about his work, he was only continuing the work of his ancestors, completing it for them, or at least bringing it to a new round. So too, with each of us, even in simple things. You make a gesture, always without thinking of it, and your companion says to you how much you look and seem like your grandfather. Haunted in our gestures by significant others, shadowed by the ancestors, we are in and through our gestures stitched into and held by a tradition. Our gestures are the habitat of a history, its embodiment, testimony that as beings in time we do belong to a community of others. The body that one is, the body that one is born with, has been crafted long before one's birth.

Haunted by significant others, the outline of a world and its landscapes of experience, the gesture as an appeal is an emotional field, a gravitational, magnetic force which attracts and holds not only you and me and the ancestral ghosts who attend us, but also mood and affect, memory and image. Indeed, the gesture is the pivot around which mood and image swing, a pivotal moment in which an image is made incarnate and a mood is given expression. The gesture is the living image charged with feeling, an erotic field whose gravitational tug is the stuff of desire and longing for the other. With the sweep of his arm, the softness of his smile, and the subtle gentleness of his bow, the old man at the door opened waves of memory and longing, affect and image, desire and loss. In his simple gesture, the old man at the door evoked a field of dreams.

Psychotherapy and the Gestural Field

It is, I believe, in this field of gestures, in this field of dreams, that so much of psychotherapy takes place. The talking cure which describes depth psychology in its origins is really about that place of conversation where the word is made flesh. Indeed, acknowledging how much the gesture is a haunted presence, it is better to say that psychotherapy is, in fact, the making of a place for the ghosts to assemble to tell their tales. The person who comes *to* therapy is the vehicle for those ghosts who come *for* therapy. The talking cure is for the sake of the ghosts who haunt the symptomatic body and its gestural field.

The symptomatic body is the locus of a loss and in this respect all psychotherapy is grief work. What the patient brings into the field of therapy is a body haunted by an absent other, a body whose gestures find no witness, no reciprocal, for their appeal. Addressed to the therapist, these gestures hold in presence an absence which yearns for some lost other, an absence which in fact invites the therapist to become that other, an absence which galvanizes a field between patient and therapist, establishing a magnetic tension between them, a field in which each infects the other with desire and longing, impregnates the other with hope and with fear. And all the while from within this magnetic, transferential field, a field brought into being not by disembodied minds who project on to each other, but by the fact that patient and therapist are embodied beings whose gestures implicate the other; all the while from within this field between them words erupt, language appears, stories are spoken.

For the ghosts, however, who haunt the symptomatic body, the words that are spoken, the stories that are made are not enough. And for the therapist who takes the side of the symptom, who attends to the ghosts who come for therapy in contrast to the person who comes to therapy, there is no choice but to be the disappointing witness, the one who in keeping the appointment with the ghosts disappoints the person. Such a therapist, is, in a paraphrase of Winnicott's fine phrase, like a transitional presence who bridges the chasm between the gestural body which no longer finds its reciprocal in the world and a new body of understanding which, if grace allows, is made between patient and therapist. In failing to be for the absent other the gesture which restores the loss, the therapist, working on the knife-edge of disappointment, allows the ghosts who haunt the symptoms their release. Like a phantom limb, which through repeated failure, shrinks into a new gestural body, the symptomatic body in the repeated failures of its haunted gestures dies, and, perhaps is reborn. In this respect, psychotherapy as grief work, as ghost work, is not about cure. On the contrary, it is about assisted dying, the craft and practice of letting go. The rituals of psychotherapy are rituals of mourning, and language, which holds such a key place in the talking cure, is central to these rituals, to this practice of letting go. In another place, I have considered in detail some of the characteristics of this language that arises in the gestural field between patient and therapist, tracing its roots to the tradition of Orpheus and his songs, and especially to the Orpheus of Rainer Maria Rilke.[5] Within that space, we practice a way of speaking which holds onto the meanings and stories made by letting go of them. We practice a way of speaking which is responsive to the gestural field as a haunting presence.

That the ghosts want their release was brought home to me quite recently via a dream told to me by a young woman whose brother died in a tragic and unexpected accident. The dream goes as follows:

I am hiking alone behind the North Star Ski Resort when I come across some ancient ice caves. They are blue and cavernous and deep. I rappel down through chamber after chamber, following the blue light. When I reach the end, there is a room with nothing but a fireplace which is lit and a rocking chair. My brother is sitting in the rocking chair. He looks strange because he has a very long, gray beard and his hair looks scraggly. I also notice that his fingernails are grotesquely long. He looks very sad. Once again, I go through the feeling that he is not really dead, but has just been here the whole time. I am not angry though. I ask him what he is doing here. He tells me calmly that he is "stuck here" and that I need to tell mom to "let him go."

The dead who haunt our dreams in search of release are like the ghosts who haunt our symptoms in search of their stories.

The significance of gesture to the practice of psychotherapy was also brought home to me from the other side. At a gathering of colleagues, I listened as one of them, also a friend, was presenting a case. The presentation was not only marked by clarity, but also by a kind of theoretical brilliance which astonished me as well as the others who were gathered. From the point of view of dynamics and psychological theory, there was no gap in my friend's comprehension of who the patient was, of what her suffering was about, or how that suffering was related to deficits in early childhood failures of empathic mirroring, failures as it were, of attunement. I understood all this from the presentation, and I also understood that my friend as a therapist was deeply attuned to his patient. But I wondered about all that theory, and I suspected that it was *not* the way in which he was present to her. Indeed, because I knew him not only as a colleague but also as a friend, I also knew that during the hour he would hold his theoretical knowledge of the patient in such a way that it would not in fact become an obstacle between them, a barrier to his empathic attunement to her. So, when he finished, I asked him a very simple question. I asked: "How are you with the patient during the hour; how do you, for example, sit in your chair?" His reply was immediate, unchecked. He leaned forward, and with his left hand he made a gesture from his heart toward the invisibly present patient who was there in the room with us. And he accompanied that gesture with these words: "I love her."

It was, as I recall it now, a touching moment. Simple, and quietly eloquent, it left us all in silence for a time. Through that gesture and its attendant words, we all felt the invisible presence of the patient in a way that the theoretical description could never match, and, installed for a moment in that field evoked by his gesture, we were humbled. I knew then that it is moments like these between patient and therapist which are healing. I knew then that in psychotherapy the ghosts ask of us these gestures of com-passion. In these gestures of com-passion we confess the limits of our comprehension, and, in doing so, we reveal our failure to be for them who they need. But in that failure we succeed. In these gestures of com-passion we release the ghosts from what we know, allowing ourselves to be with them as we are, fellow sufferers with a limited capacity to understand, and even less to heal. In letting go of what we know, we suffer a loss which resonates with who they are, absent-presences in search of what has gone away. In these gestures of com-passion we create a field of mutual mourning and each of us is released.

Beyond Psychotherapy

In concluding this essay I want to make this bold claim: the gestural field is a cosmic one, and the vibrations which a gesture establishes extend across the order of creation and even reach to the stars. To illustrate this claim, I offer the following story:

> . . . *It was a dark winter day when I made a visit to the local zoo. I have always been drawn to zoos in moments of melancholy, pulled by a loneliness and a hunger which beckons me toward the animal. Winter days, particularly in mid-week, have always been for me the best time for such visits, as they allow solitude and a private time with the animals.*
>
> *On this occasion I was going to see the gorillas. Standing in front of the cage of a large, silver -back male, I keenly felt the presence of the bars between us. The gorilla was sitting in the front corner of his cage, and I could see him only in profile. On occasion, however, (as gorillas will do with visitors) he would turn his head for a quick glance in my direction. His deeply set, dark, black eyes seemed like pools of time, and in those few brief moments of exchange I felt dizzy, as if I could swim through his eyes into another world. But the gorilla would just as quickly look away, and the spell would be broken.*
>
> *The cage was so small, especially for so large an animal, and I wondered how he could bear it. His lethargy was inescapable and I thought of the many hours of boredom he must daily endure, wondering, too, if I was reading my own sense of melancholy through him. But I had also been with animals in the wild, and the difference in behavior, in gesture, and in that imaginal space between us was pronounced. Caught up in these reveries, I had absent-mindedly withdrawn an orange from my pocket and was tossing it in the air. The gorilla turned and began to watch me. Without thinking, I tossed the orange through the bars, momentarily oblivious to the prohibition against feeding the animals. The toss of the orange through the bars covered a distance of only a few feet in real space and took perhaps only a second in real time. But the gesture and what unexpectedly followed bridged an ocean of time and space.*
>
> *One would have expected the gorilla to take the orange and retreat to the far corner of the cage to eat it. But this gorilla did not. Instead, he tossed it through the bars back to me, I caught it, and in my astonishment, I tossed it to him again. We continued like this for perhaps three exchanges,*

until this ribbon between us, this gesture of play ,was broken by the sound of a voice from the far end of the corridor. "Don't feed the animals!" When I turned toward the voice, the gorilla turned away. He retreated to the far end of the cage. He kept the orange.

I left the zoo and walked out into the city. The cold, dark, winter afternoon did little to cheer the sadness I felt at having left the gorilla inside. I was different, changed by that encounter, and even more lonely in the midst of the crowded city. The gorilla had suspended his appetite for a moment. For the sake of an encounter, he had bridged with his gesture an immense gap between our worlds. In that gesture of tossing the orange back to me, he had reached out his hand across an emptiness so vast as to be beyond measure. Together we had built a tremulous bridge of gestures. And for a brief time we stood on opposite sides of that bridge, connected in a way that seemed to acknowledge in each other our lost kinship. Even to this day, nearly twenty years later, I know that I will never forget the eyes of my winter companion on that cold day. He remembered me, and as strange as it might sound, I felt so grateful for his recognition. But I also felt how far I had come, and I knew with a great feeling of sadness that we would remain forever more on opposite sides of that bridge, and that at the best moments of my life I would be able only to stop and linger and turn around to see, once again, what was left behind. I knew all that, and I knew too that what I saw in his eyes before the spell was broken was his sadness for me.

Like the gesture of my colleague toward his patient, this too was a gesture of compassion offered to me across a great divide. How many ghosts haunt the gestural field between us and the other beings with whom we share the Earth, I cannot really fathom. But I do know that what links us to the rest of creation is the common field of the body, which, in all of its variations and permutations, is the locus or the site where we appeal to and address each other.

5

Yes, Indeed! Do Call the World the Vale of Soul Making: Reveries Toward an Archetypal Presence[1]

"They also Serve Who only Stand and Wait"[2]

". . . and what are poets for in a destitute time?" This question is posed by the nineteenth century poet Holderlin in his elegy "Bread and Wine." Considering it, Martin Heidegger, perhaps the single most important philosopher of our century, says "We hardly understand the question today." That assessment seems quite right to me. We live, Heidegger says, "In the age of the world's night, [when] the abyss of the world must be experienced and endured."

If you are fond of words, as a depth psychologist must be; if you love words and hear within them the ancient songs and rhythms of the soul, then abyss cannot fail to attract your attention. It is the place of the deep, the bottomless pit of the sea. The abyss—*bathus*— is about depth and the word is kin to grief—*penthos*— and passion and suffering—*pathos*. Within this constellation, where words are like the stars of the soul, the abyss is the depth to which we are led by the suffering of grief over loss. If the poet has something to do with calling us to attend to the abyss, then the poet in this capacity has something to do with calling us to experience and endure the deep, stirring waters of grief and suffering.

But what have we lost and why should we need to be called to the abyss and to attend to this place of grief and suffering? In *The Soul in Grief: Love, Death and Transformation*, I described how personal loss can be an opening to a larger, shared, collective sense of loss where we encounter the archetypal figure of the Orphan. In this encounter we come face to face with our deep sense of homelessness, and we discover within ourselves the gnawing hunger which we have for a lost sense of the Divine, and for the lost sense of the sacred in the ordinary. Grief is in this respect a homecoming, and this journey toward home begins, and can begin, only at the abyss, at that place where all the props of ego consciousness have fallen away and we stand naked and alone in an alien world under a darkened, winter sky.

But is not the abyss all around us on a daily basis? Do we not everyday see stories of suffering and violence, of war and deprivation? What is this strange indifference that we so often adopt in the face of these countless tragedies? Have we become so numbed to suffering and loss, and so familiar with the absence of the Divine in our world, that only some deeply moving personal loss can awaken us to the dismal fact that we are blind men and women stumbling in the darkness of the world's last nights toward oblivion?

Something seems terribly awry about the times in which we are living. The evidence of the abyss is visible, but the response that we give to it seems dangerously flawed. Do we need to be called to the abyss because we have lost our capacity to grieve? Have we forgotten how to feel and be touched by the world's suffering? Heidegger tells us that the abyss is the complete absence of the ground which frames us as mortal beings and gives us our place within the scheme of creation. Have we, in spite of all our intelligence and magnificent achievements, forgotten our place, forgotten who we are, where we come from, what we are *here* for? There are moments when I think that we need a planetary day of mourning. There are moments when I believe that the experience of grief at the abyss, and our willingness to endure it, is a necessary one if we are to return to our senses. There are moments when I dream that at the abyss our human tears of grief are mirrored in the face of a God who weeps for us.[3]

Breathing at the Abyss: Language and the Soul of the World

But what does it mean to return to our senses? In the face of this question, I trust only the poets now. Neither the politicians nor the psychologists—with rare and wonderful exceptions—neither the theologians nor the philosophers— again with rare and wonderful exceptions—linger at the abyss. Only the poet does, and only the poet who begins to see only when night comes, who begins his work as Rumi says, "When merchants eat their big meals and sleep/ their dead sleep, we night-thieves go to work." Rilke is such a poet, a night-thief, a poet for a destitute time, and at the abyss he wonders,

> Are we, perhaps, here just for saying: House
> Bridge, Fountain, Gate, Jug, Olive Tree, Window,-
> possibly: Pillar, Tower?

Imagine that! Are we here for giving voice to the world, here for the sake of being its witness, and, perhaps, possibly on occasion, its spokesperson? When we speak are we speaking up for the things of the world, giving voice to their desires, breathing with them in a con-spiracy of dreams? Is this our vocation, which we have lost, and for which we silently grieve as do the things of the world?

Gaston Bachelard, the great French master of reverie, says that poetry helps one breathe better. This claim is not just extravagant nonsense, a mere aesthetic diversion. Something of great value is present in these words, something we have lost, something we no longer remember of ourselves and about our place within the order of creation? Breath is life; it is soul, the anima mundi. When we breathe we exchange ourselves with the world around us. On the in-breath, in the moment of inspiration, we not only take in the world, we are also nourished by it, in-spired by it. And then at the pause, so slight and so subtle, in that briefest of moments before the ex-piration, when we give back to the world what it has just given to us, an alchemy occurs. Sound becomes word, rhythm becomes song, and the world blossoms into a new kind of beauty. On a bit of moving air, on this so fragile, slender, invisible thread depends the continuing act of creation. Rilke says it this way:

> For the wanderer doesn't bring from the mountain slope
> a handful of earth to the valley, untellable earth, but only
> some word he has won, a pure word, the yellow and blue
> gentian.

For Rilke, this work of giving voice to the world is heartwork. It is a descent into the depths, a move from the visible to the invisible, to that subtle realm of the imaginal which halos the visible. In these depths a reversal takes place, and we realize that we are called into speaking the world, that we are in-spired to be who we are by something other than ourselves, that we are made by the world, that the world truly does breathe its life into us, as it happened so long ago, at the beginning of time, when the breath of the Divine was breathed into mortal clay. Is it not curious, then, that it is at the abyss that we recognize that human life is truly a vocation and that the task of a human life is to be responsive to a destiny which calls one to be in service to the world? In a moment like this, we might even realize that we owe our very being to something which, as wholly other, often beckons as holy and divine.

We are drawn to the abyss when we no longer experience the presence of the Divine in the world. At the abyss, in the depths of grief and suffering, we meet the gods who have taken flight from the world. Mark Strand, a contemporary poet, captures something of the melancholy mood which attends the moment when we realize this hunger in ourselves to be called and addressed by an Otherness which is more than ourselves. In a poem entitled "The Night, The Porch," he writes:

> To stare at nothing is to learn by heart
> What all of us will be swept into, and barring oneself
> To the wind is feeling the ungraspable somewhere close by.
> Trees can sway or be still. Day or night can be what they wish.
> What we desire, more than season or weather is the comfort
> Of being strangers, at least to ourselves. This is the crux
> Of the matter, which is why even now we seem to be waiting
> For something whose appearance would be its vanishing—
> The sound, say, of a few leaves falling, or just one leaf,
> Or less. There is no end to what we can learn. The book out there
> Tells us as much, and was never written with us in mind.

The book out there was never written with us in mind! A simple sentence, and yet one which has the power to disrupt our ordinary ways of thinking and being. In spite of what we might wish to think or believe, the sun does not shine for us, nor do the stars glow in the midnight sky with us in mind. With this reversal do we not become, at least for a moment, strangers to ourselves, and, indeed, is this not what we desire—more than season or weather, what we desire is the comfort of being strangers, at least to ourselves.

To be strangers to ourselves! Why should this be? Why do we long for this? Perhaps this emptying out of ourselves is the necessary first step to becoming available to the Divine which calls us, a first step in becoming open to something as simple as the sound of just one leaf falling, or even something less than that. In emptiness something so simple can feel like a blessing, and can betray within itself some hint of the sacred. Once, at the abyss, in the depths of the winter time of mourning, I saw a spider's web haloed by the bright light of the full moon, and I knew that spiders' webs are silver stars woven on the earth.

There is a sense of great weariness in Strand's poem, as if he is giving voice to some ancient, tired place in the soul which has been too burdened by consciousness. Have we finally reached a point where we can admit that we are exhausted by what we know, by the ever increasing onslaught of information, by our theories and systems of knowledge, which now too often seem bankrupt and too thin to water the soul? In a few simple lines the poet E.E. Cummings gives us a memorable image of our deep hunger to be nourished by something more than what we know. He writes,

> since feeling is first
> who pays any attention
> to the syntax of things
> will never wholly kiss you;

Beyond meaning we long for presence. Beyond knowledge we long for something more direct and immediate with the world, for something as intimate as a kiss. When I look at Van Gogh's "Starry Night" I know that he was kissed by the stars. And then I return to the poets, to Cummings again, and say "Yes!" to these words:

> While you and i have lips and voices which
> are for kissing and to sing with
> who cares if some one-eyed son of a bitch
> invents an instrument to measure Spring with?
>
> since the thing perhaps is
> to eat flowers and not be afraid.

With the help of the poets, I am trying to suggest that an archetypal activism must start with a way of being present. Such presence is an enantiadromia, a reversal of direction, a turn from doing first to being. This reversal is a humiliation of our consciousness, a humbling of our minds which returns mind to nature, which soaks mind in the humus of the anima mundi, the world soul.

This turn about is an abysmal moment, a moment when we are brought to the edge and reminded of our hubris. It is a painful moment and one which more often than not invites grief for what we experience as absent in our lives. The danger in such a moment is that we will become busy and active in an effort to fill that absence, that we will substitute in the place of grief an activity born of fear. Already early in this century, Rilke knew this temptation, and called for a change in direction:

> *Here* is the time for the Tellable, *here* is its home
> Speak and proclaim. More than ever
> the things we can live with are falling away, and their place
> being oustingly taken up by an imageless act.

This world calls for our participation, and now more than ever, Rilke says, because we are in increasing danger of losing touch with it by acting in an imageless way. We are stuffed with our ideas about the world, and overloaded with facts about it. But we are poor when it comes to the images which dress our actions and engage us in the world, those images which bubble up from the depths of the soul and animate our encounters with the world, so that even something as simple as the arc of a leaf as it floats in the wind can inspire a sense of simple beauty. Something in us longs to be touched again by these simple aesthetic moments of the world's epiphany, longs to sense the world before we make sense of it. Something in us longs to be awakened from our anesthetic sleep.

The Call of Beauty

So "... what are poets for in a destitute time?" The great Russian novelist, Doestoevsky, once said that beauty will save the world. Hearing this claim, we should not think of beauty as what is merely pretty or handsome; we should not debase this claim by imagining beauty in terms of our modern impoverished vocabularies, which would equate, for example, the beautiful with the beauty pageant. Such a reduction would forget what Rilke cautions us to remember about beauty, that it is "nothing/ but beginning of Terror we're still just able to bear..." And if this coupling of Beauty and Terror, which silences us into a state of awe-ful- contemplation, not unlike the figures of old experienced when they met an Angel, should not be enough, then Rilke adds in the next line," and why we adore it so is because it serenely/ disdains to destroy us."

Poet and novelist are telling us that Beauty is not our creation, that Beauty is the radiance of the world's holy darkness, a wonderful phrase which I borrow from my good friend Charles Asher. Beauty is an archetypal experience, and hence one that overwhelms us in the moment. So, if we ask again what are poets for in a destitute time, then we might say that they are here for the sake of Beauty.

It is a wonder to me that it is at the abyss that we meet Beauty, at the turning points of the soul, in the depths of passion, suffering and sorrow. It is a wonder to me that Beauty can blossom from grief, as love can. It is as if only the storms of some powerful, tumultuous feeling can shake us from sleep and awaken us to the world's invisible Beauty. It is as if we need earthquakes of the soul, moments of love and loss, to rouse us from some ancient slumber.

Plato, in one of his most enticing fables, provides a context for why this moment of Beauty and its Terrors must be an abysmal moment, must carry an archetypal power, a numinous charm. The soul, he tells us, drinks from the forgetful waters of Lethe, as it approaches this life. We are, as it were, born to forget. And yet, for some, for the poets, for example, a dim remembrance of that other place remains. So Wordsworth, paraphrasing Plotinus, says,

The Soul that rises with us, our life's Star
Hath elsewhere had its setting,
And cometh from afar:
Not in entire forgetfulness...

For Plato, Beauty is the first moment of *an-amnesis*, of waking from forgetfulness, the first way in which we recover the sense of who we are, where we come from, and what we are here for. Kathleen Raine, poet herself, and the world's foremost authority on William Blake, captures this power of beauty and our need for it in our lives, in her classic essay "The Use of the Beautiful." She writes:

We are haunted by the presence of an inaccessible
knowledge, and by a sense of estrangement from some
place or state native to us; the paradise of all
mythologies, once and forever known, but lost. Of this
Paradise all are native, for it lies within ourselves,
forgotten or half forgotten.

Musing upon the beauty of a Botticelli face, Kathleen Raine adds that to experience such beauty is a "homecoming." But again the caution, the warning, which is always there: "though the way from this world to that is long and we may well fear the journey."

The poet in a destitute time leads us to the abyss, and there we join hands with Beauty and all its Terrors. In its presence we are transformed through grief over the loss of our birthright as creatures, all of us, who belong to that holy darkness of creation. We are awakened to the mysterious depths that haunt each moment of experience, and begin a journey to that other place where, as Keats noted, "Beauty is Truth, Truth Beauty."

The Rose Which In Its Blooming, Already Begins To Fade

What is the Truth of Beauty at the abyss? It is the realization of the transience of all that we love and experience. Beauty belongs to the figure of Death; it is, if you will, Death's Bride. The poet John Keats expresses this companionship quite poignantly as a lament in his "Ode to a Nightingale." Hearing the song of this bird he is led to contemplate the sorrowful difference between its beauty and our own feeble condition.

> Fade far away, dissolve, and quite forget
> What thou among the leaves hast never known,
> The weariness, the fever, and the fret
> Here, where men sit and hear each other groan;
> Where palsy shakes a few, sad, last, gray hairs,
> Where youth grows pale, and specter-thin and dies;
>
> Where but to think is to be full of sorrow
> And leadened eyed despairs,
> Where Beauty cannot keep her lustrous eyes,
> Or new love pine at them beyond tomorrow.

We grow old, we grow sick, and we die, and it is a moment like this one, a moment when we hear the simple and passing beauty of a bird's song, that we are most awakened to our condition. And in such a moment, what are we called to do? The poet at the abyss says, "Do nothing!" Only experience and endure the moment, and in this learn to love the beauty of the world in its passing. Thinking of Orpheus, that great poet whose words were so powerful and moving that they persuaded the gods and goddesses of the underworld to release his beloved Eurydice from death, Rilke asks what monument should we raise to the poet. No monument, he says. Let it be only the Rose which in its blooming already begins to fade. No monumental action, no heroic activity—only the simple witnessing of this simple presence, and one which remembers that Orpheus failed.

The poet is the true activist who dares to whisper that there is nothing to do, that there is nothing we should do. He or she is the true revolutionary, the true philosopher who inverts the relation of knowledge and being, of the mind's meaning and the soul's presence. In this respect, the poet is the one who awakens our aesthetic sense-abilities, the one who teaches us to feel again. Aesthetic in its root sense means to sense, to feel, and particularly to sense in the sense of hearing. Hearing, moreover, is kin to the word obey. What the poet asks of us, then, is that in a destitute time we hear and obey the calls of Beauty and its Terrors, that at the abyss we feel again the depths of each moment, of each encounter, that we dare to love, even in the face of loss, all that appeals to us and makes its claim upon us.

An archetypal presence begins in this place of being touched and moved by the holy darkness of the Divine in all its beauty and its terror. It begins as a way of being, and not a way of doing. It is a way of being that is responsive to the aesthetic, that is the felt and experienced demands of the other. It is about responding to the call of the other, in whom the Divine shines through, about responding because we have first listened, about being response-able, able-to-respond, because we have heard. Being first about who one is before being about what one does, archetypal activism is about character. It is about courage too, the courage not only to feel the pains of loss and grief, the sorrows of the world's dark night, but also the courage to stand at the abyss as a witness, not a judge, for what asks to be seen and spoken. Archetypal activism is the natural ethics of the soul.

At the abyss, the poet is the one who challenges us to stop for a moment, and to take stock of who we are before we act or do, to experience and endure in the experience, to stand at the edge of the abyss and all its horrors and wait. To wait even without hope, for hope would be hope for the wrong thing, as T.S. Eliot cautions. But to endure the waiting, which perhaps is made only a little more bearable by those words quoted at the beginning of this essay: "They also serve/ Who only Stand and Wait."

6

For the Moment, That's Enough: Reveries on Therapy and the Poetry of Language

The true analyst is not a sage who has come up with all the common, reassuring answers, but a troubled, restless spirit, forever in search of the more complete answer, which at any rate is not in the offing because what he actually seeks is nothing less than the meaning of life. And a lifetime will not suffice to find it; that is, without embracing ready-made solutions or certain dogmas.[1]

The situation becomes difficult, however, when the patient's nature resists a collective solution. The question then arises whether the therapist is prepared to risk having his convictions dashed and shattered against the truth of the patient. If he wants to go on treating the patient he must abandon all preconcieved notions and, for better or worse, go with him in search of the religious and philosophical ideas that best correspond to the patient's emotional states.[2]

The Gesture

He was about seventy, and maybe even seventy-five, an old man with thinning white hair, shoulders bent by age, a slight limp in his walk. Accompanied by a woman, whom I assumed to be his wife, a woman about as old as he, also with white hair, but straighter in her posture and more supple in her walk, they approached the door of the coffee shop as I was about to leave. Opening the door for them, I stepped aside to allow them to enter. But the old man took the door in his right hand and with a sweeping gesture of his left arm, accompanied by a very slight bow and a very broad smile, he ushered me across the threshold and into my day. We exchanged only one word, the thanks which I spoke as I passed them. Beyond that one word, however, something like a small miracle happened, and although I never saw them again I have remembered that moment, that brief moment, these long years.

An authentic gesture, like the old man's sweep of his arm, is the outline of a world, the chiseling of what is otherwise neutral space into a significant place. It is the seed from which a cosmos is born, a field of radiating lines and vectors which draws the participants into mutual presence. In the example, what the old man outlined with his gesture was a whole universe of manners, a landscape of civility, an old world of grace and charm whose space and time echoed an earlier, slower, more quiet rhythm. Present to that gesture, I was offered a kind of citizenship, as it were, in the world that it carved out, gifted with a sense of belonging to a common space, a community, a tradition of which somehow I was already a part but had forgotten. Beyond the man, his wife, and myself, the gesture brought with it an assembly of all those others who belonged to that old world of practiced etiquette, polite manners, genuine respect, and measured patience. Later I found myself thinking of my father and remembering those long, monthly Saturdays, when we would sit in the kitchen of his aunt and uncle, old European immigrants, and I, as a young boy, would listen to their stories. The smell of strong coffee, served in a glass, the taste of hot, freshly baked bread, the slow ticking of an ancient clock in the next room, the fading afternoon light filtered through yellow shades: all of that was enlivened again by the simple gesture, all of it made to live again as an assembly of ghosts brought to presence with a courteous bow and a sweep of an arm. That was the gift of this gesture, an appeal to enter into that world, an appeal addressed by the old man at the door to me, a stranger, and yet one who was made to feel that he belonged.

Psychotherapy as Grief Work

Psychotherapy is grief work. It is the making of a place for the ghosts to assemble to tell their tales, a place-making which takes place in the gestural field between the patient and the therapist. The symptom is a gesture made to another who is absent. The symptomatic body is the locus of a loss. What the patient brings into the field of therapy is a body haunted by an absent other, a body whose gestures find no witness, no reciprocal, for their appeal. Addressed to the therapist, these gestures hold in presence an absence which yearns for some lost other, an absence which in fact invites the therapist to become that other, an absence which galvanizes a field between patient and therapist, establishing a gravitational or magnetic tension between them in which each influences the other, transfers to the other germs of meaning as it were, a field in which each infects the other with desire and longing, impregnates the other with hope and with fear. And all the while from within this magnetic, transferential field, a field brought into being not by disembodied minds who project onto each other, but by the fact that patient and therapist are embodied beings whose gestures implicate the other, a field, then, which is generated by the resonance of flesh; all the while from within this field between them words erupt, language appears, stories are spoken.

For the ghosts, however, who haunt the symptomatic body, the words that are spoken, the stories that are made are not enough. And for the therapist who takes the side of the symptom, who attends to the ghosts who come for therapy in contrast with the person who comes to therapy, there is no choice but to be the disappointing witness, the one who in keeping the appointment with the ghosts disappoints the person. Such a therapist is, in Winnicott's fine phrase, like a transitional presence who bridges the chasm between the gestural body which no longer finds its reciprocal in the world and a new body of understanding which, if grace allows, is made between patient and therapist. In failing to be for the absent other the gesture which restores the loss, the therapist, working on the knife-edge of disappointment, allows the ghosts which haunt the symptoms their release. Like the phantom limb, which through repeated failure, shrinks into a new gestural body, the symptomatic body in the repeated failures of its haunted gestures dies and, perhaps, is reborn. In this respect, psychotherapy as grief work, as ghost work, is not about cure. On the contrary, it is about assisted dying, the craft and practice of letting go. The rituals of psychotherapy are rituals of mourning, and language, which holds such a key place in the talking cure, is central to these rituals, to this practice of letting go.

That the ghosts want this release was brought home to me quite recently in a dream, told to me by a young woman whose brother died in a tragic and unexpected accident. The dream goes as follows:

> I am hiking alone behind the Northstar Ski Resort when I come across some ancient ice caves. They are blue and cavernous and deep. I rappel down through chamber after chamber, following the blue light. When I

reach the end, there is a room with nothing but a fireplace which is lit and a rocking chair. My brother is sitting in the rocking chair. He looks strange because he has a very long, gray beard and his hair looks scraggly. I also notice that his fingernails are grotesquely long. He looks very sad. Once again, I go through the feeling that he is not really dead, but has just been here the whole time. I am not angry though. I ask him what he is doing here. He tells me calmly that he is "stuck here" and that I have to tell Mom to "let him go."

The dead who haunt our dreams in search of release are like the ghosts who haunt our symptoms.

Soul and Mind

In the *Poetics of Reverie*, Gaston Bachelard, that wonderful dreamer of words, writes that, "the soul and the mind do not have the same memory."[3] It is a phenomenologically accurate statement and one which should sensitize the practicing psychotherapist to the difference between soul and mind. Descartes erased that difference when in his *Meditations on First Philosophy* he said that he could find no distinction between them. In his synopsis of the six meditations he wrote that while ".... the human body may very easily perish, ... the mind or soul of man, between which I find no distinction, is immortal by its very nature."[4] That phrase, "between which I find no distinction," bracketed between two commas, was the gulf between cogito and flesh, mind and body, into which the soul was destined to disappear. What had been a difference became with Descartes an identity. Soul was reduced to mind, and mind was set in opposition to body.

In an earlier paper,[5] I commented on this little caesura, and noted two consequences of this slippage of meaning, this loss of difference between soul and mind. First, with this eclipse of soul by mind in the seventeenth century, the modern discipline of psychology was destined to be born without soul, was destined to be birthed as a study of mind. In this respect, I argued that ironically, "Psychology, as the speech of soul, is a science, profession, discipline without soul," and, unfaithful to its name, has betrayed its heritage. Second, I indicated that in this reduction of soul to mind, in this eclipse of their difference, Descartes parented a psychology given over to the masculine domination of the feminine. In the Latin edition of his text, mind is the masculine *mens* and soul the feminine *anima*. In the French edition mind is the masculine *l'esprit* and soul the feminine *l'ame*. In response to these consequences, I suggested that "the science, profession, and discipline of psychology needs to recover its *anima*, its soul, its feminine character."⁶

In retrospect now I regret the way in which I phrased that last statement. I regret it because it implies an action we needed to take and it forgets those historical circumstances which witnessed what Freud called "the return of the repressed." In the latter half of the nineteenth century, at the origins of psychoanalysis, in the consulting rooms of Freud's Vienna house, the soul, insisting on its difference from mind, made a dramatic, symptomatic return in the guise of the hysterics' bodies, most of whom were women. Via the symptom and the dream, soul, without our aid, eclipsed the metaphysics of Descartes.

I have taken this brief historical detour in order to suggest that soul and mind, following Bachelard, also have a different language, a different way of knowing and being in the world. At the origins of psychoanalysis, the symptom and the dream, voices of soul, other ways of knowing and being, declare that language itself is a problem. Nightly and painfully, both the dream and the symptom engage in the work of dissolution, and, in dissolving the meanings which ego-consciousness so elaborately constructs for itself and its world, soul declares that there are symptoms in our meanings, even while the telos of psychoanalysis, since its origins, has been to decipher the meaning in our symptoms. The work which inaugurates psychoanalysis is *The Interpretation of Dreams*, and in this work of interpretation the language of the dream—metaphorical, symbolic, elusive, a language of puns and plays, of detours and indirections—becomes the grammar of a text. The move is from dream to reason, from the oneric to the rational, and in so doing Freud reconquers the domain of soul for mind.

But my intention is not to offer a criticism of psychoanalysis. Rather, I want only to return to the symptom and the dream in order to show how in their phenomenology they undo our addiction to meaning, and how this work of dis-solution indicates that the language of soul differs from the language of mind.

Jungian psychology is more appreciative of this difference between soul and mind. For example, Marie-Louise von Franz notes in her book, *Alchemy*, that in alchemy ". . . the conscious mind did not follow a definite program." There is no certain path in alchemical thinking, and while the procedures are differentiated, they do not follow a rigid or fixed sequence. Moreover, this same spirit of open, searching inquiry also characterizes analysis. Thus, von Franz says that ". . .in analysis we try to get people to adopt an attitude where they do not approach the unconscious according to a program."[7] In alchemy and analysis and in the symptom and the dream, the mystery of soul undoes the clarity of mind.

A phenomenologist practices a kind of alchemical thinking in his or her fidelity to the phenomena of experience, in that naive, un-programmed openness to experience. As a phenomenologist, therefore, I am compelled to respect this difference between soul and mind, and to address the symptom and the dream on their own terms. If, from the point of view of ego-consciousness, the symptom and the dream are a radical otherness which dissolves the grounds of the ego's fixed certainties about itself and the world, then the use of ego-based language to find meaning in our symptoms, to make sense of our dreams, to discover the solutions to our sufferings, is a distortion of the radical otherness of the symptom and the dream.

The symptom and the dream, on their terms, invite us into that moment of language when things fall apart, when meaning erodes, when sense fails. They invite us into that moment when language is undone by otherness. They invite us into that moment when language fails. The poet, who in so many ways is an alchemist, and especially the poet who belongs to the tradition of Orpheus, is the one who can best teach us this moment of language.

Orpheus and the Soul

Orpheus is the figure in Greek mythology who was so adept at music that it was said of him that his songs had the power to tame the wild beasts and influence the movement of trees and stones. When his wife, Eurydice, died, Orpheus won permission to descend into the underworld to plead for her return. His lament was so moving that even the cold hearts of Hades and Persephone were warmed. But Orpheus lost Eurydice forever, when, in the last moment and in defiance of the gods, he turned to see if she was following him.

In a series of insightful essays on Orpheus, the literary critic Charles Segal notes that, "for Plato the magic of Orphic speech can persuade but cannot attain to truth."[8] For Plato that supposed inability of the poetic voice to tell the truth was reason enough to banish the poet from the polis. Freud's psychoanalysis, with its distrust of the symptom and the dream on their own terms, has continued this exile. The Orphic voice of symptom and dream would persuade the discriminating rational mind that things are otherwise than they appear, and in that persuasion would undermine the ground of truth. Enough reason, therefore, to cure the symptom and to interpret the dream!

But a later poet, one who belongs to the tradition of Orpheus, Rainer Maria Rilke, reaffirms the poet's value. In his *Sonnets to Orpheus*, he asks how we should remember Orpheus, how we should attend him, witness him. His reply is instructive. He says, in effect, that we are to raise no permanent monument to Orpheus, but let it be the rose which in its blooming also fades. For the poet, the truth is in the passing. For the poet, the truth is in the letting go. Consider whether or not in the fixed certainties of our theories, through which we as therapists reconstruct in narrative form the lives of our patients and thereby supposedly give them meaning; consider whether in doing so we monumentalize the symptom and the dream, and thereby miss their recurrent blossoming song. If the symptom is, as Greg Mogenson says, a "grave marker,"[9] if it is the locus of a loss, do the stories that we make up and believe to be true prematurely entomb and silence the dead in our narrative theories before the ghosts have had their chance to tell their tales?

Orpheus is the enduring figure of the poet whose song, whose language, had the power to comprehend, to subdue, to transform nature. His was a voice with the power to tame radical otherness, and in the classical world he represented the hope of a triumph of art over nature. But even then, in his origins, the power of Orpheus was marked by failure, for in the face of death Orpheus was not able to redeem his beloved Eurydice. Having persuaded the gods of the underworld to release his beloved, he turned at the last moment to look at her, an act forbidden by the gods. In that gesture, Eurydice slipped away from Orpheus forever; she slipped back into sleep and death from where no voice, not even that of Orpheus, could rescue her.

What is, I believe, so instructive about this tale is that it signals the limits of language in the face of radical otherness, in the face of loss and death. After the origins of psychoanalysis, moreover, this prudent hesitation about the power of language is reemphasized, because, if nothing else, the primary lesson of psychoanalysis is a radical question about the authority and authenticity of language. Despite its convictions about its theoretical models, the fact remains that the analyst who sides with the symptom and the dream is always shadowed by Orpheus's song. In his or her struggles to make sense of the suffering, to endow it with meaning, to contain it in story, the Orphic analyst is like the poet whom T.S. Eliot described so accurately in one of his four quartets. Eliot writes:

So here I am, in the middleway, having had twenty years —
Twenty years largely wasted, the years of l'entre deux guerre—

Trying to learn to use words, and every attempt
Is a wholly new start and different kind of failure
Because one has only learned to get the better of words
For the thing one no longer has to say, or the way in which
One is no longer disposed to say it. And so each venture
Is a new beginning, a raid on the inarticulate
With shabby equipment always deteriorating
In the general mess of imprecision of feeling,
Undisciplined squads of emotion. And what there is to conquer
By strength and submission, has already been discovered
Once or twice, or several times, by men whom one cannot hope
To emulate — but there is no comparison —
There is only the fight to recover what has been lost
And found and lost again and again: and now, under conditions
That seem unpropitious. But perhaps neither gain nor loss.
For us, there is only the trying. The rest is not our business.[10]

In these lines Eliot knows that language is the rose, that language blooms and fades, comes and goes, recovers what has been lost only to lose it and find it again and again. In these lines, he knows that we become the master of words only for those things we no longer have to say, for those things that no longer really matter.

There is the Orphic poet in these lines of Eliot, the recognition of the failure of language, and yet, too, something more, something which the poet Rilke also knew of Orpheus. One has only to read his *Duino Elegies* to recognize that for Rilke there are three moments in Orphic speech. There is the moment of hope in the power of speech to encompass the totality of otherness in the space of the heart, that moment so clearly visible in the Orpheus of the classical world. There is also the moment of failure of that hope, its dissolution in the face of otherness, in the face of death, a moment also visible in the Orpheus of the classical world. But also for Rilke, throughout the elegies and especially in those fifty-five sonnets to Orpheus which followed, there is the moment of recognition that in this failure lies the dignity of language, the worth of human speech, the necessity of giving voice again and again, without judgment of whether it is gain or loss, the recognition that there is after all only the trying. The elegy is a song of lament and praise, a song of loss and recovery, a voice of mourning and celebration. Listen for a moment to what Rilke says:

Who, if I cried, would hear me among the angelic orders?[11]

This is how the *Duino Elegies* begin, with a question that tears at the fabric of the soul in despair at the prospect of not being heard. And they continue in a questioning wonderment about language. In the ninth elegy Rilke asks,

Why, when this span of life might be fleeted away. . .
have to be human, and, shunning Destiny
long for Destiny? . . .

To his own question, he answers:

Not because happiness really
exists, that premature profit of imminent loss
Not out of curiosity. . .

But because being here amounts to so much, because all
this Here and Now, so fleeting, seems to require us and
strangely concerns us. Us the most fleeting of all. . .

It is this being here amidst what passes away which holds us, and which gives us our destiny. It is we, the most fleeting of all, who are called to witness the passing epiphanies of the world. True, in moments we wish that it would be otherwise; true, we hope that it could be other than how it is:

And so we keep pressing on and trying to perform it,
trying to contain it within our simple hands. . .
We'd rather
hold on to it all for ever. . .

But in the face of this all which is so fleeting; in the face of what Rilke calls that other relation, Death, we cannot contain it, we cannot hold on to it all forever. And because we cannot, then after all hope has been exhausted despair begins to turn into something else and the poet begins to wonder:

. . . Are we, perhaps, here just for saying: House,
Bridge, Fountain, Gate, Jug, Olive Tree, Window,—
possibly: Pillar, Tower?. . .

Here in the face of that other relation, here in the face of loss, we are called into speech. Or, at least, for the moment, that is what the poet wonders: Are we, he questions, here for the saying of these simple things? Perhaps. But this vocation of language in the face of loss is such awe-ful, care-ful, work. And so, Rilke adds the small but significant word, possibly, which alerts us to how care-ful we are to be in giving voice even to the simplest things of the world. Possibly! Even for something as simple as this saying of pillar or tower there is no certainty. But, slowly, as if inching his way toward some tentative claim which already quickens the pulse and beat of his heart, Rilke dares to say:

Here is the time for the Tellable, *here* is its home.
Speak and proclaim. . .

Praise the world to the angel. . .[12]

So the Orphic singer is called to speak knowing the failure. The Orphic singer is called to speak again and again, released, as it were, by the failure of this word at this moment, of this tale at this time, of this story at this juncture; the Orphic singer is released by these failures into continuous saying.

There is, I would argue, a fundamental shift in our consciousness when Orpheus draws near. Released into continuous song by the failure of our language to hold meaning in place, we are escorted beyond the vicious duality of either remaining comfortably asleep in our fixed certainties or sinking into nihilistic despair over the absence of meaning. And taken beyond these, we are invited into a way of knowing and being which teaches us to hold onto our meanings by letting go of them.

Another poet earlier than Rilke, John Keats, has given us a beautiful example of a speaking which can release what it addresses. In his "Ode to a Nightingale," Keats is made drunk by the song of the bird and hungers to be with it in the green, forested night:

Fade far away, dissolve, and quite forget
What thou among the leaves hast never known,
The weariness, the fever, and the fret
Here, where men sit and hear each other groan;
Where palsy shakes a few, sad, last, gray hairs,
Where youth grows pale, and specter-thin and dies;

Where but to think is to be full of sorrow
And leaden-eyed despairs,
Where Beauty cannot keep her lustrous eyes,
Or new love pine at them beyond tomorrow.

Deeper does the poet sink into this longing, and lulled by the beauty of the song, he compares his own song, the poem, to that of the bird:

Darkling I listen; and for many a time
I have been half in love with easeful Death,
Called him soft names in many a muséd rhyme,
To take into the air my quiet breath;
Now more than ever seems it rich to die,
To cease upon the midnight with no pain,
While thou art pouring forth thy soul abroad
In such an ecstasy!
Still wouldst thou sing, and I have ears in vain—
To thy high requiem become a sod.

The poet would cease upon the midnight, his voice stilled, and yet the bird would go on singing, pouring forth its soul in ecstasy. And that last line? It is anguish. Listen to it again:

To thy high requiem become a sod.

Of the two, the bird is the glorious singer, and how much then does the poet, the one who sings with human voice, have to recognize the failed reach of his words, their temporary and transitory nature. Listen to the next two lines and to what follows them:

Thou was not born for death, immortal bird!
No hungry generations tread thee down;
The voice I hear this passing night was heard
In ancient days by emperor and clown:
Perhaps the selfsame song that found a path
Through the sad heart of Ruth, when, sick for home
She stood in tears amid the alien corn;
The same that oftimes hath

Charmed magic casements, opening on the foam
Of perilous seas, in faery lands forlorn.

The bird's song escapes death, the poet's voice does not. Not born for
death the bird sings in pure ecstasy. But we sing and we must sing in that space
where we know not only of death as a final moment, but of each moment as a
little bit of dying, and where we know too of those not yet here, not yet born,
generations waiting in the wings, who will forget us, tread us down.
    And yet, the ode is the poet's song, reply to that of the bird, and if, so far,
Keats, like Rilke with the angel, despairs at the failure of his own voice, there is,
in the end, a release of bird and poet, and a celebration:

Forlorn! the very word is like a bell
To toll me back from thee to my sole self!
Adieu! The fancy cannot cheat so well
As she is famed to do, deceiving elf.
Adieu! adieu! thy plaintive anthem fades
Past the near meadows, over the still stream,
Up the hillside; and now 'tis buried deep
In the next valley glades:
Was it a vision, or a waking dream?
Fled is that music:— Do I wake or sleep?[13]

Adieu! What lies in that farewell? Release! Yes, that but also something
more, the recognition that while the poem is not the song of the bird— "the
fancy cannot cheat so well /As she is famed to do"— it is still the poet's song,
reply to that of the bird. In the end, then, Keats, like Rilke with the angel,
having despaired at the failure of his own voice to hold the fleeting song of
otherness or even to be heard, celebrates the singing that has been done.   At
least for the moment, does it not seem to be enough?
    Like the poet with the song of the bird, Orphic discourse releases what it
names, bids farewell to what it has so longingly hungered to capture in words.
And in that space where one holds on by letting go, we neither wake nor dream,
and there is neither gain nor loss. There is only, for the moment, the awe-ful
witnessing of a presence which is already fading.

For the Rose That In its Blooming Fades: Implications for Psychotherapy

We are with each other in the space of suffering, and we witness for each other those many losses that haunt our gestures and our dreams. And all that we ever have in this space between us is a word, dredged out of the silence, crafted with clumsy skill, a word which, like a bud on a tree, blossoms into something other and over time ripens into story. But Orpheus is always there between us, and the soft tones of his lyre tell us that the stories, the narratives we make together are only for the moment. Orpheus, drawing near, whispers that the stories that are made do not endure, and that it is the making of them which matters. So how, then, finally do we respond to the ghosts for whom the tales that we weave are not enough? The ghosts, which shimmer like ancient halos around each gesture, wait for an absent other to be restored. How do we speak to them, and with them?

It is a question, finally, not of what we say but of how we say it, and here again I return to Orpheus through Rilke. Commenting on the constellations in the starry night, Rilke wonders in one of the sonnets to Orpheus if there is such a figure as "the Rider" or "the Horseman." Is the gulf between star and Earth, man and animal, and you and me, too great for language to bridge? When horse and rider go their own ways to "meadow" and to "table," the stars, then, are "without names." The figure of "the Rider" in the night sky might then be, after all, only a picture, a construct which we place upon the stars. If that is so, then language truly does fail in the face of otherness, and suffering and death remain as foreign to us as the "nameless stars." But Rilke refuses this negation and in three lines he manages to turn what would otherwise be only despair into a wonderful sense of release.

> Even the starry union is deceptive.
> But let us now be glad awhile
> To believe the figure. That's enough.[14]

The curious paradox, then, is that Orpheus invites us to believe in the stories we make, and the songs that we sing as fictions, to believe them even while we acknowledge them as fictions. In this space of being able to make believe that one believes, we hold onto our fictions, our stories, the narrative remakings of our sufferings, of our lives, for a while, and in that while we are glad. But we hold on to them knowing that they too must pass, that within their very heart they contain already the seed of their passing, like the brilliant rose already in the moment of its full red blossoming is haunted at the edges of its petals by the pale, barely visible, hues of its fading. And yet, in some magical way, the embrace of a full presence haunted already by absence is enough. For the moment, that's enough!

More by indirection than by argument, I have tried to suggest in my remarks that in the space of psychotherapy we are offered a vision of language not as the power of naming but as the power of letting go. In doing so, I have asked the poets—Rilke, Keats, Eliot— all shadowed by the ghost of Orpheus, for assistance, not because therapy is about poetry, or because the therapist is or should be a poet. On the contrary, I have evoked their presence because they bear witness to a kind of discourse, a poetic discourse, which, I believe, better suits the informal poetry of the soul. If, as I have suggested, the symptom and the dream are the soul's work of dissolution, and if psychotherapy is indeed grief work, the work of dissolving and letting go of our stories, then we need a way of speaking which invites therapist and patient to let go of their beliefs, a way of speaking which invites therapist and patient to dissolve the stories that they craft together. Such an invitation is not too unlike the words spoken by Prospero in the epilogue of *The Tempest*. He says:

Now my charms are all overthrown,
And what strength I hav's mine own,
Which is most faint.[15]

Those words could be the confession of a therapist, the confession at the end of the work that therapist and patient have done together. The fine blend of humility and wisdom that would inspire such a confession animates the work of von Franz. To recognize and acknowledge the mystery of other-ness is to recognize and acknowledge the limits of one's knowing. Von Franz demonstrates this double recognition with the simple story of the monk who has fallen in love. Should this love be regarded either as a spiritual crisis and explained in terms of an anima projection, or should it be seen as a legitimate desire of the monk for a relation with an actual woman in the world? Of course, the conflict cannot be solved in the terms of this dichotomy of either/or, this binary logic of reason and the mind. As von Franz says, in such a moment "One is between the right and the left hand," and in that space between either this or that one is beyond ". . . the ego and all its blather." "It is consciousness," von Franz says "that creates the split and says either-or."[16] To go beyond this split the ego-mind has to let go of the certainties of either/or. And for the ego-mind this letting go is something like a dying.

So are these words of Prospero, then, a confession of failure? Perhaps. But I think not. On the contrary, I think they are more a humble confession of the limits of the power and reach of language to plunge into the depths of human suffering and give it a shape, or to hold onto the totality of life and its passing moments. And in the face of that confession what might be the response of the ghosts? I find in the following words of Prospero something of what the ghosts might whisper.

> . . . Now 'tis true,
> I must be here confin'd by you,
> Or sent to Naples. Let me not,
> Since I have my dukedom got,
> And pardon'd the deceiver, dwell
> In this bare island by your spell . . .

The therapy room, once a place of magic and of charm, a place where between patient and therapist a story was made, now has become a bare island. The ghosts ask for their release.

> But release me from my bands
> With the help of your good hands.[17]

With the release of your good hands! A gesture which holds the hands out in humble recognition that in the end life is more than the stories we make together? A gesture which in clapping brings the right and left hands together for a moment? A gesture which recognizes in celebration that what we have made together is for the moment enough? The gesture is the release and in the release therapist and patient do experience a dying, do have a small but significant epiphany of letting go. In that moment the ghosts who haunt the gestures of the symptomatic body are drawn closer to us the living, who now know something of dying. No longer then are we separated from them, strangers. On the contrary, we already know them, and they, having told their tale, depart, having been heard, no longer strangers. They are released.

Perhaps I can best summarize what I have been trying to say by returning again to a dream. It is the dream of that same young woman I spoke of before, that young woman whose brother died suddenly in a tragic accident. The dream is as follows:

I am sitting at the table of my own house. There is a knock at the door and I open it to find my brother and his girlfriend (who is still alive). He seems robustly healthy and full of his usual joviality. He says he can only stay for a short time because they need to be on their way. It is then that I notice the large, pyramidal yet rounded green hat that he is wearing. I ask how they are doing. My brother's girlfriend tells me that they are doing just fine except for the fact that they don't have money. Gleeful to be able to be of some assistance, I run to get my wallet and give them all the cash contained therein. I realize that they are about to leave and I really want them to stay just a little bit longer. My brother knows this without me speaking and he says, "Come with me, I have something to show you which I don't even think you know exists." I follow him up the stairs. We walk up and up flights of stairs which I no longer recognize as parts of my house. It gradually becomes darker and darker as we ascend. Soon I am aware of ghost-like figures passing me up and down the stairs. They are dressed in eighteenth century garb and pay no attention whatsoever to my presence. When we reach the top, there is a well-lit room that looks much like an artist's studio. All the people that I know who have died are lounging around, talking or occupied in parlor-type games. I see my grandfather and my uncle and many others whom I didn't even remember "losing." I hug them all and it feels good. My brother tells me, "This is part of your own house and you can visit here anytime you like."

The dead who haunt our dreams, like the ghosts who haunt our symptoms, know the value of release. We would give them what we think they need— money or our stories— but they teach us otherwise and lead us elsewhere, beyond our offerings of money and of meaning. And in that moment, when we give up our words, when we surrender our gifts, we remember we have lost them and we grieve. Then they find their release and we find ours. Our vocation to language is to speak with the dead and of them in such a way as to free them from the imposition of our meanings.

Afterward: An Image

Winds move, music moves
Only in time: but that which is only living
Can only die. Words, after speech, reach

Into the silence. Only by the form, the pattern,
Can words or music reach
The stillness, as a Chinese jar still
Moves perpetually in its stillness.
Not the stillness of the violin, while the note lasts,
Not that only, but the coexistence,
Or say that the end precedes the beginning,
And the end and the beginning were always there
Before the beginning and after the end.
And all is always now. Words strain,
Crack and sometimes break, under the burden,
Under the tension, slip, slide, perish,
Decay with imprecision, will not stay in place,
Will not stay still.[18]

We can no more hold otherness with the word than we can hold water in the palm of the hand without it dripping away. There in one's open hand, those few drops seep out between one's fingers. And although a moment comes when one might want to squeeze one's hand together, the better to hold the remaining water, one can only hold it, the water, the word, the story, gently, with open hand, while it continues to slip away.

Once, many years ago, I saw in a church, an old church, in Canterbury, England these words engraved in stone:

How vain, how foolish to build on hopes this side the grave.
For soon the rose that blooms,
Will fade by death,
Beyond the power of human skills to save.

Vanity? Foolishness? Yes! Language, giving voice to the world, is a foolish gesture. And yet, as the poet knows, it is in this very foolishness that the dignity and the worth of our being lies. For Rilke, we are neither angel who has no need to speak, nor beast who has no power to do so. We lie between them, called to give voice to what does pass away, to witness the moment, even while it, like the water in the palm of one's hand, slips away. But for the moment, that's enough.

7

Alchemy and the Subtle
Body of Metaphor

Introduction

In *Memories, Dreams, Reflections,* Jung openly confesses that his
confrontation with the unconscious persuasively convinced him of the objectivity
of the psyche. It is closer, however, to the true spirit of Jung's experience, to its
phenomenology, to speak about the *autochthonous* character of the psyche rather
than its objectivity, because the latter term still carries the baggage of a Cartesian
metaphysics which splits subject and object and leads to a psychology of
projection. For Jung, Philemon, for example, is not a projection of his psyche;
rather, he is an inhabitant of the land of soul. In ecology, autochthonous describes
an indigenous plant or animal, and in its Greek origins the word contains the
suffix *khthon* meaning earth. Thus, an "autokhthon" is "one sprung from the
land itself."[1] Philemon, then, is indigenous to the psyche, one who from the
earliest times belongs to the soil of the soul, part of the tribe of that country
there before our time of colonization, that time of ego-consciousness when we
have already taken possession of the soul. The soul is another country, as different
from mind as it is from matter, and in this sense it makes perfect sense for Jung
to say that Philemon " brought home to me the crucial insight that there are
things in the psyche which I do not produce, which produce themselves and
have their own life." Philemon taught Jung a most significant and profound
lesson when he said to him that he (Jung) mistakenly "treated thoughts as if

(he) generated them"; and in contrast to this view Philemon said to Jung that "thoughts were like animals in the forest, or people in a room, or birds in the air." He then added, "if you should see people in a room, you would not think that you had made those people or that you were responsible for them."[2]

Jung in his best moments is a radical phenomenologist. In these moments he manages to exorcise the ghost of Descartes to attend to those subtle bodies of the imaginal realm which are between matter and mind. Those subtle bodies, like Philemon, have less substance to them than things, but more substance than thoughts. Philemon is no bloodless abstraction. But neither is he a matter of measurement or calculation. A radical phenomenology, like one can find in the later works of Maurice Merleau-Ponty, or the poetic works of Gaston Bachelard, or the metabletic works or J.H. van den Berg, is in service to Philemon and his tribe. It is devoted to those subtle bodies which are *neither* facts *nor* ideas. It is a work of the heart which is neither that of mind nor eye, a poetics of the soul's landscape where a mind feels its way into those imaginal presences who always haunt the margins of the sensible world. It is my belief that Jung practiced this radical phenomenology most daringly in his studies of alchemy. In doing so, I would argue that Jung, correctly so, enlarged his psychology and even transformed it into a cosmology. The transformation of lead into gold is the release of soul into its imaginal realm, its liberation from entrapment in the leaden literalism of scientific fact, or the suffocating dogmatism of a philosophical idea. Philemon, via Jung, disturbs the modern mind. He is the harbinger of the kind of consciousness that heralds the end of any psychology which would separate soul from cosmos. According to Paracelsus the soul is a star.[3] Philemon is a figure who teaches us, as he did Jung, that when one has a cosmology one does not need a psychology.

The Politics of Projection

More than twenty years ago, Albert Kreinheder wrote an insightful essay entitled "Alchemy and the Subtle Body." Bemoaning the small and narrow mindedness of much of contemporary psychology he wrote the following:

> It's not enough to get to work on time, to firm up the waist line, to balance the checkbook, and learn how to smile like a nice person. If that's all there is, we're still the same little earthworms, getting older every day, and no wondrous new birth has taken place within us. It would be so much nicer to have a miracle.

Philemon is a small miracle. But consider for a moment Jung's encounters with Philemon from the point of view of that contemporary psychotherapy which Kreinheder describes. It is not too difficult to imagine its effort to make sense of Philemon by reducing him to a projection of Jung's psyche, and, even worse, treating him as a symptom, as a hallucination. This kind of sensibility, especially when compared to that of the alchemists of old, can make us "worm-like literalists, sensible to the verge of stupidity." "Miracles," Kreinheder says, "never happen to sensible people."[4]

Projection is one of those notions which rests upon our unacknowledged stupidity. More so, it is one of those notions whose use can explain away what might otherwise be a miracle.

Of the many sins it conceals, the one I want to attend to is the way in which projection is the psychological counterpart of a politics of capitalism. My point is that the historical roots of the notion of projection are inseparably entangled with those that have nourished the European nation state and its politics of economic colonialism. The Cartesian dualism of an interior, subjective knowing mind sealed off from an exterior, objective world to be known and exploited repeats itself in the European movements of expansion into the New World. The subjugation of soul and its indigenous inhabitants, like Philemon, by the ego mind is of a piece with the domination of the native peoples of the New World by European powers. It is no accident that the appearance of psychology in its modern sense as a separate discipline coincides with the rise of the modern nation state, or that the hegemony of European nation states in the colonization of the New World coincides with the creation of the modern ego.[5]

The powerful murals of Diego Rivera in the "Palacio nacional" in Mexico City are a disturbing reminder of the terrible effects of this legacy of exploitation, a legacy which continues in more subtle but no less effective form in the therapy room whose models of treatment uncritically make use of the notion of projection. Projection is a colonialism of the soul, an imperialism of the ego mind against the soul. In October, 1492, Columbus anticipated the later voyages of Descartes, who in November, 1619, embarked upon them in a series of three dreams. His dreams lead to the enslavement of those autochthonous inhabitants of soul no less than those earlier journeys enchained the indigenous peoples of the New World.

Psychology cannot remain unaware of its continuing contribution to a politics practiced without a sense of soul, anymore than it can remain unaware of the cultural historical roots and political implications of its own theories and practices. Andrew Samuels reminds us of this point in his important book, *The Political Psyche.* In this work, he brings depth psychology and politics into dialogue. He offers his work as a "contribution to the long-standing ambition of depth psychology to develop a form of political and cultural analysis that would, in Freud's words, 'understand the riddles of the world.'"[6] Samuel's book persuasively applies the insights of clinical practice to politics and the exigencies of politics to clinical practice.

In addition, however, to this moment of application, there is another moment in this dialogue between the political and the psychological. Michel Foucault addresses this moment in the following remarks:

> Post-modernism assumes the task of reinvestigating the crisis and trauma at the very heart of modernity; the post-modern (is) a testament to the fact that the end of modernity is . . . a symptom as it were of its own unconscious infancy which needs to be retrieved and reworked if we are not to be condemned to an obsessional fixation upon, and compulsive repetition of, the sense of its ending. In this respect, the task of a post-modern imagination might be to envision the end of modernity as a possibility of rebeginning.[7]

This essay is less an application of the principles of depth psychology to the practice of politics, and more a critical, cultural-historical examination of those principles, especially the notion of projection. My intention is to show that the uncritical use of a term like projection already implies a politics of imperialism which functions at an unconscious level in the theories and practices of depth psychology.

In this move to deconstruct the origins of depth psychology for the sake of a new beginning, I am not suggesting that the idea of projection is either wrong or false. In its presence and in its effects it is demonstrably real. Moreover, we see it exercised daily in the practice of politics. Rather, I am arguing for a mindfulness about its heritage and a recognition of the consequences which follow upon its use. Jung's encounters with Philemon suggest the possibility of another way of knowing the world and being in it which has nothing to do with the notion of projection. It is a way of knowing and being which takes us beyond that dichotomy of subject and object which necessitates the very idea of projection. The telos of my argument is that Philemon carries us beyond a psychology of projection into a cosmology of synchronicities.

The Gestural Body

Disembodied minds project; ensouled bodies establish an interactive, gestural field. Merleau-Ponty's phenomenology of perception lays the foundation for what I would call a gestural metaphysics. The gestural body is a magnetic, gravitational, erotic field which sweeps the other into the orbit of its intentions and desires, and which, reciprocally, is swept up by the gestures of that other. Together, in mutuality and below any explicit conscious awareness, you and I create a landscape of experience. The actor on the stage whispers a line and the audience, almost imperceptibly, already leans into the softly spoken words. The whisper and inclination of the audience belong together; one is not the cause of the other. "The gesture is the outline of a world, the chiseling of what is otherwise a neutral space into a significant place."[8] Animate flesh impregnates animate flesh. Together we establish an ambience and create a mood. The gestural body which solicits and seduces the other is the threnody of the Cartesian dream of reason. It is the undoing of that dream which would place the mind inside the body like a pilot is inside the ship. And the symptomatic body which inaugurates the therapy room of depth psychology is this gestural body in disguise. "The symptomatic body is the locus of a loss. What the patient brings into the field of therapy is a body haunted by an absent other, a body whose gestures find no witness, no reciprocal for their appeal."[9] At a cultural-historical level this absent other was the world which had already faded into the distance of a measured objectivity for a spectator-self ensconced within a body made over in the image of a machine.

To think and to theorize in terms of projection is to practice a psychology rooted in Cartesian metaphysics which discounts the gestures of the animate flesh. This abandonment of the flesh establishes the codes by which the modern mind and its shipwrecks— those figures of soul haunting the symptomatic body— are described: a spectator self, imprisoned in a body made into a specimen, observing in distance and neutrality a world turned into a spectacle for its exploitation and use.[10]

Projection rests upon a philosophy of space which separates the inside from the outside, a dualism of interiority and exteriority which identifies the interior with mind or consciousness and the exterior with the world, a world without qualities, a world drained of its erotic complexities, a world of matter that has been de-animated. It is a way of thinking and being which produces the following kind of declaration:

It is my mind, with its store of images, which gives the world color and sound; . . . and "experience" is, in its more simple form, an exceedingly complex structure of mental images. Thus there is in a certain sense nothing which is directly experienced except the mind itself. So thick and deceptive is this fog about us that we had to invent the exact sciences in order to catch at least a glimmer of this so called "real" nature of things.[11]

The passage is not from Descartes. On the contrary, it is from Jung and it clearly illustrates that his psychology is haunted by a dualism of inside and outside, leaving soul without world and the world without soul. It is no surprise, therefore, to read in Jung that "projection is an . . . automatic process whereby a content that is unconscious to the subject transfers itself to an object, so that it seems to belong to the object."[12] Beauty is in the eye of the beholder and Philemon shudders with rage.[13]

A psychology of projection is at odds with a psychology which acknowledges the autochthonous characters of soul. And yet this tension is not about an "either-or." Projection as a psychological experience does exist. But as von Franz reminds us, "what may or may not be described as projection today is still largely a question of judgment. . . so that in my opinion psychologists should use the greatest caution and discretion in dealing with this concept."[14]

Greeting Philemon

Who is Philemon? And *what* is he? What kind of being is he and to what landscape does he belong? Autochthonous, he dwells in the land of soul, but now it is a question of *how* he dwells there. How Philemon is tells us who and what he is.

Jung reports that he talks to Philemon as if he were another person. And he does so while walking in his garden. Jung speaks with Philemon while they walk together. Their relationship is peripatetic. Jung and Philemon have a walk-about.

This small detail is not trivial because it tells us that for Jung there is a differentiation between himself and Philemon but not a separation. Philemon is different from Jung, a someone else, an-other, and yet in their walk-about they are related. Philemon addresses Jung and Jung replies. Jung speaks to Philemon and Philemon listens. In this other-ness, Philemon has his own reality. We can, however, easily imagine that for Jung Philemon's presence is not like that of the flowers in the garden, or the stones on the path, or the birds in the tree. Philemon is present in a different way. His presence is more subtle.

What shall we call this subtle presence of Philemon who is *neither a* factual object in the world (like those stones or those birds *can* be), *nor* a subjective idea in Jung's mind which he projects onto the world? What is the nature of this subtle body of Philemon who is *neither* a thing *nor* a thought? Philemon haunts the garden of Jung. He plays on the border of the real and the ideal, hovering like some great being of light, a vibration that at one moment seems substantive like a particle and at another moment without substance like a wave. Philemon is an imaginal being, one of those invisible guests in the felicitous phrase of Mary Watkins.[15] Philemon, I would claim, is the subtle body of metaphor.

Metaphor is a *third* between the two of things and thoughts. It is the halo which surrounds even perceptual things, like stones on a path, when in a moment of reverie they display their elusive charm and reveal their presence as mineral beings who know the patience of endurance and the peace of waiting. In such moments, one can long to be the stone because its imaginal presence is so strong, because its metaphorical character has been welcomed, because one has allowed oneself to be drawn out of the separation and isolation of one's subjectivity to be penetrated by the spell of its animate presence. "The sea observed is a reverie," Victor Hugo once said, and around it waves of desire or storms of emotion can appear.[16] A radical phenomenology of the sensuous world, as Merleau-Ponty's phenomenology presents, releases the imaginal trapped in the literalism of facts or the dogmatism of thoughts. It reveals that the real is most radically the subtle body of metaphor.

As an autochthonous character of soul Philemon is an imaginal being, a metaphorical presence in the world. He is not *a* metaphor. Rather he is that kind of presence which a metaphor brings, a figural presence whose texture is neither that of fact nor idea, and a presence which requires of us that delight in and attunement to the play of language and experience. A psychology of projection resting in a dualism which rationalizes mind and literalizes matter loses the sense of this kind of presence, this third between things and thoughts. It eclipses the imaginal realm of experience and leaves only a void in the space between matter and mind. Indeed, the primary consequence of the Cartesian dream of reason is this eclipse of the world's imaginal body, this eclipse of soul and the indigenous figures who belong to its landscape. Philemon and his kin are uprooted by the reasonable mind which de-animates the world and transforms the flesh of soul into a mechanism. Philemon and his kin are perhaps the first refugees of modernity, displaced and homeless wanderers who appear at the gateway of ego-consciousness in the ragged and tattered disguise of a symptom, or in the chaotic form of a dream, whose alien, mad logic terrorizes the reasonable mind. Philemon and his kin rise up out of that void between matter and mind, and in ghostly form, like a mist, announce their presence.

In a superb, historical irony, the Cartesian dream of reason begins in 1619 with three dreams, nightmares really, which disturb Descartes' sleep. These haunting wraiths of the soul are the harbingers of what will come out of those dreams to vex the sleep of our world. They are an early anticipation by the soul of its own banishment by the ego mind, protestations of what is to come and will come when Descartes works out his project. They are the shadow side of the 1641 opus, *Meditations on First Philosophy* , where Descartes writes that "the human body may easily perish, but the mind or soul of man, *between which I find no distinction,* is immortal by its very nature."[17]

This erasure of difference between mind and soul is the colonization of soul by mind. In both the Latin and French editions of his text, Descartes continually shows his preferences for those terms which translate as mind or spirit over those which translate as soul. In Latin, *Mens*—the masculine spirit or mind— subdues *Anima*— the feminine soul. And in French, the masculine *l'esprit* conquers the feminine *l'ame.* Moreover, it is important to notice that this eclipse of difference between soul and mind, and the triumph of the latter over the former, is situated in relation to Descartes' vision of the body. The mind is immortal, the body is not. But this mortal body which perishes is not for Descartes the animate, ensouled flesh. On the contrary, it is a mechanism, its perishability illustrated by the idea of the watch whose mainspring has broken. To perish, then, is not so much to die as it is to fall apart. Into that void between matter and mind, the feminine soul as animate flesh disappears. Torn between matter and mind, the soul falls apart and slouches toward Yeat's Bethlehem and Freud's Vienna, waiting to be re-born in his therapy room.

Philemon as an autochthonous character of soul demands a redemption of that lost third, the realm of the imaginal between things and thoughts. Philemon himself, as well as his tribe— the figures of the dream and the ghosts who haunt our symptoms— is not only an animate presence in the world; he is also the animate presence of the world.[18] Philemon is an example of the world's subtle body, a reality which is neither a fact nor an idea. To encounter him and his kin requires, then, a kind of consciousness attuned to metaphor. Writing of this subtle body, Nathan Schwartz-Salant says that, "The question is not whether or not the subtle body exists, but whether or not its existence can be perceived." By perceived he means a vision which is more than a matter of what meets the eyeball. He means another kind of consciousness, one "not concerned with ordinary perceptions, but with imaginal ones." "Those who can *see*, will do so," he adds; "those who cannot will remain skeptical."[19]

Alchemy is the kind of consciousness which predates the skepticism of Descartes' dreams. Jung's alchemical studies offer another way of greeting Philemon, apart from that skepticism and doubt of the imaginal which leads to a psychology of projection.

Alchemy and the Subtle Body of Metaphor

The literary critic, Howard Nemerov tells the following brief story to illustrate the character of metaphor.

> While I am thinking about metaphor, a flock of purple finches arrives on the lawn. Since I haven't seen these birds for some years, I am only fairly sure of their being in fact purple finches, so I get down Peterson's *Field Guide* and read his description: "Male:About the size of House Sparrow, rosy-red, brightest on head and rump." That checks quite well, but his next remark— "a Sparrow dipped in raspberry juice"— is decisive: it fits. I look out the window again, and now I *know* that I am seeing purple finches.
>
> That's very simple. So simple, indeed, that I hesitate to look any further into the matter, for as soon as I do I shall see its simplicity is not altogether canny. Why should I be made certain of what a purple finch is by being lead to contemplate a sparrow dipped in raspberry juice? Have I ever dipped a sparrow in raspberry juice? Has anyone? And yet there it is, quite certain and quite right. Peterson and I and the finches are in agreement."[20]

A purple finch is a sparrow dipped in raspberry juice! The power of the metaphor is that it opens a vision of the world which is neither empirically true nor false. The metaphor is not a factual description of the world. Indeed, if in a fit of empirical frenzy Nemerov managed to enter the garden and seize in his hands a purple finch, his hands would not drip with juice.

In the Cartesian dream of reason, what is not an empirical fact in the world must be a rational idea of the mind. But the purple finch which Nemerov sees is not an idea in his head. He is looking at the bird in the garden. The metaphor which opens Nemerov's vision is neither a fact in the world nor an idea in the mind. A metaphor is a power which releases the imaginal sense of things.

Winston Churchill, that great master of the English language and of metaphor, once described Mussolini as "that utensil." Does one not see through that image the empty buffoonery of Mussolini?

Alchemy was and is a way of thinking which installs one in this *neither-nor* domain of metaphor. Within this domain any absolute separation of inner and outer, of mind and matter, of consciousness and nature is dissolved. David Fideler makes the same point in the following fashion. "Alchemy," he says, "is rooted in an uncritical way of knowing, in which there is no fundamental difference between the alchemist and the rest of nature."[21]

Fideler's use of the term "uncritical" refers to a way of knowing which suspends the judgmental activity of an ego mind that distances and separates itself from what it would know. In fact, in speaking of no fundamental difference, Fideler, I would argue, is suggesting that alchemy is a way of knowing where consciousness or spirit belongs to matter or nature, a way of knowing which recognizes that spirit matters and that matter yearns to be in-spired. Alchemy is and was a way of knowing and being which holds difference within relation. It does not deny the tension of difference between consciousness or spirit and matter or nature. Quite the contrary, in accepting this tension alchemy depicts a way of knowing through intimacy and relation rather than through separation and distance. A metaphor dis-solves separation between knower and known; it holds us in relation with the other without erasing the difference between us. The contemporary physicist, like his alchemist counterpart of old, recognizes that his presence as observer affects what is observed. That recognition, however, does not eclipse the difference between them.

The *neither-nor* logic of metaphor, the logic of the third between matter and mind, the realm of soul, requires that one must give up the notion of being able to attribute with final certainty that the epiphany of meaning belongs *either* on the side of consciousness as experience, *or* on the side of the world as an event. The *either-or* logic of mind is undone in the *neither-nor* logic of soul. The density of facts and the clarity of ideas are dis-solved and confused in the softer texture and diaphanous mist of the imaginal. Indeed, the work of soul, like that of alchemy, is about dis-solutions rather than solutions. The dream, for example, is a nightly alchemical work which dis-solves or undoes the fixed solutions of the daily ego-mind. And metaphor does in daylight what the dream does at night. It is a piece of soul work, a waking dream, or what I would call, following Bachelard, a reverie, one of whose benefits is to free us into the imaginal depths of the world. Indeed, the depths of the world which metaphor reveals extends to the stars. "At the end," Bachelard says, "imagining a cosmos is the most natural destiny of reverie."[22]

Alchemy's opus—the transformation of lead into gold— is metaphor's work of releasing the spirit of things from their leaden literalism. In this regard, the alchemist is like the poet, who is a maker and master of metaphor. Both alchemist and poet are *metaphoricans*, one of nature and the other of the word. The alchemist and the maker of metaphor practice a poetic science of the natural world, not an empirical one. Therefore, when the poet Emily Dickinson says, "Tell all the truth, but tell it slant," she could be speaking also of the alchemist's vision.[23] For alchemist and poet the imaginal reveals itself to an oblique vision which alludes, like a metaphor does, to something which always remains elusive. The imaginal is not captured by the focused stare of the empirical sciences, or the clear and distinct ideas of the Cartesian mind. I imagine that Jung walks with Philemon in his garden and *side by side* they converse, perhaps, on occasion, stealing a glance at each other, leaving the other in mystery.

In an alchemical work entitled *De chimea* there is the famous illustration of the winged and wingless birds. The winged bird is above the wingless one and each is eating the other's tail. The text says that the wingless bird prevents the winged bird from soaring away. But we can also say that the winged bird in its efforts to fly away slightly elevates the wingless one.

The illustration is perhaps the best and simplest way to indicate the central issue of alchemy:the tension of spirit and matter. Alchemy, as I said earlier, is a kind of consciousness which holds this tension and in holding it the subtle body of the third, the soul, the realm of the imaginal, which is neither that of spirit, consciousness, mind, nor matter, nature, body is born.

Commenting on this central issue, von Franz notes that this tension where we cannot decide whether something belongs to the realm of mind or matter is an eternal problem.[24] But in fact, it is not even correct to say problem because the term implies a solution. Indeed, von Franz is indicating that when one takes up the claims of the soul there is no solution. A solution to the tension of spirit and matter happens only when one denies the tension; it happens only when one separates the winged and wingless birds. Then the clarity of a two is achieved, the clarity of a dualism, which allows one to say with certainty that a particular occurrence is either a subjective, psychological experience projected onto the world, or an objective event in the world cleansed of our participation. But in achieving that clarity what is lost is that creative tension which reveals the desire, longing, hunger on the part of spirit to matter, and that equally strong hunger on the part of matter to be in-spired.

Alchemy redeems the subtle imaginal body of the world, Philemon's landscape.[25]   More than once, Jung makes it quite clear that the domain of alchemy is this region between spirit and matter, this domain of neither-nor. In *Psychology and Alchemy*, for example, he writes:

> . . . it always remains an obscure point whether the ultimate transformations in the alchemical process ought to be sought more in the material or more in the spiritual realm . Actually, however, the question is wrongly put: there was no "either-or" for that age, but there did exist an intermediate realm between mind and matter, i.e., a psychic realm of subtle bodies whose characteristic it is to manifest themselves in mental as well as material form. This is the only view that makes sense of alchemical ways of thought, which must otherwise appear non-sensical.[26]

In reverie before his fires the alchemist witnessed the conjunctio of spirit and matter. The psychic realm of subtle bodies which is realized in that act of witnessing is neither matter nor mind. On the contrary, as a footnote appended to the above text poignantly indicates "(Anima) is a subtle, imperceptible smoke."[27] Smoke and vapors, dust and mist:these are the stuff that soul is made on. The subtle body of alchemy, like the subtle body of metaphor, is the stuff of mood, an ambience which pervades and penetrates the field. The imaginal is neither in us nor in the world. It surrounds us, like light or wind. Philemon in his subtle, imaginal body is an aroma, a perfume.

Philemon, Jung, and Phenomenology

It is difficult, if not impossible, to distinguish with any finality between a projection and an autochthonous figure of the soul. In telling us about Philemon, Jung wants us to appreciate him as an autochthonous character of soul and not a projection. We have no grounds to disbelieve him. Moreover, the issue here is not an either-or, for as von Franz so wisely notes regarding the term projection, its use "depends on the state I am in."[28] In this essay I have attempted to show the historical context of that state. Its use coincides with an eclipse of the imaginal as a third between matter and mind, with a de-animation of the flesh that transforms the vital, gestural body into a mechanism, and with a broken connection between the ensouled sensuous body and the sense-able world.

The Cartesian dream of reason, with its metaphysics of an inside-mind-space and an outside-world-space, is a moment in the history of the soul when this eclipse of the imaginal became acute. We are still living within that dream,

as is Jung's psychology. The notion of projection and its use bears witness to
this fact. But the possibility of projection is certainly older that this dream.
Indeed, perhaps, as von Franz notes, it is as ancient as consciousness itself.
Speaking of a monk who has fallen in love, she asks whether his love should be
regarded *either* as a spiritual crisis and explained in terms of an anima projection,
or as a legitimate desire for a relation with an actual woman in the world. Wisely
she cautions that this conflict cannot be solved rationally. She writes: "The
only way the self can manifest is through conflict." One must roast in the
conflict, like the salamander in alchemy roasts in the flames. One must endure
in the difficult third place where the conflict is neither this nor that. "It is
consciousness," she says " that creates the split and says either/or." And then,
most astonishingly, she adds that "to meet one's insoluble and eternal conflict is
to meet God, which would be the end of the ego with all its blather." This
moment is "the moment of surrender. . . where Job says he will put his hand on
his mouth and not argue about God."[29]

Autochthonous characters of soul are also moments which invite surrender.
The Cartesian dream of reason is a response to that moment which has refused
the invitation to surrender. Modern ego-consciousness rests upon this refusal
and in that refusal lies both its power and its shadow. It is what has allowed the
ego mind to keep itself distant, separate, and apart from the world, and to bend
it and the soul to its own will.[30]

In one respect, Jung's psychology has been an attempt to come to terms
with this refusal, an attempt to go beyond the psychology of projection which
arises in the void between mind and matter. "Man, with his consciousness, is a
disturbing factor in the order of nature; one could really question whether man
was a good invention on the part of nature or not." This is von Franz who adds,
"one aim of analysis is to get consciousness to function again according to
nature."[31] Jung's studies of alchemy and his notion of synchronicity tend in that
direction. They move toward a psychology which is in fact no longer a psychology
in the modern sense of an interior soul or self, but a cosmology where the self
is a star. They move toward a consciousness which surrenders to its participation
in the order of creation.

In this move, Jung's psychology converges with phenomenology, especially
with a phenomenology like that of Merleau-Ponty. In an early work,
Phenomenology of Perception, Merleau-Ponty shows how the cogito is flesh, a
sensuous consciousness impregnated by the sense-able things of the world. And
in his final work, *The Visible and the Invisible*, he describes the body-world
relation as a chiasm or crossing where the world is the *telos* of the sensing-

sensitive flesh.

Between these two works, there are numerous, significant essays like "The Philosopher and His Shadow," a work whose very title evokes the suggestive image of the light of reason carrying its own darkness. Thinking is an embodied gesture, always embedded within and arising from a specific situation. Thinking is always carried into its thoughts by a body already seduced by the allure, the charm of the world, by the spell of the sensuous to borrow a title from David Abram's richly evocative book on Merleau-Ponty. In addition, there is the late essay "Eye and Mind," perhaps Merleau-Ponty's best work, where he tells us that the painter takes his body with him. In effect, he is saying that there is the miracle of painting, and the everyday epiphanies of vision, because vision fulfills itself only through the visible, because the cogito-incarnate realizes itself only in, and through, and as the world. Between body and world lies the field of eros, a bond of desire which already inscribes the mind with a hunger for this otherness of the world. And if we ask what is this world which seduces the passionate mind to embrace it; what are these things of the world— the trees, the mountains, the stones; the stars, the oceans, the clouds; the birds, the animals, the flowers; the roads, the houses, and the gardens —, we discover that they are pregnancies of possibilities, swollen seeds of promise ready to release their fruitful mysteries in our presence.

In *Psychological Life: from Science to Metaphor*, I drew on this work of Merleau-Ponty, as well as that of J.H. van den Berg, to declare how a phenomenology of the sensuous world reveals the world's metaphorical character.[32] In its metaphorical structure, we find a world where we encounter things not as facts to be discovered, or as screens for our mental projections, but as invitations, or even temptations, or as occasions to participate in the world's continuous unfolding and realization. A more recent work, *The Orphan and the Angel: Grief and the Reveries of Love*,[33] draws upon the poetic phenomenology of Gaston Bachelard to show how reverie is the mood of this radical phenomenology which liberates the imaginal presence of the world, frees it from the dead literalism of fact and the un-inspired dogmatism of thought.

An incarnate consciousness is a first, necessary step toward the recovery of the imaginal as real, and the real as imaginal. Starting with a body that is already mindful of the world, with a mind that is already kissed by things, phenomenology allows one to appreciate the metaphorical structure of reality and the metaphorical character of our experience. Soaked within this appreciation, we are able to be responsive to the third between material facts and mental ideas, the third of the imaginal, where metaphorical consciousness dwells. And such a consciousness is indispensable for encountering someone like Philemon who will not yield himself to the literal minded or to a thinking that is too rational.

In this regard, Jung's psychology needs phenomenology. It needs its radical epistemology which goes beyond the Cartesian dream of reason. Indeed, it needs it because ghosts are powerful beings, and even someone like Jung could not so easily exorcise the ghost of Descartes. His psychology, in fact, is always moving between one uncritically rooted in projection and one that acknowledges the autonomy of soul. Thus, one will find in the very same passage about the subtle bodies of alchemy quoted earlier this statement: "... the existence of this intermediate realm (subtle bodies) comes to a stop the moment we try to investigate matter in and for itself, apart from all projection. . ."[34]   Or, one will find a statement like this : " . . . the real root of alchemy is to be sought in the projections of individual investigators."[35]   In these passages, Jung not only defends projection, he also makes it a condition for the appearance of the subtle realm.

I would argue, however, that those moments when Jung's psychology is humbled by the autonomy of the soul are the ones where the alchemical opus of transforming lead into gold continues, and where his psychology is most radical and realizes its own destiny. They are the moments when he steps out of our Cartesian consciousness which splits spirit and matter, mind and nature, into a consciousness attuned to the synchronicities of spirit-matter. Indeed, I would claim that it is no accident that after his long studies of alchemy Jung announced this principle of synchronicity, for it is the *telos* of that journey from a psychology of separation based in projection to a cosmology of relations based in synchronicity. The third of metaphor between matter and mind, the realm of the imaginal is a sychronistic field. We encounter Philemon and his kin when our consciousness, weaned of the literal and released into the figural, situates us in the field between the literal and the logical.

Open to the Miracle: From Psychology to Cosmology

A metaphor is a small miracle, a momentary tear in the fabric of the quotidian round, a moment when a vision which erupts between us is neither a psychological experience nor a material event. It is the kind of moment which recognizes and appreciates the subtle body of the world, the kind of moment which can occur, for example, when in a state of reverie, of empathic attunement to the world, I say of the smile which marks the countenance of a loved one that it is a facial orgasm, or of the wind which slightly stirs the trees that it is the sky's ocean. It is a moment of beauty really, a moment when one is awe struck by the fecundity of the world, by its glorious ripeness and outpouring generosity. Those marvelous paintings of old which show the Angel in encounter with us always impress this point of being awe-struck, struck dumb, because we are truly capable only of silence in this moment where we witness the conjunction of spirit and matter, of mind or consciousness and nature. These small miracles, which open to us that third of the imaginal between spirit and matter, are moments when that arc which bridges the earthy animal passion of out material existence, and the heavenly angelic beauty of our spirit, energizes our humanity, delivers us from ourselves, and releases us into the cosmos.

It is no accident, I believe, that Jung acknowledges that in former times moments of synchronicity were known as miracles.[36] A metaphor is a moment of synchronicity and such a moment, as von Franz notes, situates us in the between of the imaginal. Synchronicity, she writes, is more than a new idea. It is "the manifestation of a concrete living principle which can not be described as dead matter, or as 'only' psychic (with the implication of not being connected with matter)." With the eruption of this concrete living principle, we are in that same place of neither/nor, the third of metaphor. Moreover, when von Franz adds that synchronicity "is a power which brings forth acts of creation in time,"[37] we are again in the mood of metaphor, because, as we have already said, the vision of metaphor is the way in which we continue the work of creation, releasing the promise of the world into its fulfillment.

The alchemists of old were adepts in this release, witnesses to the conjunction of spirit and matter. They lived in the subtle field of neither/nor, as Jung himself acknowledged, and in doing so they occasioned moments of synchronicity, occasional miracles. Indeed, the principle task of alchemy was the redemption of matter, the release of those divine sparks of spirit which had fallen from the heavens. The *telos* of Jung's psychology was, I believe, always a sacred cosmology where soul finds its home again in the order of creation. The passageway of this journey lies between eye and mind, between the empiricism of facts and the rationalism of ideas. A scared cosmology requires the poetic vision of the soul. It calls for that kind of consciousness which, in delivering us from the literal and the logical, lives in the realization of the metaphorical. The synchronicity of metaphor occasions a moment when the veil of creation lifts to reveal the sacred face of the ordinary, the miraculous in the mundane. Philemon belongs to such moments. He resides in them, just beyond the curtain, waiting for us, over there in the field.

Postscript: Philemon and the Angel: A Confession

When I had finished this essay, I was thinking of Philemon, about the subtle body of metaphor, about his place in the world as an imaginal being. But something was not quite right, and I felt a bit uneasy about this claim. Was it right, or better, fair, to describe him as an imaginal presence in the world? My unease had to do with the question of whether this claim was already too much, whether it had already yoked Philemon too closely to us and kept him a prisoner of our psychologies and the human realm to which they belong. Did the claim eclipse the radical other-ness of Philemon? To borrow for a moment a philosophical mode of expression, I wondered if the claim did not rob Philemon of his ontological status as something wholly other and apart from the human psyche. The claim, of course, has an epistemological weight, since it is only through the human psyche that the experience of the world and all its appearances takes place. But epistemological claims should not occlude ontological differences, and it is Philemon's difference from us which is at the heart of this claim. From an epistemological perspective the imaginal is and must, of course, always be a psychological experience. But from an ontological point of view the imaginal is not the psychological. In this regard, Philemon is *not* a psychological being. Indeed, the point of my essay is that he leads us beyond psychology into a cosmology where different orders of being intersect with us and we with them.[38]

Musing along these lines, I thought about the Angel, and recalled how in an earlier publication I refused to call the Angel an imaginal being.[39] Guided by Rilke's appreciation of the Angel who in its radiant alterity is a mirror who draws back into itself its own beauty, I understood how this absolute otherness can reveal itself as a kind of terrible indifference to us. This radical other-ness is in fact the basis for Rilke's claim that every Angel is terrible. In the face of this other-ness, then, it seems to me too poor of us to call them imaginal beings, too insensitive, and even, perhaps, too arrogant. And I recalled at this moment the consequence of an encounter with beings like Angels who belong to and come from other orders of creation. In their awe-ful presence, we are struck dumb, and silence is often the norm.

Between the claim and the silence, then, what are we to choose?

The great paintings of Angels from Medieval Christendom depict these other beings and the painted image is a claim. And Rilke has taught us not only to appreciate our power to claim, but also to value it as a sign of *our* difference.

For Rilke we are called to speak and proclaim; we are called into the claim. Language is our vocation and we are asked to speak, not only *to* the angel— "Praise the world to the Angel/Tell him things"[40]—but even *of* the Angel. What seems important here is the recognition that the claim is not the being who is proclaimed. The Angel is not the painting; the Angel is not the image, nor the word. And yet, still, the image or the word alludes to the being who is other. The claim alludes to an other-ness which seems elusive, two words whose roots mean to play.[41] What seems important, then, is a proclaiming— Philemon is an imaginal being— which plays with other-ness. What seems important is a kind of proclaiming which never takes itself too seriously. It is a way of speaking which recognizes that for the moment, that's enough.[42]

These reveries on Philemon and Angels were interrupted by the appearance of a friend and colleague at that threshold of my office. He came in and we began a conversation. In the midst of it, I "saw" my wife crossing the path outside my office, and I knew she had come, as promised, to see me for a moment before I began an evening class. I halted my conversation with my friend, and ran outside to greet her, but she was not there. I called her name, thinking that she had disappeared behind the row of hedges on the far side of my office. But there was no response. Completely mystified by her absence, I returned to my office. At that moment, the phone rang, and it was my wife. She was calling to tell me that she would be unable to arrive at my office on time and that she was keenly disappointed. Both of us were strongly anticipating this meeting, as brief as it would be. We were missing each other and longed to be together, even for a moment.

On the way to my evening class, I realized for the first time, that, given the position of the chair in my office, I could not have seen with my bodily eyes my wife crossing the path. On the contrary, I had seen her with an imaginal eye, that third eye which is open to that realm which is neither factual nor rational. In that moment, her presence was of that subtle sort which belongs to an-other realm of experience, to that third realm which I had been calling in this essay the imaginal.

In that circuitous way of thinking characteristic of reverie, it occurred to me that I had also just witnessed an occasion of bi-locality, which quantum physics ascribes to quantum objects in that state called "superposition." At the quantum level matter is highly energized—matter, we might say, is truly in-spired— and in this state an electron can occupy more than one orbital level simultaneously. Since we too are material beings, is it possible that in in-spired states of desire and eros we can be in more than one place simultaneously?

Sinking deeper into reverie, I then remembered that another aspect of superposition is that a photon, a particle of light, not only can travel along two paths at the same time, but also traverse space in the same way that Thomas Aquinas described the movement of Angels. When an Angel's movement is discontinuous, he said, "it does not cross all the intermediate places between its starting place and its term."[43] Its movement between two places is instantaneous, and one cannot say where it was in between those two places, like one cannot say with any certainty where a photon has been between, for example, its emission from the sun and its impact on Earth. In between, it is non-localized, anywhere or everywhere as it were. Moreover, the state of superposition of quantum objects is a condition best described in terms of neither-nor. Indeed, the famous example of Schroedinger's cat who is neither dead nor alive is a classic example of superposition. Quantum objects in superposition are in that same metaphorical state which, I said, describes Philemon's presence. At this moment, an awe-ful conclusion pressed itself upon me: the imaginal is a quantum reality, a quantum field. Quantum physics and imaginal psychology are two sides of the same coin. Philemon and his kind are expressions of that other-ness where soul, spirit, and matter meet, where physics and psychology join.

It is the principle of synchronocity which yokes the imaginal psyche and quantum matter. Philemon is an experience-event that one can describe only as neither psychological nor physical, a metaphorical presence, which this principle of synchronicity addresses. Moreover, since synchronicity is described by Jung as acts of creation in time, creation is continuous, and thus it no longer makes sense to ask about the origins and endings of creation. These questions are dissolved and one can say only of creation, of Philemon, of photons, of the imaginal-quantum order, that it *is* because it always was and because it always was it will continue to be. In that place of synchronicity, in that place where an experience-event is neither physical nor psychological, in that place of metaphorical presence, that place of imaginal-quantum beings, Philemon and his kind, like Angels, are beyond time, are eternal.

A-musing reveries, wild musings prompted by this experience of bi-locality evoked the Angel, and I wondered why in relation to my concerns about Philemon the Angel had appeared. I wondered about the connection between Philemon, the Angel, and this experience of bi-locality. Was it a moment of synchronicity? In speaking of synchronicity, von Franz has used the quotidian example of a telephone call from someone about whom one is thinking in that moment. It seems to me that this was such a moment, an opening in the world's fabric through which the imaginal erupted.

But still, why? Why at that moment when I had been musing about Philemon and the Angel, concerned that I might have done him a dis-service by calling him an imaginal being? I have no answer. But I do have a feeling and the feeling is that this experience was Philemon's way of cautioning me at the end of this essay not to forget the difference between us. It was, I believe, his way of saying, "Be care-ful not to take the claims of your psychology too seriously."[44]

8

On Angels and Other
Anomalies of the Imaginal Life

The Witness and the Critic

Reverie has always been for me something of a temperamental style, which is why, I guess, I was from very early on called a daydreamer. Then I was too young to appreciate the apt loveliness of the word, but in time I came to value the vision of someone who dreams the day, which is a wonderful privilege really, an honor and a gift. Dreaming the world while awake, an appropriate if brief description of reverie, seeing the world through a veil of dreams--its dreams--, allowing things to blossom with their secrets and mysteries, the daydreamer in reverie regards the world with soft eyes. Still later, when I was studying phenomenology, I began to sense how the daydreamer and phenomenologist are kin. For what is phenomenology if it is not the capacity to dream with the world?

Young daydreamers are drawn to become phenomenologists, just as phenomenologists can be described as old daydreamers. In either guise the curious fact is that each is always slightly out of step with the explanations given for the things of the world. For a daydreamer, and for a phenomenologist, an explanation always has the effect of taking him or her away from how things are in themselves, simply in their presence as they appear and in their difference from other things. When, for example, someone knows that ice and steam are, in spite of their appearances, the same thing—molecules of H_2O—, then one is at serious risk of not seeing the ice or the steam as they are on their own terms. Knowing the facts in this case can close one's eyes to their difference: the steam which rises from a hot cup of coffee is not the same as those ice cubes which float in some cold tea. Ice and steam even belong to different landscapes of the world. The former is more at home on cold wintry mornings; the latter on hot summer afternoons.

A daydreaming phenomenologist is loyal to differences. This loyalty requires a kind of patience, the best virtue which a daydreamer has and, not surprisingly, the one which a fact-minded person often finds so irritating. This patience characterizes the style of what I call the witness, the one who stands up for the things of the world, especially for those small things which often go unnoticed, like the play of light and shadow in a grove of trees, or the early-morning song of a bird.

For a witness these small epiphanies of the world always have something of an attic quality to them, that place of reverie so beautifully explored by Gaston Bachelard in *The Poetics of Reverie*. Writing out of this space of attic reverie in *The Soul in Grief: Love, Death, and Transformation*, I wondered what strange alchemy must transpire in this place which, farthest from the ground of our daily concerns, is the first to receive the warmth of the morning sun and then later the light of the stars and the glow of the moon. In the alchemy of reverie the hard edges of the world are dissolved as things reveal their secrets and announce their dreams. In this place, the witness knows the world in a different way than does the critic, and, taking leave of him, frees the world into its awe-ful mysteries. On one such occasion, I saw how a rose so fully desired to be itself that it opened beyond its own boundaries, drinking in the light, becoming pure light itself before its pedals would begin to fall away. In that moment, I realized a wonderful secret of the world: that a rose is a flowering of the sun, the light's way of becoming blossom and seed, odor and color, texture and visibility.

Witness and critic are two different styles and temperaments, each of which reveals and conceals the world in its own particular fashion. In the face of the world's multiplicity, for example, the witness eschews judgments for as long as possible, the better to let things declare themselves before we silence them with how we know them. The witness is one who loves the world, the one for whom knowing flows from being, from being in love. For the critic it is the other way around: being follows from knowing; how things are depends upon how we know them. The scientific- technological way of knowing the world is a good illustration of the style of the critic. This way of knowing the world gives us great power over it, but it also shapes our way of being in the world: consumers of it ensconced in a practical, matter of fact mind.

It is not, however, a question of being either a witness or a critic. We are always something of each, just as love always has something of power in it, and power, if one is careful, can cradle love. Nevertheless, I do lean in my life and work toward the side of the witness because the critic has been so much in the ascendant that the witness's way of knowing the world and being in it, the way of love, the path of the daydreamer and phenomenologist has become endangered.

Looking at Medieval Paintings

Looking at paintings can be an occasion for reverie and for change. An occasion if the painting is more than what we look at; if it is also a moment which reflects how we are looking.

Medieval paintings are such an occasion. Mirroring back how we are looking, they can challenge some very basic, unexamined assumptions about how we regard ourselves and how we construct our notions of what is real. A stroll through a gallery of medieval paintings can be a kind of therapeutic reverie. The self who enters the gallery is undone, as the paintings become an instrument for an archeology of one's vision. Standing before these paintings one can discover forgotten possibilities, other ways of seeing and knowing which over time have fallen into disuse. A medieval painting can be a checkpoint at a border crossing between two worlds. Looking at these paintings can be a journey into a different landscape of experience where the usual habits and customs of one's style of being in and knowing the world are transformed.

There are many things in the territory of a medieval painting to challenge one's vision. Angels, for example, abound within its borders. They are everywhere, dominating the spaces which they share with our medieval ancestors, before we lost sight of them. Magnificent beings, these angels announce by their presence the continuity between the divine and the human realms. They are, as their name indicates, messengers, beings who connect us and keep us in touch with the glory and the wisdom of another order of reality. They tell us things, as so many of the annunciation paintings demonstrate. In particular, I have always loved those paintings where the angel, announcing to Mary that she is to be the mother of God, speaks to her through a trumpet-like tube which connects the Angel's mouth to the Virgin's ear. It is a strikingly beautiful image and a powerfully persuasive way to suggest that the angel impregnates us with the word.

In the presence of these images, I realize that in the medieval cosmos we are summoned to listen, called to obey, and for a moment I am wistful for how much of ourselves we have lost in becoming deaf to all those appeals from the side of the world which no longer reach us. In the presence of these trumpeting angels who voice their appearance, I fall into a kind of reverie where I feel the difference between living through the ear of attunement that is called to listen and to obey, and the eye of mastery through which we have come to dominate the world from afar. And when the reverie ends and the gallery in which I am standing returns, I am left with a strange sense of loss and longing.

In *Technology as Symptom and Dream*, I showed how the fifteenth century invention of linear perspective in art became a cultural convention of mind through which we learned to become a distant spectator of the world. Since that time we have increasingly forged a vision which has allowed us to dominate nature, and presumably ourselves as well, through the observer's eye. In the presence of these angels, however, something of the servant who lives through the ear haunts me, like a phantom hovering just beyond my reach. I begin to recognize the limits of a despotic eye which knows and treats the world as a spectacle, and I feel again the price I pay for a way of knowing and being which forgets that life is a vocation, that one is chosen to be who and what one is at least as much as one might think one chooses it. In a moment like this I hear that lost part of myself which yearns to be that servant again, which yearns to be addressed by something other than myself, which yearns to surrender in service to a vocation. Then the absence of the angel is a cold space in an empty world.

They are gone, these angels of an annunciation. They have disappeared from the landscapes of our world, fled from our vision. And it is painting which charts their departure. By the early eighteenth century those powerful angels of annunciation that one sees for example in the works of da Vinci, or Giotto, or Simone Martini, or Fra Angelico, have deteriorated into chubby, baby-faced, pink-bodied cupids. In a painting by Joseph-Marie Vien entitled, "The Merchant of Love," these remnants of the angels of annunciation are being plucked from a basket, like a commodity for purchase. The angel has now become an object of possession, something to amuse us, a bauble in service to our vanities. No wonder, then, that in our time the poet Rilke will ask who, if he cried out, would hear him among the angelic orders. His *Duino Elegies* are a song of lamentation over this loss, a register of our sorrow over their absence. Now we stand bereft of their presence, in a place of loneliness between their magnificent splendor and awesome beauty and the shy, sleepy dumbness of the animal, whose advantage over us is that it is content within its world, a cosmos of containment, while we, as Rilke notes, are not at all at home in our infinite universe and our overly interpreted world.

What then are we to do should we meet an angel, Rilke asks? By the end of his *Elegies* the song of lamentation has become one of praise for our condition of being neither angel nor animal. "Tell him things," he advises. Speak and proclaim the world. Say to the angel such simple things as house, bridge, fountain, gate, jug, olive tree, window, possibly: pillar or tower.

Standing before a painting, a reverie like I am describing can happen. In their power to change us, paintings can create fields of reverie where conversations with the dead who always accompany us in the landscape of the imaginal can take place. And so, on occasion, I do see these Angels of Annunciation through Rilke's eyes, and when he whispers to me, "tell them things," I know that for now in this moment he is right. But I also feel the elegiac quality of his knowledge, because I cannot forget that our speaking to the angel comes out of a sense of loss. Once, long ago, the angel told us things. Now we are to tell them. On a cloudy, rainy Saturday afternoon in an art gallery, so radical a change like this asks to be witnessed. It is almost as if these Angels of Annunciation are speaking again, appealing to us now to feel the sharp poignancy of this difference. Then: "The Angel of the Lord declared unto Mary and she conceived of the Holy Ghost." Now: "Tell them things!"

The Golden Firmament and the Blue Sky

As a daydreaming phenomenologist, I am for better or worse a witness for what has been lost, forgotten, left behind, or otherwise marginalized and neglected, a witness for those lost things which still remain and haunt the outer margins of the experienced world. For their sake, and in service to them, I write in a mood of reverie and with a sense of love. Forgotten angels require this kind of witnessing, loving presence, and it seems to me that we have an ethical obligation toward them. Standing before these paintings which record their presence, I am obliged to suspend my habitual, critical ways of knowing and being in favor of becoming that witness who welcomes the angel. Otherwise the angel becomes only a curious oddity of a time long past, a quaint and naive expression of a benighted age, a fiction no more real then than it is today. To see the angel then and now I have to look with eyes which can glimpse what lingers in the shadows and half-light of our bright reason.

The sky in medieval paintings is another occasion for reverie, reflection, and transformation, another occasion to check our vision to see how we see ourselves and the world. But I hesitate here even to use the word sky, preferring something like firmament, because the former already carries the assumptions of our way of knowing the world and being in it.

What is at issue here is the difference in color between the golden firmament of the heavens and the blue sky of the world. Here, maybe even more than with the angel, a medieval painting, like Duccio's "Christ Entering Jerusalem," can pose a question to our usual and familiar ways of constructing reality. With the angel, we are confronted with an absence in our current experience, but the blue sky—the blueness itself of the blue sky—is evident to our senses. Surely the medieval painter was expressing only some artistic convention, and just as surely they, like ourselves, saw the blue sky above them.

This is the view of no less an authority than Kenneth Clark. In his master work, *Civilization*, he notes that medieval men and women saw the world clearly enough, but they preferred to believe in what they saw as symbolic of an ideal order. But can one truly separate seeing from believing? Was the medieval mind so divided against itself that it lived in one world and knew another? Clark's remark has the effect of making the different medieval mind and its world too much like our own split modern mind and the fragmented world in which we live—a world where the perceived differences between ice and steam are subsumed under the symbolic ideal of H_2O. If we agree with Clark, we run the risk of colonizing the medieval world by the modern mind, of erasing the differences between them. Then it becomes only a matter of knowing the facts which surround the use of gold, of knowing, for example, the influence of Byzantine art on the thirteenth century Italian painter Duccio's use of gold. While such facts are the legitimate concern of cultural and art historians, knowledge of them can separate me (as well as the historian) from the experience of the golden firmament of heaven. Armed with these facts, I can put everything back in its rightful place: the sky is really blue and always blue: now, then, and forever.

Reverie, however, opens another way of knowing and being. The golden firmament is first simply what it is, and it asks of us only a simple and direct question: what is it like to be and to live in a world where the heavens are gold? Before a medieval painting like Simone Martini's "The Road To Calvary" we are asked to imagine this difference: above our heads not an open infinite blue sky, but a golden heaven which domes the world.

The golden dome of heaven is not a reality circumscribed by our empirical categories of time and space. It is an imaginal reality, and as such a possibility of human experience which is present and available at all times. One finds it, therefore, not only in the twelfth and thirteenth centuries, but also earlier and throughout the medieval period. In addition, even in the late thirteenth and early fourteenth centuries, when Giotto's masterpiece, the "Arena Chapel in

Padua," depicts the blue sky, Cimabue's paintings are depicting the golden firmament. Giotto and Cimabue are contemporaries, but they live in different worlds.

I am defending in this essay that domain of reality which Henry Corbin calls the "mundus imaginalis." It is a place which is neither that of sense perception nor that of the conceptual categories of the mind, but no less real on that account. It is a region of subtle bodies where the spirit matters and matter is inspired, a landscape whose organ of reception is that of the active imagination. In the introduction to Corbin's book on the Sufi imagination of Ibn 'Arabi, *Alone with the Alone*, the Shakespeare scholar Harold Bloom reminds us that this imaginal world is as much an aesthetic domain as it is a spiritual one. And so, the imaginal world is also that far country watched over by the poets from Shakespeare and Milton to Coleridge, Wordsworth, Shelley, Keats, Blake and a host of others. Indeed, Bloom notes that this imaginal world has at times had no name other than poetry itself.

Imagining a cosmos where the heavens are gold, standing as a witness for this other reality, frees our world into its true depths where beauty precedes meaning. Is this not what Keats meant when he said "Truth is Beauty, Beauty is Truth?" It is a terrible kind of beauty and an awe-ful truth to be sure, which is what Rilke meant when he said that beauty is, after all, only the first moment of terror we are just able to bear. To read Keats' "Ode to a Nightingale" is to experience with the poet this awe-ful truth of the beautiful.

Freeing the golden firmament of heaven from its encasement within a consciousness that has lost touch with beauty and with terror, the universe of the wide blue sky is cracked open, and the blueness of the blue sky, now more than a self-evident fact, itself becomes a marvelous beauty and an occasion for reverie. In such a moment one has come home to the world.

More often than not, however, we live without passport to that other country where beauty and its terrors, love and its shadows, death and its griefs awaken the soul and lift the veil from our eyes to reveal the imaginal realm. Without passport the blue sky remains a wide-open space of measurement and calculation, a world of infinite expanse waiting for our exploration. In that space we trace the arc which stretches from Galileo's 1609 observations of the moon to the 1969 Apollo moon landing. When we live in this way, we are in a different world, and we are different from who and how we are when we dwell beneath the golden dome of heaven. In this domain we are in the realm of the divine which secures our world and gives it its place.

Angels belong to this kind of cosmos. Indeed they have no place in the open and empty expanses of an infinite universe. This is why one of the first Russian cosmonauts, Yuri Gagarian, was correct when in 1959 he said of his journey into space that he saw no angels there. We should not have been shocked by his remark. But we were because we did not recognize the shift between worlds. We heard only what he said and not who was saying it, a modern man who lives beneath the fact of a blue sky, a sky which no longer harbors the heavens, that abode where the choir of Angels sing.

Looking at medieval paintings, I know that angels had to disappear when the golden firmament of heaven began to fade into a blue sky. Beneath the golden dome of heaven I am gathered and tucked within a sacred, symbolic cosmos; under the blue sky I am living in a secular, factual world. The angels who dwell in the golden firmament of heaven do not respond to our rational and empirical ways of knowing and being. The imaginal world is visible only to a vision that sees through the facts and penetrates the veil of ideas with which the mind clothes the world. Immersed in reverie before these paintings, I know that such a vision was not only once real, but also is real today.

Imaginal Vision and the Customs of Hospitality

We live in dark times because we have largely lost our capacity for an imaginal way of knowing and being and have largely forgotten how to appreciate the imaginal depths of the world. Beneath the golden cosmos, the critic in us wants to ask, "Was not the Medieval sky blue?" And to this question the critic expects the witness in us to answer "Yes"—for what else can be said in the face of the evidence of the blue sky? Alongside this self-evident fact, the golden firmament of heaven does not matter. It is only an artistic convention, a mere conceit, a piece of fiction with no real substance beside the heavy density of the fact. And even if the witness in us would dare to say "No!" to the critic's question, nothing would really change. The critic would merely shrug convinced of the naïveté of the witness, convinced that the daydreaming phenomenologist is hopelessly out of touch with the way things really are, a wooly headed romantic whose sense of things is useless and unproductive.

But, of course, the golden firmament of the heavens does matter, and the witness who welcomes its presence is not naive. The witness simply begins in a different place than does the critic. Without judgment about the truth or falsity of an experience, the witness begins with a welcoming sense of wonder and even generosity, which allows things to be what they are as they are. Is a dream true or false, correct or incorrect? A poem? A work of art? Indeed, what happens to the dream, or the poem, or the work of art if we begin in this way? In this either/ or form these questions force the dream or the poem or the work of art to speak on our terms, before they have had their chance to declare themselves and speak on their terms. For the witness these questions are premature. They are even impolite and inhospitable. Pressured by these kinds of inquiries, the golden firmament fades away and angels disappear. Do we not need to weep for this disappearance? And do we not have to mourn for our part in this loss? Angels and their kind have not taken leave of us; we have abandoned them.

We mourn because we have dared to love, and we love again because we have dared to grieve. Mourning can revitalize our capacity to know the world by loving it, not unlike, I think, the painter and the poet must do. Each, I believe, faces the world in a spirit of loving wonderment, and in reply the world whispers something of its secrets. Something of this exchange is present, I believe, in these few lines of E.E. Cummings. He writes: "While you and i have lips and voices which/are for kissing and to sing with/who cares if some one-eyed son of a bitch/invents an instrument to measure Spring with?" The thing, he says, a few lines later is "to eat flowers and not be afraid." Imagine knowing Spring in this way, by eating flowers, by taking Spring within ourselves in an act of intimacy and of love which no instrument can equal!

This spirit of loving wonderment which opens the imaginal sense of the world describes the attitude of hospitality. It is the custom which rules in the domain of the imaginal. To enter into that domain requires that one learn the ways of hospitality. The Roman poet, Ovid, tells a wonderful story of hospitality in *Metamorphoses*.

In Ovid's tale two gods, Jupiter and Mercury, disguised as strangers, are wandering the earth but do not find any place of rest or welcome until they arrive at the very humble dwelling of two old people, Philemon and Baucis. Philemon and Baucis are living in an un-godly age, in a world not too unlike our own where there is no recognition of the divine. But these two old people are the hosts who offer hospitality, withholding nothing of their meagre stock of goods. Baucis even proposes that she and her husband offer the strangers their one and only valuable possession, a goose which they have been saving for a special occasion as a sacrifice to the gods. In this moment of generosity, the gods reveal themselves. Then the humble abode of Philemon and Baucis is transformed into a temple, and these two old people are made the priest and priestess of this sanctuary forever. At the same time a flood destroys the un-godly human race.

Wolfgang Giegerich has written a splendid article about this tale in which he argues that these transformations are not "magical miracles." On the contrary, these transformations are a radical shift in perspective or attitude, a transformation of consciousness in which we are "moved from one view of things to another, from a preliminary, superficial view of the world as positive fact to one capable of perceiving the divine essence even in the most simple event."

A chief value of Ovid's tale, and Giegerich's reading of it, is that it helps us appreciate not only that the imaginal is real, but also that the real is radically imaginal. The imaginal is the grounding of the world; it has, therefore, ontological priority over the empirical and the rational. As such, however, it is not some other world apart from this one. No! To borrow a line from the poet Coleridge, it is an other world that now is. There is only this world, the world in which we live and have our being. But this one and only world is numinous and holy. The old practices of hospitality disclose the world in this way, as sacred and strange. Practicing hospitality the world truly does becomes the "vale of soul making." In their gestures of hospitality, Philemon and Baucis practice soul making. They do so by lingering in the moment, by staying with the strangers who are made guests without judgment, evaluation, or criticism. Hospitality is this kind of devotion to things as they are. It is presence to the present moment which frees the image in the event, de-literalizes the factual character of the event, and dissolves preconceived ideas about what this moment is or should be.

Hospitality does not postpone the moment. Offering the strangers made guests their one and only possession, the fatted goose, Philemon and Baucis cast aside any worry, care, or concern about tomorrow. Their hospitality does not hold anything back. Their hospitable presence is a way of knowing the world and being in it which does not live on credit, does not live on borrowed time, on time stolen from the past or the future. Staying in the moment, hospitality eschews any nostalgic longing for yesterday, as much as it avoids any kind of yearning for some utopia of tomorrow. Lingering in the moment, hospitality refuses to put any kind of narrative structure on the moment, refuses the temptations to question the moment in terms of its origins or development, as much as it refuses to question it in terms of its purpose or utility. In hospitality, time follows the rhythms of the soul and not those of the mind. Moments are not strung out on a line where sequence means consequence, where the past is the cause of the present and the future is a present which is being caused now. In hospitality, moments have a timeless, archetypal quality to them.

Hospitality is an attitude of patient waiting, an attitude which knows, as the poet Eliot says, how to wait without hope, because it knows that hope would be hope for the wrong thing, because it knows that this hope would empty the moment of its hidden presence. But while hospitality waits without hope, without care, or concern, or anxious worry, it does wait with love. Ovid's tale makes this clear, for the goose which Philemon and Baucis offer is the bird of Aphrodite, the goddess of love. Also, Philemon's very name means the loving or hospitable one, and Baucis's name means the tender or affectionate one. Philemon and Baucis, then, are the hospitable ones because they nourish the moment with love, because they feed the strangers who are made guests with love. Indeed, is not love the prerequisite for lingering in the moment? Giegerich believes so, which is why he insists in this tale "Love makes the difference."

In response to this kind of loving hospitality, the moment freely gives of its own fullness: the gods show their faces. Gestures of hospitality liberate the imaginal sense of the world, and endow the individual moment with a numinous quality. Giegerich says, therefore, that "what this story is actually about is how, within common reality and precisely out of it, the divine emerges, how everyday reality blossoms into divine beauty." Hospitality allows the sacred to show itself through the profane, the extra-ordinary through the ordinary, the divine through the mundane.

When through gestures of hospitality we release the imaginal depths of the world, we do come to realize that the world truly is ordinarily sacred, that the world really is the vale of soul making. In such moments angels might appear, and the dome of heaven might be gold.

9

Psychology is Useless;
Or, It Should Be

Idle Reveries

In December 1817, the poet John Keats wrote a letter to his brothers in which he coined the phrase "negative capability." He defined it as the ability "of being in un-certainties, Mysteries, doubts, without any irritable reaching after fact and reason."[1]

I read these words and I wonder why this notion of negative capability draws me into its web. I am no poet, and yet the poets have been my preferred companions for more than the thirty years that I have been a psychologist. Have they been my teachers because as a psychologist I have been formed by the traditions of phenomenology and depth psychology, particularly the works of Freud and Jung? Is there within these traditions some measure of hospitality toward the artist in general and the poet in particular?

For phenomenology the reply to this question seems straightforward. As a phenomenologist I practice a kind of fidelity to experience. This fidelity or hospitality makes no initial judgment about whether an experience is true or false, right or wrong, more or less real or valuable than some other experience. Phenomenology is not about comparisons. It is about the appreciation of differences. Van Gogh's "Starry Night" is an experience of the cosmos which has as much validity as the vision of the heavens through a telescope does. That one is an image and the other a fact does not matter. The phenomenologist is a witness and not a critic of experiences,[2] and for a phenomenologist what appears matters first before one asks what it might mean. Presence, for a phenomenologist, precedes meaning.

With depth psychology the reply to the question is, perhaps, more ambiguous. At times, depth psychology is tempted toward a reductive interpretation of a work of art, as Freud, for example, is in his essay "The Moses of Michelangelo."[3] And yet, I cannot forget that late in his life Freud was awarded the Goethe prize for literature, an award which he greatly valued. I know too that he deserved that award, because he did invent a whole new genre of writing. In Freud's hands, the case history reads more like a detective story than a factual medical history. Indeed, it is not even history in the sense that the historian practices this craft. In Freud's hands, the case history is a piece of fiction[4] which, like Van Gogh's painting, for example, lies in order to tell the truth.

I am drawn to this notion of negative capability because it sits well with me as a phenomenologist and depth psychologist. For me the poet's capacity for negative capability is like the phenomenologist's epoche, and like the depth psychologist's openness to that domain of experience whose reality like that of a dream is neither true nor false. In addition, I am attracted to the poet because of what I sense is an idleness which is not only welcomed but also cultivated as a way of knowing and being which is unconcerned about fact or reason. For me, poet, phenomenologist, and depth psychologist are companions in idleness, an idleness so deeply embedded in the bone that each of them can let go of that irritability which spawns impatience in the face of mystery, doubt, and ambiguity. For poet, phenomenologist, and depth psychologist presence does precede meaning because of a patience which can linger in the moment and wait for the presence in the present to appear. Poet, phenomenologist, and depth psychologist are witnesses of epiphanies. Each, in his or her best moments, lives in surprise.

Tutored by Gaston Bachelard (1971), I have learned to call this idleness attendant upon epiphanies reverie, and through him I have learned to appreciate how reverie authors a solitude which allows one to contemplate the world "without counting the minutes."[5] The fruit of this capacity to idle away an hour or two while dreaming with one's eyes wide open is a "contact with possibilities which destiny has not been able to make use of."[6] Suspending for a moment the facts which we have about things and the ideas which we know of them, mysteries are born. Reverie, Bachelard notes, enlarges our lives "by letting us in on the secrets of the universe."[7]

In moments of reverie, I wonder about facts and reasons. What are they? Facts are about things, and things have what a colleague and friend once called "punchability." I can count facts and I can count on them. They yield themselves to measurement and observation. Water is H_2O. That is a fact. Sunlight is a spectrum of colors. That is a fact. The earth moves. That too is a fact. And so is the fact that the sky is blue.

Once, however, not so long ago, I saw the golden dome of heaven above the earth. I saw it on a cloudy, rainy Sunday afternoon when I was idling away an hour or so looking at medieval paintings in the National Art Gallery in London. About that moment I wrote that the impatient critic in us would ask, "Was not the Medieval sky blue?"[8] Alongside this self evident fact, what answer other than an affirmative one could be given? Alongside the heavy density of this fact, the golden firmament of heaven does not matter. It is only an artistic convention, a mere conceit, an amusing fiction.

And the moving earth? Of that fact Bachelard says that "Even if reason, after long work, comes to prove that the earth turns, it is no less true that such a declaration is *oneirically absurd*." The words in italic are Bachelard's way of saying that the dream opens the same space as that of reverie, and that for the poet in his or her reveries the earth does not move. "One does not dream," he adds, "with taught ideas."[9]

Facts and things, ideas and reason—these are not the material out of which the golden dome of heaven, or the waters of baptism imbued with the holy spirit, or the rainbow as a sign of God's covenant are made. No! It is closer to the truth of our existence to say with the poet that "We are such stuff/ As dreams are made on,"[10] flimsy stuff, wispy, diaphanous, and fragile, subtle shapes, "like soap bubbles," the poet Antonio Machado says, "almost without weight."[11] This is the clime that Keats is exploring with his notion of negative capability, that subtle realm of reality which is neither fact nor idea.

The Poet

In *The Poetics of Reverie*, Bachelard confesses that he is not the same man when he is reading a book of philosophy as he is when he reading the poets. I would imagine that the same would be said about reading a book of science. Facts and concepts require a way of knowing and being which is different from the realm of experience opened by the poet. The philosopher and the scientist not only know the world in a different way than does the poet. They live in different worlds. Facts require an empirical sensibility, and to gather them one must have a keen observing eye which best takes the world's measure the more distant it can be from it.[12] Concepts, on the other hand, require a rational sensibility, a respect for meaning and some dedication to the idea that the mind can order the world's chaos. But between matter and mind, between matters of fact and ideas of reason, there is a whole other universe where the poet dwells, a domain of reality that yields its secrets to an aesthetic sensibility.

The psychologist, I would claim, dwells there. Or, at least he or she should, if psychology is worthy of its name, the speech of the soul. The psychologist should dwell there, even as failed poet, if psychology is a discipline which responds to the autonomy of Soul and does not discard it into that abyss between matter and mind. Forgotten in the abyss, Soul is either reduced to physiological facts rooted in the biology of the flesh, or confined in concepts which chart, for example, its rise and decline in developmental theories and theories of psychopathology. But at best, such theories are only and forever ideational maps for a territory where maps are finally useless.

In the domain of Soul, it is more appropriate that the psychologist be a failed poet than a good scientist. As a discipline of Soul, it is more proper that psychology be closer to the arts than to the sciences or philosophy. Even from within the abyss, it seems more fitting that the language of psychology echo the aesthetic voice of Soul, the voice of dream and fantasy, mood and feeling, image and vision, symptom and symbol, than attempt the precision of science and its empirical speech, or the clarity of philosophy and its rational tones. When we shout too loudly into the emptiness of the abyss, we hear only our own voice. It seems more suitable that psychology follow the path of the soul and *its* ways of knowing and being, even though these ways are subtle and elusive rather than rigid and fixed, rhetorical and persuasive rather than empirical and proven, metaphorical and figural rather than methodical and literal.

In his autobiography, *Memories, Dreams, Reflections,*[13] Carl Jung describes his own struggle to honor the autonomy of Soul and its artist's voice. Even he who insisted on the "objectivity" of the psyche refused to hear its aes-thetic claims. In the chapter entitled "Confrontations with the Unconscious," Jung says that when he was writing down his fantasies which seemed overwhelming and strange and quite odd, he asked himself, "What am I really doing? Certainly this has nothing to do with science. But then what is it?" He then heard a voice which said, "It is art."

Jung goes on to report that the voice which re-sponded to his questions was that of a woman, indeed very much like that of a former patient, a "talented psychopath who had a strong transference to me." "She had become a living figure within my mind," he adds, and, as he continues, he says that he was "greatly intrigued by the fact that a woman should interfere with me from within." He realizes that "she must be the 'soul'" and explains his experience in terms of the notion of the anima. Continuing, he confesses that were he to take his fantasies as art, he would have "felt no moral obligation toward them." Without such an obligation, "The anima might then have easily seduced me into believing that I was a misunderstood artist, and that my so-called artistic nature gave me the right to neglect reality." In a very clear statement of his position toward these fantasies which the anima claims are art, Jung describes the technique which he used "for stripping them of their power."[14]

In these passages Jung hears the artist soul as a seductive feminine voice which in its appeal threatens to take him away from what is real. This voice is not the voice of science. It is an emotional voice and, by implication, not a reasonable one. Feeling no moral obligation to this voice, he is nevertheless intrigued by this power of the woman to interfere with him. Jung's response is to strip her of her powers.

I would, however, be remiss in my own obligations to this material were I to neglect the very positive value of Jung's technique of engaging the unconscious. Jung is describing here a form of active imagination, and what is essential about this technique is that it takes the figures of the unconscious seriously, as autonomous realities, while also acknowledging the necessity of the individual's conscious point of view, less the person be overwhelmed by these figures of Soul. It is not the procedure, therefore, which is in question. Rather, it is the issue which gives rise to it, the issue of psychology as an art.

The events which Jung is describing took place in 1913. When I read these passages I marvel at the disjunction between them and the spirit of Jung's work. I know that he does not intend to say that that domain of experience which negative capability opens is a reality that makes no moral claim upon us. One has only to read in *Memories, Dreams, Reflections* of his encounters with Philemon to appreciate the moral obligation which Jung felt in relation to this figure. Philemon is an autonomous reality of Soul, an imaginal presence, a distinct ontological being who does not belong to the realms of either fact or reason, a being who belongs to the same tribe, for example, as Hamlet or the other dramatic personae of Shakespeare.[15] Indeed, there really is no way to avoid the moral claims which the soul of art makes upon us. The claims of art do seduce us. The poet does inspire. The musician does transport us to another level of being. The painter does show us another and different way to see. Each opens that space of negative capability which parts the veil of conventional wisdom, and in those moments we are stirred in the depths of Soul before touched at the surface of mind. And that possibility is dangerous to and subversive of the established order. If psychologists who practice out of the depths of Soul also belong to this tribe, then they too are dangerous. Or they should be.

Quite near the end of his life, Jung returned to this earlier confrontation with the artist soul, and in a poignant way admits how much he had sacrificed for the sake of making his work acceptable. In a letter which he wrote in October, 1954 to Aniela Jaffe, he thanks her for an essay she had sent to him on Hermann Broch's novel, *Der Tod des Vergil* (*The Death of Vergil*). Then he says that he has wondered "about my reluctance which on all sorts of pretexts has hitherto held me back from letting this *Tod des Vergil* approach me too closely."

The span of time between the events described in 1913 and 1954 is forty-one years, a major portion of one's lifetime, and still Jung is reluctant to let the artist get too close. In the very next sentence we learn why. "I was *jealous* of Broch," he writes, "because he has succeeded in doing what I had forbid myself on pain of death."

Here is a man nearing the end of his life, seventy-nine years of age, who confesses that he has heard, and perhaps has always heard, "a voice whispering to me that I could make it [his psychological work] 'aesthetic,'" and who refused because he feared that "I would have produced nothing but a heap of shards which could never have been turned into a pot." In words that echo painful realization, he adds that "In spite of this ever present realization the artist homunculus in me has nourished all sorts of resentments and has obviously taken it very badly that I didn't press the poet's wreath on his head." And then, in a telling P.S., written as it were as an after-thought, as something which comes after one is done with thinking and reasoning, the resentment gives way to the sadness as Jung asks, "Anyway why did it have to be the death of the poet?"[16]

Why, indeed? Why did the poet have to die? Not Vergil, but the poet in Jung, the voice of his own psyche which asked so early on that he acknowledge the negative capabilities of Soul, that attitude which welcomes mystery, doubt, uncertainty without any impatient hurrying after fact or reason. Was it the image of a heap of shards as his only legacy which warned him away? Was it some fear of losing his way if he allowed himself to listen too closely to the cunning, seductive voice of the wily feminine? Did Jung lash himself to the mast of science, like some modern day Odysseus in order to resist this siren song? I do not know. I only know that no matter how often I read this passage, I never become so accustomed to it that I am not moved by the lament which Jung expresses for the death of the poet that he was and was called to be in crafting a psychology in service to Soul and its aesthetic values.

Had Jung pressed the poet's wreath upon his head, would the keen and many valuable insights of his work have become so widely known? Would it have had the same pervasive and enduring effect on our culture and our ways of knowing and being? Perhaps not. On the other hand, what has been the price of Jung's refusal to get too close to the poet of the Soul? Has psychology missed something essential to its nature? Has it degenerated into an inferior science, even into a new creed and dogma with all sorts of pseudo-certainties, dubious facts, and largely irrelevant ideas about the nature of Soul? Has it become mired in the therapy room as a mode of treatment and missed the chance to be a spokesperson for the autonomous reality of Soul, its imaginal landscapes and aesthetic values?

The Imaginal World and Aesthetic Sensibility

In this essay I have been exploring a difference between three ways of knowing and being. Keats' notion of negative capability is the abyss at whose edge the poet dwells, and where the psychologist as failed poet belongs. On one side of this abyss is the scientist with his or her facts and measurements. On the other, the philosopher with his or her reasons and ideas.

Poet, philosopher, scientist! This alignment is neither a hierarchy nor a value judgment. I speak of them as types, as different styles of presence, different attunements to the world, and different ways of saying what the world asks of us. They are different sensibilities, and it is this issue of sensibility, of how each type senses the world before he or she makes sense of it, which inspires this essay. The facts which negative capability eschews are generated by an empirical sensibility, and the reasons by a rational one. At the abyss, therefore, the poet, and the psychologist as failed poet, are concerned neither with facts nor reasons. At the abyss, poet, and psychologist as failed poet, are witnesses with an aesthetic sensibility for the moment. For the moment, and not for anything beyond it. For the sense of the moment, for sensing it, and not yet for making sense of it. For the moment in its presence and not yet for any explanation of it.

Of the many poets who have been my companion on this journey to hear the voice of Soul, three present themselves at this moment as spokespersons of an aesthetic sensibility. In four simple lines, E. E. Cummings tells us that in the abyss of negative capability it is feeling which is our guide.

> since feeling is first
> who pays any attention
> to the syntax of things
> will never wholly kiss you[17]

When I read these lines, I can not help but recall Freud's syntax of the kiss. Discussing the aim of the sexual instinct, he describes a kiss as contact "between the mucous membrane of the lips of the two people concerned."[18] As a fact that is correct. But whoever kisses with such an attitude will, indeed, never wholly kiss you.

The soul of words lies nestled in their etymologies, and Cummings captures something of the soul of an aesthetic sensibility. Aesthetic means to sense or to feel, and ironically today we are perhaps most familiar with its sense via its absence. An-aesthetic is without sense or feeling. It is the state of numbness which prepares one for surgery, the condition of oblivion too which marks our an-aesthetic culture where violence has become so much the norm that we need increasing doses of it masked as entertainment in order to be jerked into some semblance of feeling.

The second poet is John Keats. In "Ode to a Nightingale" he hears the song of the bird and it throws him into melancholic despair. Can he, poor poet, even hope to come close to that song? Here in this vale of soul making which is the world, Keats knows only,

> The weariness, the fever, and the fret
> Here, where men sit and hear each other groan;
> Where palsy shakes a few, sad, last gray hairs,
> Where youth grows pale, and spectre-thin and dies
> Where but to think is to be full of sorrow
> And leaden-eyed despairs,
> Where Beauty cannot keep her lustrous eyes,
> Or new Love pine at them beyond to-morrow.

Despite his melancholy, he continues to listen. In spite of his sorrow, he obeys the call of the bird, and in doing so he realizes that the key difference between his poem and the song of the bird is that the latter is immortal:

> Thou wast not born for death, immortal bird!
> No hungry generations tread thee down;
> The voice I hear this passing night was heard
> In ancient days by emperor and clown:
> Perhaps the self-same song that found a path
> Through the sad heart of Ruth, when, sick for home

She stood in tears amid the alien corn[19]

Of the two, the bird is the eternal singer. In the ambiance of his song, the poet who sings with a human voice must re-cognize the failed reach of his words, their temporary and transitory nature.

In the attitude of negative capability, Keats senses and feels the song of the bird so deeply that it impregnates him with the sense of his mortality. He listens to the beauty of its song, obeys its call and hears the whisper of death. At its deepest level, the sense of the aesthetic is about listening, and to listen is related to the word to obey. At the abyss, the poet's aesthetic sensibility is a way of listening to the call of the world and obeying and responding to it even in the face of death. At the abyss, a word whose own etymology relates it to grief and suffering, the poet's aesthetic sensibility makes him or her a witness who listens to the world's depths, to those depths where what has been forgotten, marginalized, or otherwise neglected, makes its appeal for his or her voice.[20] With a voice fragile, weak, haunted by the knowledge of death, transitory and for the moment, the poet speaks what he or she has heard. The poet responds, and even in the face of death continues the unfinished and ongoing work of creation. The poet responds because an aesthetic sensibility is response-able, able to respond because it has listened and obeyed. Being a witness is in this sense an ethical act, perhaps the first ethical act, perhaps the highest.

There is no perennial philosophy here, no eternal wisdom in the poem. There is no way to cheat death here, no heroic action to take, no program to establish. There is no illusion that what we say and speak will conquer death's kingdom. Not even Orpheus, eponymous poet, could do that. There is only the act of witnessing the moment and being responsive to it. But for the moment that's enough.[21]

The third poet, Rilke, knows this territory of the temporary, and how the aesthetic sensibility of the witness is the proper response to the world and its fleeting moments, to the world which looks for "rescue through something in us, the most fleeting of all."[22] In reverie over Orpheus, Rilke asks again and again what monument we are to leave to him. "Set up no stone to his memory," he says. "Just let the rose bloom each year for his sake."[23] This is the other face of negative capability's capacity not to hurry after some fact or reason in order to still into permanence the world's passing moments. It is the ability to love the moment in its passing, to love the rose, we might say, which in its blooming is already beginning to fade. Considering the starry night sky, Rilke wonders about the constellations. "See the sky," he says. "Is there no constellation/called 'Rider'?" He allows himself to hope for a moment that the otherness of creation, these nameless and alien stars, can be brought into the ken of human language, made fixed and certain by our ideas of them. But in the end he forgoes that hope because he knows that "Even the starry union is deceptive." What we would secure in permanence forever slips away, like water in the palm of one's hand. And yet, like Keats, like the poet at the abyss, like the witness, Rilke immediately adds "But let us now be glad a while/to believe the figure. That's enough."[24]

The poet at the abyss, and the psychologist as failed poet who should be there with the poet, is witness to subtle realms. Not fixed in fact, these subtle realms are as elusive as dreams. Not imprisoned in concepts, they are as fragile as dust. Henry Corbin, the great Islamic scholar of Sufi mysticism, and a thinker who deeply influenced Jung's work, has termed this subtle world the "mundus imaginalis."[25] This imaginal world is an intermediate world, a hinge or pivot between the intellectual and the sensible worlds, a world which is neither that of fact nor reason, a world "where the spiritual takes body and the body becomes spiritual,"[26] a world whose organ of knowledge is the heart. Of course, this is not the physiological organ, the heart as a pump, the factual heart which is the only heart we know and in which we believe. On the contrary, it is the heart which is the locus of an active imagination, "the *place* of theophanic visions, the scene on which visionary events and symbolic histories *appear* in their true reality."[27]

But the Sufi mystics of long ago are far from our ken, as far as the alchemists of ancient days are, those magicians of matter who in states of reverie before the fire practiced their own kind of negative capability and witnessed the subtle shapes and textures of the natural world, like the salamander roasting in the flames, or the green lion devouring the golden sun. Jung more than anyone has done much to rescue this lost art of visionary gnosis.[28] But even he more often than not abandoned that state of negative capability and forced the mystery of this other world of subtle bodies into that familiar conceptual scheme where these visions are projections of an interior, subjective psyche onto matter.

In his best moments, however, when Jung escapes the Cartesian heritage which dominates so much of depth psychology, he acknowledged that "there was no 'either-or' for that age, but there did exist an intermediate realm between mind and matter, a psychic realm of subtle bodies."[29] In a telling footnote to this notion of subtle bodies, Jung identifies them with the *Anima*, which is "a subtle perceptible smoke."

The work from which these passages are taken, *Psychology and Alchemy*, was originally published in 1944. Subtle bodies belong to the landscape of Soul, to the *Anima*, that same realm from which he was addressed in 1913 with the claim that what he was doing was art. It would seem that alchemy was a bridge between that event of refusal in 1913 and the words of lament about the death of the poet in 1954. It appears that through his studies of the arts of alchemy, Jung was able to acknowledge that psychology practices the arts of the Soul whose reality is a matter of smoke and mirrors.[30]

We do not have to return, however, to the mystic or the alchemist to recover the true arts of the Soul. Closer to home are the hysterics who crossed the threshold into Freud's and Jung's consulting rooms. Their symptoms were mysteries which yielded their secrets neither to fact nor reason. Shipwrecked survivors of the Cartesian dream of reason, bastard daughters of Descartes' dualism of matter and mind, they rose up out of the abyss pregnant with the visions and the passions of Soul.[31] Their bodies were alchemical vessels where the work of symptom and dream were dissolving the facts of medicine and the reasons of philosophy. These hysterics were silenced poets, their symptoms the unfinished artistry of the Soul, which demanded from Freud and Jung a kind of negative capability

Mystic, alchemist, and hysteric, are guides who return psychology to the poet, because poet, mystic, alchemist, and hysteric all dwell in one way or another within that same epistemological space of negative capability, that imaginal world of Soul where the "heart has its reasons which reason itself does not know."[32] In his introduction to Corbin's book on Sufi mysticism, Harold Bloom, Shakespeare scholar and literary critic, writes that the imaginal world, which is opened to ordinary perception in moments of reverie when one can be in negative capability, is "generous enough to embrace . . . the aesthetic."[33] Is psychology humble enough to acknowledge the aesthetic claims of Soul? "It is art," the voice of Soul said to Jung. Is psychology able to respond to this claim, to recognize that its facts and reasons are works of art, neither more true nor false than a Mozart symphony, or a Rilke poem, or a Shakespeare play? Can it accept that its findings and theories are stories, allusions to that elusive invisible presence which always haunts the visible, a presence which the artist captures for a moment which is, however, enough? In the land of Soul does the psychologist have the heart to be the failed poet companion of the mystic and the poet, the suffering hysteric and the hoary alchemist?

Psychology is Useless

Now it is time for confession. The title of my essay is a rhetorical device, a piece of hyperbole, designed to capture the attention of the reader, to seduce the reader into the act of reading. Is it true that psychology is useless? Yes! I stand by the claim, but now with this addendum. In another letter written in April 1819, John Keats says, "Call the world if you Please 'The Vale of Soul Making.'" "Then," he adds, "you will find out the use of the world."[34] The psychologist is not useful in the same way that a heart surgeon with his or her skill is useful. Nor is the psychologist useful in the same way that a politician might be. On the contrary, the psychologist is as useless as a dream, as practical as a fantasy, as helpful as a moment of reverie. And yet, in this practice of uselessness, the psychologist discovers the use of the world, *its* purpose and true value. The soul of the world makes its aesthetic claim upon us, and we are called into its service, called to shape its sounds into music, its colors into painting, its rhythms into poems, and through our own sufferings to hear its anguished cries.

The psychologist as witness is one who stands by. The psychologist as witness is one who knows that "They also serve who only stand and wait."[35] These words were spoken by the poet John Milton in his blindness as he dictated to his daughters *Paradise Lost.* The useless psychologist, with the poet and the alchemist, with the mystic and the hysteric, is in his or her best moments when he or she gives up the temptations to be usefully insightful, or brightly meaningful, or even diagnostically helpful, a guide for the blind on the journey home. He or she knows only that we have lost our way. Look at Van Gogh's "Starry Night," for example, and you will know that too. Or read a poem out loud, feeling the cadence of the poet's words, and you will know. Or drop into useless reverie for a moment and when the Soul of the world touches you, you will know and sense the call to come home.

10

On Not Being Useful:
The Pleasures of Reverie

I am sitting in my garden. It is early morning and the cool breeze has a blueness to it, the blue color of the open sky, a blue so blue that only the grass is more green. The birds are already in full song. In this moment, I have no thoughts, and it is only later, as I sit at my computer, that this moment of reverie becomes a reflection. Ensconced in reverie my consciousness, that reflective sense of awareness which knows that it knows, slips away for a moment, and, by an act of natural grace, the I that I am is dissolved into the coolness of the morning, into the colors of sky and grass, into the melodies of the birds.

In *The Poetics of Reverie*, Gaston Bachelard writes, "Reverie helps us inhabit . . . the happiness of the world." It does so because it has the power to "rid us of our history . . . to liberate us from our name." On those occasions when the morning garden invites a reverie, I do feel cleansed of the burden of the "I." But it is a bittersweet experience. While reverie frees me into the openness of the world, it also taps some deep pool of longing and fills me with a sense of something lost and left behind. Like some magnetic or gravitational force of the soul, a moment of reverie attracts to itself all those other moments in time when the boundary between myself and the world dissolved. And so, in this garden reverie a child who once was is now present again, not as an act of memory, but as a presence haunting the garden, in the smells and sounds and textures of the cool, morning breeze. In this moment of reverie, I sense that it is not I who remembers him. Rather it is he of long ago who visits me, who arises in this garden place because he belongs here, because he has been waiting here for this moment, for my return. And for a moment I wonder if he is dreaming me, if I am a temporary condensation of these morning garden mists, these cool breezes from the ocean, the songs of the birds becoming conscious of themselves in time.

The first days of summer vacation were always a special occasion. I would awaken very early in the morning, and, before anyone else in the house stirred, I would slip out the door and enter the world. Those days were always beautiful, and something in me knew that if I were early enough, and careful and patient, I would see the world in its un-guardedness before it was enclosed within my family's plans for the day. Something in me knew that if I could wait for a moment longer, linger without any sense of hurriedness, I would sense again the greenness of my blood, the blueness of my soul, the light cloudiness of my being.

The world was always quiet then, as if it had just awakened from a wonderful dream of itself. I loved this early morning peace of the world, this sense of un-self-conscious presence of the day uncluttered by the busyness of our activities, not yet burdened by our intentions and schedules. In these moments just before the first rays of light expelled the darkness of night, the grass was always soaked in dew, and, magnified by those tiny crystalline prisms of nature, the green of blade and leaf was extraordinary. And surrounding it all was the light, a woven veil of soft, buttery yellow.

Those were the blue honey days of the world, days of liquid amber, days when the world had taste, and when its sweet smell was also a riot of colors, that deep, rich morning green, a fresh, lush greenness, a smell-color that was profligate in its shameless abundance. They were sensuous days, polymorphously perverse days with a diaphanous texture to them, with a feel of lightness, as if the day in its beginning was the gentle hand of a lover softly touching one's cheek. The breeze was that lover's kiss, the kiss of the world's early morning. How richly animate all this was, how harmonious: eye and ear, nose and skin attuned to each other and to the world, color dripping with aroma, the sound of quiet matched by the gentleness of the world's touch.

In moments of reverie I sometimes dream that my vocation in life was born in those halycon days and lost. I look at my life and work and know in some dim way that I have tried all my life to re-capture in words that soft, buttery yellow of the morning light and the blue honey of the world. Have I failed? Would I have come closer to my vocation had I been a painter because the painter knows the world as color before it is meaning, knows the world in its first shy blush, as it were, before it is wrapped within a word? I do not know. What I do know, however, is that reverie is a melancholy affair, and that its quality of sorrow paradoxically contains a seed of joy. If, in moments of reverie, I discover that I have forgotten my vocation, then in these same moments I realize that in my failures I have also been true to it. I realize that it has been the trying which has mattered.

Sitting on a bench amidst all this luxury, a moment always came when I would turn my gaze toward the ground. Brown and dry, somewhat barren in comparison with the rich color of grass and tree, the dirt was nevertheless alive and full of deep mysteries. The black ants knew those secrets, and, fascinated by their order and precision, I would watch them march toward their tiny entrances into the underworld. I wanted to be carried by them into those dark, mysterious caverns, but they took no notice of me or my wishes. Many years later, after I discovered Rilke's *Duino Elegies* and read how the Angel in its beauty and glory is indifferent to us, I understood that the ants were also angels, dark angels of the underworld, splendidly indifferent to us, and rightly so. Even then, so long ago now, I knew in some dim way that the world had become too human, too full of us and our intentions. The ants were early teachers of humility.

In those moments, I felt a kinship with the world and all that surrounded me, a part of all that simple splendor. I felt grateful and received, welcomed by the green grass, black ant, quiet sound, gentle breeze. In a way I could not then give words to, I felt as if I had come home. Today, my garden reverie is another homecoming. The paradox, however, is that home is to be found neither then in the memory of those days of long ago, nor now in the reverie in the garden where those moments from another time linger as a perfume which scents the morning light and the cool breeze. The paradox of reverie, its bittersweet quality of melancholy, is that it takes me home by awakening me to my sense of homelessness.

"Home," T. S. Eliot writes, "is where we start from." Yes, that seems true. But it is also not true, because home is also the place toward which we are journeying. In this sense, reverie takes us out of time, at least out of historical time, time as a line of moments, horizontal time, and installs us in a timeless time, a vertical time where moments are qualities of the soul and not measures of the mind. In reverie we slip into that place where the eternal quality of the world shines through the veil of the here and now. It is a moment when home as heritage shines as a destiny. My good friend Kathleen Raine, Blake scholar and poet in her own right, calls this moment "the paradise of all mythologies once and forever known but lost." And, she continues, "Of this Paradise, all are native."

But of what value are these moments? Of what use is reverie? The questions are valid, but they can be answered only when we know who asks them. In a letter to his brothers written in December 1817, poet John Keats described a state of being which he called "negative capability." It is, he wrote, a state when "man is capable of being in uncertainties, Mysteries, doubts, without any irritable reaching after fact and reason." It is the irritable one in us who asks these questions about use and value, the impatient one who I have called the critic in another essay and whom I compared with the witness. In that essay, "On Angels and Other Anomalies of the Imaginal Life," I wondered about the disappearance of Angels and the golden firmament of the heavens seen in medieval paintings. I argued that Angels and the golden dome disappear and stay hidden, replaced by a merely blue sky, when we ask first not what is there, but what the *there* means, when we eclipse presence by a need for meaning. Reverie is a matter of hospitality, I wrote, and hospitality a matter of staying in the moment, of being able to suspend for a moment the "irritable reaching after fact and reason."

Reverie is useless and how utterly wonderful it is because of that. We need the artist for these moments. We need the poets to help us remember, in large measure because the artist, especially in our culture, is, thankfully, useless. I am a psychologist steeped in the traditions of phenomenology and depth psychology, but I grieve on those occasions when psychology is, or strives to be, useful, or worse meaningful, or still worse helpful. These temptations are, I believe, its moments of greatest danger. In my best moments as a teacher, writer, or therapist, when there is something at work like natural grace, I have been neither useful, nor helpful, nor even meaningful. Reverie is not useful; it is a pleasure. Reverie is not an activity; it is a gift. And the gift which it brings, as well as the pleasure, is that in cleansing us of our names, it grants for a time the boon of knowing, as the poet Wordsworth notes, that "Not in entire forgetfulness,/And not in utter nakedness,/ But trailing clouds of glory do we come/ From God, who is our home:/ Heaven lies about us in our infancy!"

What the poet in these lines calls God, the philosopher might call Being, and the psychologist Soul. It is not the name, however, which matters. It is the experience that we are funded by something other than ourselves to which we owe, at least, some acknowledgement and recognition. But we have largely forgotten this gift with the terrible consequence that we continue to place ourselves, as well as the rest of creation, in mortal danger.

"Call the world if you please 'The Vale of Soul-Making.' Then you will find out the use of the world." This was written by Keats in another letter to his brother in April 1819. Less than a year earlier Mary Shelley, wife of poet Percy Bysshe Shelley, had published her novel *Frankenstein*. The proximity has always intrigued me and I have often wondered if letter and novel share a secret symmetry concerning the early division between a poetic sensibility and a technological one, between a witness with an aesthetic sense who tastes the blue honey of the world in a moment of reverie and the empirical critic who knows for a fact that honey is not blue and that the world is neither sweet nor has taste, at least not in a way that is useful or which truly matters.

For Keats, the use of the world is its purpose which is to be distinguished from our own preoccupation with how the world is, or might be made, useful. The difference is one of attitude, a subtle difference about where and how one is present to things. *In Technology as Symptom and Dream*, I described how our fact-minded sense of the world requires a distance between us and the things of the world, how the technological world and its achievements originates in a separation between us as spectators of the world who take its measure, and the world as a spectacle for our observation and use. In *The Soul in Grief: Love, Death and Transformation*, I went in the other direction and described how reverie dissolves that separation and opens the aesthetic depths of the world because it places us in the midst of things, in a proximity so close that there is a kind of con-spiracy between us and the world, a breathing together born in a nearness to things that makes it quite impossible for us to be mere observers from afar.

Reflecting on painting, phenomenologist Maurice Merleau-Ponty said, "There really is inspiration and expiration of Being, action and passion so slightly discernible that it becomes impossible to distinguish between what sees and what is seen, what paints and what is painted." Merleau-Ponty then quotes artist Paul Klee who said, "I think that the painter must be penetrated by the universe and not want to penetrate it. . . . Perhaps I paint to break out." Imagine that! Reading these lines, I think of Van Gogh's "Starry Night," and I wonder who is painting. Is it the artist painting the night sky in its radiant, almost too bright splendor? Or are the stars painting themselves through the artist? A bit of both is at work here, a sensuous coupling between two bodies, that of the artist and that of the world, drawn together, as it were, in some kind of erotic attraction for each other, as if the world needs us to fall into moments of reverie in order to complete itself, and as if we need to sense the world's need for us in order to fulfill who we are.

The word aesthetic contains this connotation of a sensuous co-mingling. In its etymological roots, where the seeds of the soul of words continue to germinate, aesthetic means to sense or to feel, especially in the sense of to hear, which is cousin and kin to the word obey. Within the aesthetic sensibility of a reverie we are called by the world, attentive and attuned to its hushed voices, as a lover might be to a beloved, impregnated by its desires to know and reveal itself, agents in its service. "Earth, isn't this what you want: an invisible/re-arising in us?" poet Rainer Maria Rilke asks. And this question is preceded by another, even more surprising one: "Are we, perhaps, here just for saying: House,/ Bridge, Fountain, Gate, Jug, Olive Tree, Window,-/possibly: Pillar, Tower?" One word in these few lines—possibly— just this one word, tells us how seductive is this appeal to be the world's lover, and how fraught with responsibility and even danger, as all love is, is the task of giving voice to what we have heard, to being the spokesperson for the world and its silent dreams of speaking. Reverie puts us in that place where we can be responsible not for but to the world's purpose. It positions us so we might be response-able, able to respond, because we have listened.

Mary Shelley's Victor Frankenstein is a deaf man. Throughout the novel he refuses at every turn to listen, even to the appeals of the pitiable creature he has made, who in his loneliness begs his creator for a mate. Today the word "Frankenstein," this single word, is common coin to describe any handiwork of the human will that controls its creator. Is Shelley's creation the face and figure of an early warning, the shadow who haunts us when we forget to listen to the use of the world, when we grow deaf and indifferent to its purpose, when we forget the vocation to be lovers? Letter and novel! One an appeal, the other a dire warning?

The difference between an aesthetic and empirical sensibility is not, however, any more a judgment than that between witness and critic. The poet is not superior to the scientist. The pleasures of reverie are not a higher value than the powers of technology. These are not my claims. We are witness and critic, fact-minded empiricists and aesthetic dreamers. I am speaking only on behalf of what we have forgotten, seeking to redress the imbalance which exists in favor of the empirical over the aesthetic, which places truth not only over beauty but also apart from it, and which accords meaning a primacy over presence. In reverie presence precedes meaning, and beauty is the first epiphany of the world's truth. That moment of beauty, that moment when, for example, one sees a spider's web framed in moonlight as a cold blue-silver star hanging in the far distance of space, can also be, and often is, a terrible moment. "For Beauty's nothing/but beginning of Terror we're still just able to bear," Rilke writes. Terror because the epiphany of beauty is always an awakening, an an-amanesis as Plato says, an end of forgetfulness which stirs the soul from sleep and starts its journey home. Meditating on a Botticelli face, Kathleen Raine, whose life and work have been in defense of these ancient springs of the world's holy splendor, says beauty is a "homecoming." In these epiphanies of terrible-beauty, the world shines with a luminosity, and we know that we have come from elsewhere and that this world is truly the vale of soul making, the arena in which we make ourselves ready for the return.

Reverie is homework and I am insisting, then, on our right to this work, on our right to be useless, to waste time, if you wish, to be in service to nothing other than the moment as it calls, to the small epiphanies and miracles of everyday life. In this space the dichotomies between poet and scientist, the aesthetic and the empirical, the pleasures of reverie and the powers of technology, presence and meaning dissolve, and for a moment we recognize that "Beauty is truth, truth beauty." That is Keats speaking. But physicist Michiyo Kaku admits as much when he says the equations of physics are the poems of nature.

Faith is the bird that feels the light
And sings when the dawn is still dark.

These are the words of Indian poet Rabindranath Tagore. They nicely sum up what I have tried to address in this essay. Not so much about faith, but about the song, the words drawn from us when it is still dark, when we are still in darkness, and drawn by that aesthetic sensibility which is already attuned to the world's dawning luminosity even before the evidence is available, even before we have empirical proof. They remind me of the words of another poet, E. E. Cummings, who writes:

Since feeling is first
who pays any attention
to the syntax of things
will never wholly kiss you

Reverie dims for a moment something of our consciousness, of our desire to know the world and how it works, its rules, its syntax. It opens for us a place which satisfies, if only for a moment, our desire to let go of what we know of the world so that we might be known by it, and known so deeply that this being known feels like an embrace, like the world's kiss. It satisfies some deep longing for a kind of absorption that restores for a moment our identity with the elements of creation, with light and air, star and stone, tree and bird, wave and wind. Reverie opens us to the early mornings of the world when the world's luminosity was not yet so bright, nor the light of our minds so intense, a time outside of time before the lines of separation between us and nature were so sharp and so clearly defined. It opens us to the timeless and eternal qualities of the world before we have paved the world in the concrete facts of our knowledge. It opens us also to the timeless dimensions of ourselves before, as Kathleen Raine so aptly puts it, our separate identities have grown over us "like a skin, or shroud."

Once, not so long ago, I stood on the knife-edge of one of those early mornings of the world. The hills were still dark, but their edges were already ribboned with color, a purple hue crowning their jagged peaks. It was a rare moment when the world was deciding whether it would slip back into sleep or stretch itself to become another dawn. In that moment I sensed that the sunrise is never guaranteed, that each dawn is a decision made again and again by the world itself. Just awake enough in that last second before that choice was made, I felt that everything which I continuously anticipate, the entire round world of all creation, could fold back into eternal night. I was motionless within that moment, wrapped in its stillness, waiting for the world to renew itself again. In that moment I was empty; I was only an empty waiting.

At first I hardly noticed—the sound was soft, singular, far away. But a few notes of a bird were just enough to rouse me from my empty waiting. An anticipation began to build as the solitary singer became a chorus. And then, something like a small miracle happened: in the hills light exploded in joyful song. Song and light had begun and in this first moment of the new day it seemed as if the entire space of the world would not be large enough to hold this swelling song of the spreading light.

When God made the world saying, "Let there be Light," birds must have been singing. This is a secret that the morning song of the bird teaches at each dawn: Light is Song, Song is Light! When dawn comes, birds sing, and song is brought into the world. When birds sing, dawn comes, and light is brought into the world. Song and light are one and the same. The song of the bird is the voice of the light; the light of the world is the rhythm of creation. Light sings the world into being, and song lightens the world.

But, again, I confess to the critic within me that these secrets are of no use. I surrender to his judgment that they are truly useless. And yet without these secrets which lie in the aesthetic depths of the world opened by reverie, I am something less than human, something less than what I am called to be. It is not enough to be a good citizen, to pay one's bills on time, to obey the law and live by the rules. Of course, these things matter. But they are not enough. We are addressed by another voice, called to continue the act of creation by being a witness, a simple witness, for those epiphanies of beauty and terror which reveal the hidden face of the divine in the flower, for example, whose phototropism is a form of prayer. In reverie we learn how to pray in such a way that we make ourselves ready to hear the true purpose of the world.

11

The Backward Glance:
Rilke and the Ways of the Heart

Prelude

I am sitting here at my computer, the day already quite far along in its journey toward the night, and thinking about this article, knowing that the deadline, itself a curious word to describe the art and process of writing, is fast approaching. It is not that I do not know what I want to say, for the backward glance has been a gesture that has haunted me for many years and has been a theme of many lectures and articles. Rather, it is the title as I wrote it just now. It warns me to be wary of following dead lines. It makes me pause to wonder who has written those words and who is writing this article.

The backward glance presumes a pause, an arrest of one's forward motion in the world, even if only for the briefest of moments. Who makes such a pause now? I do. But who is this "I" who seems so familiar with this gesture? In this moment I realize something that I have never seen before. It is myself as phenomenologist for whom the pause is the natural pre-condition for the gesture of the backward glance.

What is phenomenology if it is not the art of lingering in the moment? Lingering in the moment is the prelude to the backward glance, and phenomenology taught me this art. Or, perhaps, it is nearer to the truth of the experience to say that, when I encountered phenomenology many years ago in the person of my friend and teacher J. H. van den Berg, it awakened the dormant tendencies of my own heart and soul. To linger in the moment, to be content with idling away an hour or two in reverie,[1] an attitude that is so easily judged and dismissed as wasting time, even perhaps on occasion to allow oneself to be useless,[2] is the gift of phenomenology.

When one lingers in the moment, mysteries unfold. Each moment becomes a haunting and one begins to experience the invisible and subtle shapes and forms that shine through the visible, that sustain it and give it its holy terrors and its sensuous charms. Lingering in the moment, each moment is stretched beyond its boundaries, until suddenly the moment itself falls out of historical time into some timeless realm. The horizontal line of time collapses and one falls into vertical time, where moments belong together not by virtue of any causal connection, but because of an emotional affinity and kinship amongst them. So, one day while sitting with my back against the cold, damp, stone wall of an old and ancient French Gothic church in Venasque, a tiny village in the Luberon valley of southern France, the warm sun on my face and the quality of the air and the light opened a portal to another world that I once knew but had forgotten, a world that does and does not belong to my biographical history.[3]

In such a moment, one is neither in time and space nor outside time and space. Rather one is in a nowhere realm, a no-where world that is now-here. To linger as a phenomenologist in the moment is to open oneself to these breakthroughs of the timeless into the timebound, breakthroughs that are experienced as ontological surprises, that is, as breakdowns of our usual and familiar ways of knowing the world and being in it. And in this regard I realize that I am as much a depth psychologist in debt to the work of Carl Jung as I am a phenomenologist so much in debt to my old friend and teacher J. H. van den Berg.

Phenomenologist and depth psychologist, then, gather around the title of this essay. They pause there, lingering in the moment that seems to promise some epiphany. Or, perhaps it is better to say that I am drawn here in these two guises, and that I am stopped by some soft whisper, which hints that something more is to come. And there is more. There is Rilke, who is a poet.

What does the poet bring to the backward glance, whose prelude is a lingering before a fall? The poet brings the heart and its ways of knowing and being, the heart that Pascal said had "its reasons which reason itself does not know."[4] The heart, too, that the poetry of the Sufi mystics celebrated as the organ of perception for the subtle worlds of the imaginal realm that are no-where now-here.[5] The mind races ahead, but the heart waits. It lingers, just long enough on occasion to be penetrated by the mysteries of the world, by the numinous presence of the sacred in the ordinary, when, for example, the song of the bird at dawn reveals a great secret of the world: that light and song are one and the same; that the song of the bird is the voice of the morning light.

I know this presence of the poet. Having found my way into psychology through philosophy many years ago, I say now that I have found my way out through poetry. Not that I am no longer a psychologist! Rather, along this arc from philosophy to poetry, I have learned that psychology is a way station, a rest stop, at times an oasis, a halfway house between worlds. Rilke, among many others, has been a sure guide here. So too, Kathleen Raine, poet, teacher, friend.

So, even here at the beginning, I pause, because the few words that announce the title are themselves a pregnancy of possibilities. Here at this threshold, even before I begin, there is a haunting, as if these three guises of phenomenologist, depth psychologist, and poet are the portals through which the ghostly presences of Van den Berg, Jung, Raine, and Rilke come to claim authorship of this work. I turn for a moment, glance over my left shoulder, and I feel their presence. They hover here with me, whispering the words that asked to be said, suggesting this or that turn of phrase. This pregnant pause, this brief glance, this dangerous gesture makes me even wonder for whom this work is being done. Whom does it serve?

In his autobiography, *Memories, Dreams, Reflections,* Jung confesses, that "In the Tower at Bollingen it is as if one lived in many centuries simultaneously." "There is nothing here to disturb the dead," he adds, and in this place the souls of his ancestors are sustained as he goes about the work of answering "for them the questions that their lives once left behind."[6] For Jung it is the ancestors for whom the work is done. It is the dead of long ago, stretching down the long hallway of time, who ask us to linger in the moment, and who solicit from us this turning.

The backward glance is the beginning of a vocation. It is a moment when one can be given the gift of a calling that designs the destiny of a life. This is the sense of Jung's reflections, but I know it, too, in my heart. This is what Van den Berg gave to me—questions that have sustained me over time. He also gave me a way of being with these questions, a way of going about this work of being a phenomenologist. He did not teach me merely to look at the world with open eyes. Any phenomenologist could have done that. No! His lesson was far more subtle. To re-gard the world, to look again, to linger with open eyes that love the world. This is what he gave me, a way of seeing the world that shifts the locus of vision from eye to heart. In doing so, he prepared me for the poets, who practice this kind of vision.

In his poem, "Turning Point," Rilke says, "Work of the eyes is done, now / go and do heart-work. . ."[7] This heart-work is a work of transformation, and the heart that Rilke speaks of here is a kind of alchemical vessel whose processes mirror those of the physical heart. Just as the physical heart transforms venous blood into arterial blood with the air of the world, the alchemical heart transforms the dense material of the seen world into its more subtle forms with the breath of the word. This mirroring is, I believe, the secret intuited by the phenomenologist Gaston Bachelard, whose *Poetics of Reverie* is a heart's sure guide in the art of lingering. For Bachelard, poetry helps one breathe better because through it word and world flow into each other. "The man who reaches the glory of [this] breathing," Bachelard says, "breathes cosmically."[8] To practice the art of lingering in the moment as prelude to the backward glance is heartwork, which is good for one's physical well-being.

For Rilke this transformation of matter into language is the very function of poetry itself. Before the word is spoken, we pause, take a breath, and draw into ourselves the open world that lies there in front of our gaze. And then, inspired by the world we speak. But who is speaking in this moment? Is it us or the world? For Rilke there is no doubt. "Earth," he asks, "isn't this what you want: an invisible/re-arising in us?"[9] In the Ninth Elegy Rilke offers us the image of the wanderer who brings back from the mountain slope not some handful of earth, "but only some word he has won, a pure word, the yellow and blue gentian."[10] Things want to become invisible in this way. They want to realize this destiny of transformation, to ex-pire in the breath of language, to become in words their subtle form.

It is through the language of the heart that the world of nature is transformed. It is also through the eyes of the heart that the dead become present to us, and through these same eyes that the dead and the living are changed into the more subtle shapes of an imaginal presence. So Van den Berg, who still lives, is already for me also a lingering presence who haunts my work and gives to it its style. So too, Kathleen Raine, who also still lives. In this imaginal landscape, they are kin of my soul whose abode is my heart, and in this way they join the dead, Rilke and Jung, to companion me along the way.

The backward glance is a gesture that exposes the heart and opens it to this subtle, imaginal world that is no-where/now-here. To linger in the moment is the prelude to this act, and in this pause you let go of your mind and risk yourself to the heart and its ways of knowing and being. It is a gnosis rooted in the etymology of the word, which relates heart to memory. As an act of heartwork, the backward glance initiates the work of re-membering, a work that is a journey of homecoming to that no-where/now-here imaginal place where one's biography falls into the larger stories of creation. The awe-full beauty of this moment, which begins with the pause that lingers, is the discovery that what matters in a human life is not only what we know, or might yet discover, but what we have forgotten, left behind, neglected, marginalized, and otherwise abandoned. And the awe-full terror of this moment of the heart's awakening is the realization that we are all pilgrims on a journey to no-where, orphans between worlds on a journey of homecoming.

"Prelude" derives from a root that means to play ahead of or in advance of the opening of a work, usually in the sense of an artistic performance. I want to stay within the mood of this word as this prelude nears its end and the work of this essay is about to begin. I want to keep the spirit of play and the spirit of art in the work, and so I will organize this essay around several scenes of the backward glance. Indeed, in this spirit of play, my intention in what follows is to make a scene, or several scenes. Before, however, the curtain falls on this prelude a final word about it needs to be said.

Just as I have lingered for a moment at this threshold to see who accompanies me as the writer, this prelude invites the reader to wonder who is reading, who is present in the moment when one stops along the way and lingers. The invitation is to enter into a style of reading that goes through the heart. As such, this invitation is into a way of knowing that is about neither facts nor ideas, a gnosis that is an aesthetic sensibility, a gnosis that opens one to feeling those more elusive presences that haunt the imaginal world. It is a gnosis where one is capable of being touched and moved by the otherness of this world where the dead and the living have already been transformed into matters of and for the heart. It is a gnosis whose arc begins in a turning where you lose your mind for the sake of the heart.

Scene One: The Man on the Hill

The *Duino Elegies* is, perhaps, Rilke's most famous poem. Filled with numerous figures like Angels and animals, lovers and children who die young, acrobats and wanderers, the figure that captures the essence of this poem is, I believe, the one that appears at the end of the eighth elegy. It is the image of a man on a hill that overlooks his valley, the final hill that shows him his home for the last time.

Who is this man? He is each of us, the one who obviously has turned around for the sake of a final glance. All of us know such moments, and we often live them with some passing sense of sorrow. Rilke's poem, however, burns the image of this moment into the soul. His poem turns this gesture into a poetic act through a simple question that he inserts into this turning: "Who's turned us round like this, so that we always / do what we may, retain the attitude / of someone who is departing?" To underscore the impact of this image-question, Rilke says that just like this man on the hill "will turn and stop and linger, / we live our lives, forever taking leave."[11]

The eighth elegy is a hymn of mourning. There is a very strong feeling tone of lament for something that we have lost along the way, not only in our personal lives, but also in our collective lives as human beings. One reads this elegy and hears a continuous sigh for what we have become, "spectators" who look at the world from a distance, who are never nestled within things long enough in order to look out from them. For us as spectators the world is a display, crowded with "empty, indifferent things, pseudo-things, dummy-life," as he says in a letter a year before his death.[12]

In contrast with the spectator we have become, Rilke praises the animal, within whom "there lies the weight and care of a great sadness." The curious thing about this praise is that this sorrow of the animal is for us, as if the animal somehow knows our spectator condition and mirrors for us what we have lost. Thus Rilke says, "For that which often overwhelms us clings / to him as well, —a kind of memory / that what we're pressing after now was once / nearer and truer and attached to us / with infinite tenderness." Compared to that time and place, a place that Rilke calls our "first home," and which I would call a landscape of the soul, that no-where world now-here, this time and place that is our second home where we are spectators "seems ambiguous and draughty."[13]

In this elegy the backward glance turns us toward this original home, which the animal remembers for us and which we ourselves dimly recall. This other time and place is what beckons us, this calling of that world that once was but never has been, that no-where now-here, that soulscape which is not for the eyes of a spectator, that homeland of the heart.

But who belongs to that homeland of the heart? Who dwells there with the power to turn us round and make us aware that we are always looking at things as if for the last time? These questions take us into the core of Rilke's work and life. To get there, however, we have to go by way of a different question. The gesture itself of a backward glance indicates that there is no direct vision of whomever it is who turns us in this way. The spectator's forward gaze has to be given up for the backward glance. The question of who turns us in this fashion has to yield to the question of who has heart for such a turning.

The eighth elegy says the child does, sometimes. On occasion, the child can get quietly lost within that first home, but he or she is always dragged back again to the timebound world. In some of the other elegies and in other poems, Rilke portrays this quiet presence of the child to this first home as that faraway look that we sometimes see on a child's face. Moreover, he even wonders if the child who dies young preserves something of that first home, which makes the death of a young child even a cause for some sad joy. Rilke challenges us in this way to re-imagine our lives, and as difficult as this image may be, it is not so without merit that we can dismiss it. I do not want to soften Rilke's image by taking it as only a symbol. Rilke is speaking about the actual death of a young child. Nevertheless, the image does have a symbolic resonance. We are admonished, after all, to become again like children if we are to enter that other time-place, the Kingdom of Heaven.

Lovers too may have the heart for this turning, but Rilke is too cautious about love to accept its lasting value. Thus, he rebukes lovers for getting in the way of each other. "Lovers-were not the other present, always spoiling the view!— draw near to it and wonder...," he writes. "Behind the other, as though through oversight, the thing's revealed...But no one gets beyond/ the other, and so world returns once more."[14]

Although Rilke considers children and lovers as possible candidates for this heartwork of turning, for this change of heart that is the backward glance, the image of the man on the hill overlooking the valley for the last time, the one who is always on the verge of departing, cancels these possibilities, or at least postpones them. A poem, like a dream, demands fidelity to the images, especially for a phenomenologist. The one on the hill is a man, not a child. And he is alone, not with a lover. Who, then, finally has heart for this gesture of re-gard, the courage, a word etymologically related to heart, for the backward glance? "Or someone dies and *is* it."[15] Rilke says this too in the eighth elegy, and the italics are his.

Recall Jung's words about the Tower at Bollingen, that place where he did the work of the ancestors. Those words have the same spirit that is present in so much of Rilke's poetry. His work and his life bear continuous witness to the claim that we owe life a death, and that it is only in living life from the side of death that we most truly exist as human beings. Indeed, the *Elegies* celebrate our place between Angel and Animal and mark that domain as our privilege because, neither like the Angel who is eternal, nor the Animal, which perishes, we die. We perish, as it were, with awareness, a condition which also marks a boundary between the spectators we have become and the innocent child who, in dying young, dies perhaps before knowing what has been lost.

This difference is crucial for Rilke, because the awareness of death also deepens love. While Rilke is eloquent about the difficulties of love, it remains for him our highest calling. He says, "only from the side of death...is it possible to do justice to love." He also says, "It lies in the nature of every ultimate love that, sooner or later, it is only able to reach the loved one in the infinite."[16] At the heart of love for Rilke beats a passion, a hunger, a desire for the infinite. Thus, in spite of the rebuke that lovers spoil the view for each other, the paradoxical thing about love is that it is only through the other that we glimpse the divine.

So who has the heart for this work of turning? Those who have risked the difficulties of loving, even loving in the face of loss. That is who we are with the man on the hill, lovers whose vision looks upon the world with the attitude of departing, lovers who see things always as if for the last time. If it is the dead who call us home, then it is lovers who have risked the terrors of loving in the face of death whose hearts are attuned to those voices that solicit the backward glance. The next two scenes play out this theme through two of Rilke's most compelling poems about love and death.

Scene Two: The Return of the Dead

"Requiem for a Friend" is a poem Rilke wrote for Paula Modersohn who died on November 21, 1907, less than three weeks after giving birth to a daughter. Her death disturbed Rilke because he saw in her life and death a vocation that was crushed by the conventional forces of marriage. Paula was a painter, and if it is true that through her Rilke saw something of his own conflict between communal life and the solitude required for creative work, it was still her struggle to hold the tension of work and love that haunted him.

In the opening lines of the poem, Rilke makes it quite clear that she is exceptional among the dead. "Only you / return; brush past me, loiter, try to knock / against something, so that the sound reveals your presence." Others who have died seem ". . . so contented / so soon at home in being dead, so cheerful, / so unlike their reputation." Paula, however, is not at home in her death, prompting Rilke to say, "I'm sure you have gone astray / if you are moved to homesickness for anything / in this dimension." Addressing her again, he says, "the gravity of some old discontent / has dragged you back to measurable time."[17] Her return is an appeal to Rilke, a pleading, he says, that "penetrates me, / to my very bones, and cuts at me like a saw." "What is it that you want?" he asks.[18]

The poem, a conversation between the poet who is alive and the failed artist who has died, is whispered in the night, amongst shadows and mirrors. Rilke confesses to Paula that he has in fact held onto her through the mirror, a presence through the image, which is real but free of the weight of earthly life. But that mirror presence is so different from how she is now present to Rilke that he wonders, somewhat angrily, if she has denied herself the fruits of her death. "I thought you were much further on," he says earlier, but her return fragments this hope.[19] He is forced to attend to her appeal

"Come into the candlelight" he says. "I'm not afraid / to look the dead in the face." But this invitation and Rilke's boldly courageous claim does not capture the attitude of her haunting return. On the contrary, Paula's return from the dead requires Rilke to look back in order to understand her appeals to him. In the candlelight, he is silent with her for a time, until an invitation arises from that silence: "Look at this rose on the corner of my desk: / isn't the light around it just as timid / as the light on you?" Bathed in the same subtle light, Paula and the rose share the same tension. "It too should not be here, / it should have bloomed or faded in the garden, outside, never involved with me."[20] But it is here, there on Rilke's desk, and in response to its presence he knows that he is called to let it rise up within his heart and take on its subtle form through the breath of the word.

Should we be here? Yes!—for being here does matter, and about this fact Rilke has no doubts as the *Duino Elegies* make clear. It is only that death reminds us that we have come from elsewhere, that we have fallen into time from some other world, a journey into birth, which death reverses and closes as a homecoming. This memory sits in our hearts as a longing. It sits in our hearts too as a calling. ". . . time / is like a relapse after a long illness" Rilke says.[21] A relapse not a recovery! A relapse into the sickness of forgetting, whose prescription is the vocation to remember.

Paula's return from the dead is an appeal for mourning: "That's what you had to come for: to retrieve / the lament that we omitted."[22] This requiem, however, is not just for her. It is also for Rilke himself, and for all of us. The dead return to awaken us and in this return they invite us to re-gard again everthing in life that we have just simply passed by. So Rilke wonders whether for the sake of Paula he must travel again. He also asks, "Did you leave / some Thing behind, some place, that cannot bear your absence?" He says too that "I will go to watch the animals / . . . which hold me for a while/and let me go, serenely, without judgment." And, he adds, "I will have the gardners come to me and recite / many flowers, and in the small clay pots / of their melodious names I will bring back/ some remnant of the hundred fragrances." All this he will do and more: "And fruits: I will buy fruits, and in their sweetness / that country's earth and sky will live again."[23]

A catalogue of simple, common, ordinary things and actions. Rilke will do all of this, not just for Paula but also for himself and for all of us. He will return to these things and to these actions that he has done so many times with new re-gard. The dead, like Paula, who have struggled to hold the tension of life and work, return and turn us around, and in their presence we stop for a moment, linger, and take that second look. These dead are our teachers, the ones who initiate the backward glance and inform it as a ritual of mourning. They teach us that we are called to love and to work while knowing that we will and must fail. In this regard, these dead teach us that mourning lies at the core of the human heart, that the backward glance envisions the world through eyes of lament.

Scene Three: The Rose that Fades

Orpheus is the eponomous poet, the one whose name when spoken is the presence of poetry itself. For Rilke, Orpheus is the figure who shows us that eyes of lament exercise the mournful heart. Through Orpheus we see that the backward glance opens the heart to the transitory nature of the world, to the fleeting character of all that we hold close to the heart and cherish. No matter what we do the things that we love pass away. Not even art, with its hopefully timeless forms, can triumph over mutability and the certainty of death. Only in the moment and for the moment do we sometimes create a fragile and temporary haven in the midst of loss.

In his *Sonnets to Orpheus*, Rilke celebrates this paradox of evident mutability and desired permanence that Orpheus embodies. Orpheus is the one who both fades and endures. Thus, in the final sonnet, Rilke says, "And if the earthly has forgotten you, / say to the still earth: I flow. / To the rapid water speak: I am."[24] Orpheus is who and what he is in his flowing, and in this guise he is emblem for who and what we are called to be. Orpheus: *Ich rinne*-I flow; *Ich bin*-I am! Rilke and each of us in the presence of Orpheus: We change, therefore, we are! We die, therefore, we live! This is the Orphic celebration for Rilke, this seed of joy in the heart of lament, this ejaculation of life in the face of loss. Through Orpheus, Rilke transcends the dichotomy of the eternal and the temporal; he surrenders that longing for the timeless in the midst of the timebound, and that despair in the folds of time for the eternal. Through Orpheus, Rilke celebrates the paradox that we can love the world and others because they do pass away; love the rose, which in its blooming is already beginning to fade. Indeed, even for Orpheus himself there can be no record that fails to honor the tension of this paradox. Thus, Rilke says, "Set up no stone to his memory./ Just let the rose bloom each year for his sake."[25]

Rilke's vision of Orpheus is a metaphysics of the heart and its ways of knowing and being, a phrase that I use here intentionally to counter the metaphysics of the mind and its ways of knowing and being. The former embraces death as the other side of life, while the later flees it. The former nourishes an epistemology of love; the latter spawns an epistemology of power. The lover's lingering backward glance is the emblematic posture of this metaphysics of the heart; the spectator's forward penetrating gaze the posture of the metaphysics of the mind.

In "Orpheus.Eurydice.Hermes," Rilke best sums up his poetic vision.[26] The poem re-tells the classic story of Orpheus' descent to the underworld to rescue his beloved Eurydice from death. With Rilke, however, the tale is told from Eurydice's point of view, and in doing so Rilke allows us to glimpse how the supposed failure of the backward glance is our fate. At the last moment, Orpheus stops, and turns round to see if Eurydice, guided by Hermes, is following. In this turning, Orpheus disobeys the commands of the gods, and he loses Eurydice once again, this time forever.

I do not know if it is true that poetry here attains to a unique level of wisdom, but it seems that this tale of disobedience leaves no doubt that the gods wisely forbid the backward glance. They know Orpheus must fail, and that through the failure he, and through him we, will come to know that the timeless is to be made here in the timebound through loving in the face of loss. Angels are eternal and animals perish, but we die. But because we die we also love in ways that they cannot do. In "Orpheus. Eurydice. Hermes" the backward glance reveals that death is the bride of love. This is why Paula returns. This is why the dead return and solicit the backward glance: to open the eyes of the heart so that we can see through the eyes of love and loss.

Scene Four: The Call of Destiny

The backward glance is instruction in the art of holding on by letting go. Orpheus' failure to make love eternal is his success in making love a human act that spans the timeless and the timebound, an act that transforms fate into a vocation, an act that releases each lover to his/her destiny and in doing so manifests the eternal no-where now-here. This is why Rilke says in the Requiem that the only thing that is wrong is "not to enlarge the freedom of a love / with all the inner freedom one can summon." This is why he says," We need, in love, to practice only this: / letting each other go. For holding on/comes easily; we do not need to learn it."[27]

In the moment when Orpheus turns, he lets go of Eurydice, just as in her death she has already let go of him. There are, I think, no other lines of poetry that capture this moment of Eurydice's release than those that Rilke pens for the moment of Orpheus' turning. In her death she had already passed beyond being Orpheus' possession: "She was no longer that woman with blue eyes / who once had echoed through the poet's songs. . ." Already in her death, she had closed within herself, ". . . had come into a new virginity." Multiplying the images of her intensified, new interiority, Rilke says, "She was already loosened like long hair, / poured out like fallen rain, shared like a limitless supply." And as if to underscore the significance of this transformation into her own destiny, Rilke adds as a single line, set off from the previous lines and those that are to follow, "She was already root."[28]

Orpheus had descended into the underworld to rescue from death the woman that he knew and loved. Eurydice, however, is not that woman. When he turns and Hermes puts out his hand to stop Eurydice, and, according to Rilke, tells us with sorrow in his voice that Orpheus has turned, Eurydice, unable to understand, softly whispers, " *Who?*" [29]

Eurydice then turns round and follows her own path into her destiny. She descends with Hermes back into the timeless underworld, while Orpheus returns alone to the world of time. But he too finds in this return after the turning round of his backward glance his own destiny. In the last sonnet of the first part of *Sonnets to Orpheus*, Rilke tells us that Orpheus outsings the enraged cries of the maenads. Although in the end they do destroy him, the vibrations of his songs linger: ". . . in lions and rocks / and in trees and birds. There you are still singing."[30]

The backward glance-so simple, so fraught with peril! A lesson arranged by the gods! A teaching that humbles the mind by opening the heart to the presence of death. A gift brought by the dead who return to show us how to love the moment because it flows away, like water held in the palm of one's hand. Orpheus is the archetypal image of this gesture: his "failure" our hope; his songs, which linger after his death, our joy. Moreover, in his lingering songs the destiny of Orpheus, which he is given in a backward glance that only seemingly fails, becomes our vocation. "Only because at last enmity rent and scattered you / are we now the hearers and a mouth of Nature."[31] In the backward glance we hear through the heart's lament over loss the singing of the world. Then the backward glance becomes a homecoming, homework that is also heartwork, a song of lament that swells into a hymn of joy.

Afterword

The prelude is finished, the scenes are done, the curtain has fallen, the lights have been dimmed. But someone lingers in the corner, inviting a final backward glance.

In a letter that he wrote in 1918 shortly after the war, Rilke says that, "The scale of the human heart no longer applies and yet it was once the unit of the earth, and of Heaven, and of all heights and depths."[32] We have forgotten the gnosis of the heart. Our hearts no longer seem large enough to be the measure of the heights and depths that bless and wound a human life. At this exit should we not wonder if our hearts are failing today because we have no re-gard for the world and have grown deaf to its appeals to stop and turn and linger. Perhaps we need to learn the backward glance as a gesture of mourning so that we can be released into song.

12

On Being a Fool:
In Defense of the Pathetic Heart

The Heart Has Its Reasons

Blaise Pascal, 17th century polymath, younger contemporary of Descartes, and in so many ways his philosophical antithesis, gazed at the starry night sky and experienced its endless space with dread. Pascal's anxiety in the face of all that emptiness is a modern condition. Indeed, even within his own time, there were still those who saw within the heavens the abode of Angels and who heard therein the music of the cosmic spheres. How the heavens have grown silent, cold, dark, and empty, and how Angels have been banished from them, have been interests of mine for more than a quarter century. This difference between a musical cosmos and an empty, infinite universe records a radical shift in the human condition.

We are the inheritors of this change, and in this essay I want to describe the loss of heart and its consequences, which this change has produced. I want to follow Pascal and awaken the heart in our time, when mind, unhinged from nature, has all but taken leave of its senses and drifts in a cold, dark universe, whose stars no longer seem to be beacons for our journey home.

In his short, posthumously published treatise, *Pensees,* Pascal wrote that "The heart has its reasons which reason cannot know."[1] I read these lines and imagine them to be a defense of the heart in the face of the mind's dread, as its telescopic eyes penetrate more and more deeply into the vast abyss of space. I read Pascal's words in this way because at roughly the same time that he was attempting this defense of the heart, the heart itself was under attack. In 1628, William Harvey, English court physician to King Charles I, in defining the heart as a pump, privileged the systolic moment of its rhythm, that moment when the heart is empty of blood. In this same period, the devotion to the Sacred Heart of Christ began, when Christ appeared to Margaret Mary Alacoque, a Visitation nun cloistered in a small convent in southern France. On this occasion, Christ showed her his bleeding heart and asked why the human heart had become so empty of its capacity to receive His love.[2]

Pascal's defense was, I suggest, a prophetic acknowledgment of how the emptying of the heavens by a mind divorced from nature would find its mirror in the emptying of the human heart. His words, I imagine, were an attempt to rescue the human heart from the Cartesian mind. In the face of the empty heavens, the human heart was being emptied of its capacity to love. "I think, therefore, I am," Descartes proclaimed. "The heart has its reasons which reason cannot know," Pascal whispered. Pascal's voice was too soft. Reason shielded itself against the terrors of the lonely heart, drained of love and filled with dread, in the face of an empty void.

This shift from heaven to heart, from the dread that is visible in the dark abyss of empty space to the chambers of the heart whose anxiety is less visible, has allowed our loss of heart and our increasing incapacity to love to remain more hidden. It has also kept our dread and anxiety more unspeakable, because that which has no visible face is more difficult to name.

The trace of this dread, however, haunts us. Daily, in small doses, our hearts break, and we attend to their broken condition in strange ways. The broken heart is a metaphor that matters, but we forget its reality by focusing on the pumping heart as matter that is not a metaphor. The ways in which the heart loves and is shattered in love, as Goodchild[3] describes in her extraordinary book, become mere tropes, when measured against the image of the heart as a pump. This strategy amounts to substance abuse, because the pumping heart, regarded as only a material organ, loses its symbolic resonance. It becomes matter without spirit, an organ, which is no longer a seat of in-spiration. Without this locus of the heart, our in-spirations, this breathing in of the divine enmeshed within nature, this moment of being touched by the numinous that beats at the heart of even the most ordinary events, become the manic enthusiasms of our consumer culture. Overwhelmed, the heart that has been reduced to the pump beats faster and faster as it tries to contain the holy spirit, the divine wind that blows through the soul of the world.

Cardiognosis as Method

The heart that is only a pump is a heart that has lost its soul. The Angel of the organ, we might say, has taken flight. Sadly, however, the Angel of the heart, like the Angels of all creation, have had no place to go, since the Heavens have been emptied of their presence.[4] The historical events that I have presented above are a track of this loss, and in this essay I want to stay with that loss in order to feel its grief.

We grieve because we have dared to love, and we love again because we have allowed ourselves to grieve.[5] Grief endured can be the beginning of "cardiognosis,"[6] a way of knowing that is neither about mind nor measurement. It is a gnosis that begins in grief over loss, in a sorrow attuned to absences that haunt presence, in a sadness whose archetypal background is rooted in the myth of the fall from paradise, a sadness then which is sensitive to all that has been left behind.

When we are present in this fashion we are witnesses for what has been forgotten, witnesses who, summoned by what has been left behind, engage in the work of an-amnesis, of un-forgetting, of awakening, an awakening that starts with the gesture of a backward glance. In this backward glance, we begin to see in a different way. Through the tears of the heart, we begin to see that knowing is about loving and not about power, and that its practice requires a surrender of oneself to what one wishes to know, a surrender that places oneself in intimate proximity with the desired other, and not at a distance that allows dominance and control. In this way of knowing, we know as we let ourselves be known.[7] Although this way of knowing and being is neither about the empiricism of facts nor the logic of reason, it is a legitimate way of knowing the world and being in it. It is a gnosis familiar to the artist and the lover, the mystic and the poet, childhood and madness.

Cardiognosis is an attempt to recover the soul of the heart, its Angel, by awakening the heart of the soul. A primary aspect of this gnosis of the heart concerns time and memory. For the heart, what has been forgotten does not lie in a past that is behind one on the line of time. For the heart, time is not a river, and events do not flow from a past that is behind toward a future that lies ahead, somewhere up river. Time is not a consecutive history of events. Indeed, for the heart the causal links among historical events are not what matters. Pascal, Harvey, and Descartes shared the early part of the 17th century, and Descartes knew of Harvey's work. But Descartes was a quarter century dead when Margaret Mary Alacoque had her visions. For the heart, time is not horizontal, as it is for the reasoning mind. On the contrary, in the heart time is vertical, like falling rain, which makes the river of history possible.

The heart's vertical time is, perhaps, best imaged as a spiral, or a vortex, or a whirlpool, which sweeps within its currents all those moments, characters, and occasions, which have an emotional affinity with each other, which belong together by virtue of their tribal kinship. In this swirl, the line of time is bent into memories that turn round each other at different levels, held together by an emotional gravity, by a shared pathos, which goes beyond facts and beyond logical reasons. These connections of remembrances are not about a "Cogito," not the work of a thinking mind. Rather, these connections arise more or less spontaneously, while the thinking mind is off guard, seduced into a state of reverie. Thus, the kinship among Pascal, Descartes, Harvey, and Margaret Mary Alacoque stirs the depths of the heart before it touches the surface of the mind. And in the grip of this way of knowing and being, we become witnesses to something once known but forgotten, not critics who struggle to make sense of it all. The memories of the heart make sense of us before we even attempt to make sense of them. "The heart has its reasons which reason cannot know."

Insofar as the gnosis of the heart is about re-membering, about awakening to what has been lost, forgotten, marginalized, or otherwise neglected, heart-work always has a mood of melancholy, as if in this witnessing of loss one is awakening to some ancient grief. In another place,[8] I have written of these affinities among heart-work, grief, reverie, vertical time, and memory, and here I wish only to add that this way of the heart is very much in neglect today. As noted above, it seems to be a way of being practiced only by poets, lovers, and madmen/women, like those hysterics of former times who carried across the threshold of Freud's and Jung's consulting rooms a soul that had lost its heart. In a world where heart has largely been silenced by a mind no longer in love with or in awe of Angels, it seems imperative to recover the heart's ways of knowing and being. The crises of our times, which increasingly place all of us at the edge of an abyss of terrors too unthinkable, will not be addressed only in political or economic terms. They need a heartfelt response, which might allow us, as Sardello says,[9] to face the world with soul. We need to dare to imagine what we and the world might become, if we let ourselves lose our minds and surrender to our hearts.

The Path of Tears and Laughter

In the language of the heart, tears are the syntax of grief. As blood is to the heart as pump, tears are to that other heart that has its reasons that reason does not know. Nietzsche once observed that man is the animal who laughs. But we are also the animal who cries. Laughter and tears are what make us human, and the capacity for each is also what makes us capable of receiving the divine. Both are, if you wish, tropisms of the heart's soul, natural inclinations that arise within a heart that is moved and touched by and attuned to the other beyond any reasonable measure of restraint.

Do Angels laugh or cry? Perhaps, though, when I read Rilke I sense that they are incapable of love, which so often is the occasion that moves us to tears and joy. The opening lines of the first of his *Duino Elegies* plaintively ask if the Angel would hear our cry, and the second elegy suggests that, because of their perfect beauty, which leaves them so self contained, they would not. Drawing their beauty back into their own faces, they are mirrors for themselves, content within their own being, indifferent to us. Without the capacity to love— or is it for the Angel the absence of any necessity to love?— I doubt that they either laugh or cry.

Yet, something in my own heart tells me that this is not so, and that angels do weep, and perhaps on occasion also laugh. I know that they envy us, that they wish, for example, that "they had beards to enjoy the pleasure of the sound / Of scraping the passage of time from faces / worn with sorrows, lighted with joys."[10] So, maybe they do love, and laugh, and weep. Tears and laughter, then, might not only make us human, they also might be the bonds that tie us to Angels and even web us into all creation.

I know, for example, that animals weep and smile, because I have seen it. Once, on a cold, winter morning, just before dawn, I saw a tear in the eye of a great horse that had galloped up to me in a meadow. Call it the effect of the cold, if you wish, or the projection of my own inner state, but recognize that if you do, then you would not have seen with me the appeal in this tearful eye for some momentary rescue from a loneliness shared between us.

On another occasion, I also saw tears welling up in the eyes of a caged gorilla. In that moment, I felt that the tears of this great, silent beast were in remembrance of a bond that we once shared and that we ourselves had broken. I knew in my heart that his tears were for me, for us—remembrance and an appeal to come home.

Finally, once in the midst of a sorrow so total that it was beyond any human gesture of comfort, I saw a cat smile. For a moment my grief was suspended and my heart felt the joy of laughter.

It seems, then, that we should admit that tears and laughter make us human because they do knit us into the web of creation. When we cry or laugh, we are, momentarily, out of our minds, and outside ourselves in this way we are joined to a mystery larger than ourselves. In tears and laughter, the heart overflows the boundaries of complex and convention. Tears and laughter are like harmonic resonances that attune us to others, vibrations on the web of Being that place us in sympathy with all creation.

The Pathetic Heart

Henry Corbin, the foremost western scholar of Sufi mysticism, tells us that sym-pathy is a "condition and mode of perception," which belongs to the subtle heart.[11] The prefix, "sym," means "like," while the stem, "pathy," comes from "pathos," which means feeling, emotion, passion, suffering. This stem is also joined with the prefix "com," meaning "with," and gives us our word com-passion. Sym-pathy and com-passion, then, are the ways of the heart, which make us like others and bring us near to them. In our feeling, passionate, and suffering hearts we are in communion with others who are like us.

The stem, "pathy," also yields the word pathetic. At the root of sym-pathy and com-passion, therefore, lies a pathetic heart. Sym-pathy and com-passion are, we might say, the flowers that blossom from a pathetic cardiognosis. To be in the world and to know it with heart is to be pathetic. Surely, however, this flies in the face of our complexes and conventions. To be seen as pathetic is an insult and injury to one's pride, and conventional wisdom applies it as a term of derision and abuse. The soul of the word, however, tells a different tale. If we are to follow the path of the heart, we must pause at this pathetic place and consider what being pathetic can teach us about the ways of the heart that have been largely forgotten.

When one is called pathetic, the experience is not pleasant. The term carries the connotation of being weak, pitiful, and inadequate. One does not care to be perceived in this fashion. It is an insult and injury to one's pride. The soul of the word, however, lies deeper than the ego's wounded pride: Pathetic / pathos: filled with passion! From this perspective, what appears as insult to mind is in fact a recognition that in one's pathetic state one is filled with passion, that in this state one's heart is able to be moved by emotion, touched by suffering, that one is capable of feeling. In this moment, one might, then, feel grateful, even thankful, for being seen as pathetic. In the pathetic state, one is being a witness for values lost and forgotten, for passion, feeling, suffering, and emotion as fundamental attributes of a way of knowing and being, which web each of us within bonds of sym-pathy and com-passion not only with one's fellow creatures, but with all creation. From the perspective of the ego-mind with its persona mask of complex and convention, the pathetic state may seem to mark one as a clown or a fool. But from the perspective of the soul of the heart, this does not matter. For if clown or fool, then these are but disguises of the guerrilla fighter in service to the heart of the soul. As such, one must be content with the knowledge that one is doing good work, not unlike the poet Rumi's image of the soul as a night-thief that does its work, "When merchants eat their big meals and sleep/their dead sleep."[12]

The tendency to dismiss or to have one's pathetic condition dismissed is understandable, because, as root of the sym-pathetic and com-passionate heart, the pathetic heart challenges the empty heart and the isolation it has fallen into. The pathetic heart painfully awakens the empty heart to its broken connection with the starry night. One's pathetic heart betrays how we have forgotten that we are fundamentally in kinship through passion and not reason, and how, in this kinship, we are available to being penetrated by the pathos of other beings, able to be in sym-pathy with the passions of others and nature. For clown or fool in service to the heart's ways of knowing and being, the pathetic state is Pascal's line hurled in the face of those who no longer remember that the heart does have its reasons that reason does not know.

For the sake of this heart, one must even become a saboteur on occasion. One must evoke and provoke moments of awakening, perhaps even daring to lie and declare that one once did see a cat smile. Such provocations are like pieces of art that disturb the night sleep of fat merchants. They offer opportunities to greet the smug smiles worn on the faces of complex and convention with the warning that one risks a broken heart when one is no longer capable of being pathetic.

Being pathetic, I would suggest, is the primary function of a psychology that practices cardiognosis. Being a saboteur, a clown, or a fool, are, I would suggest, the required postures and gestures of the one who would practice a psychology rooted in the heart's ways of knowing and being. Saboteur, clown, fool, in service to the awakened heart, know that being pathetic is no fallacy. He or she knows that the pathetic fallacy, defined as the attribution of human qualities and feelings to things, a projection of our poor, impoverished psyches onto an empty, in-animate world, is not an attribution at all. He or she knows that it is an attunement to and a witnessing of the vital pathos that connects all beings, from stones to stars, from animals to Angels, from humans to the divine.

The saboteur, clown, or fool, does not impose the pathetic heart on anyone, so much as he or she stages occasions for its appearance. The heart's ways of knowing and being require that saboteur, clown, fool be a witness who, in service to the heart, undoes the mind and then walks away. He or she lingers just long enough on these occasions only to be a witness for the defense. He or she lingers close to things and stays there just long enough to invite and to allow the heart to be impregnated by the passions of the silent invisibles and become their voice. The witness for the pathetic heart does only this, nothing more. He or she proves nothing, offers no reasonable system, and is even content to be regarded as useless.[13] The pathetic witness is a patient waiting in the moment, which then erupts in a wild, joyous act on behalf of the silence in the chatter, the invisibles in the visible, the small miracles in the heart of the simple and the ordinary, the forgotten, marginalized and neglected ways of the subtle passions of the feeling heart.

The Scandalous Rose

Proclus, the fifth century neo-Platonist philosopher gives a beautiful example of the attunement of the pathetic heart to an otherwise ordinary moment. In its heliotropic movement, a flower manifests its affinity with the sun. In this tropism or inclination, the flower and the sun exchange their mutual regard for each other. This turning of the flower, he says, is a conversion toward its "Angel, "an action that is an expression of the pathos between them, the feeling of the one for the other. Helio-tropism is a helio-pathy; the rhythms of nature are tides of passion. Out of this pathetic resonance, a bond of sym-pathy is made between flower and sun. Imagine how upsetting all this can be to the mind that has taken flight from the pathetic heart. The flower, in its turning, shamelessly displays its attraction for the sun, an erotic act performed in public for all to see, even the children. Scandalous!

Proclus' example is repeated in an observation once made by the poet Rilke. On that occasion, he saw how a rose had fully opened its petals to the exuberance of the sun's morning light. His description of that fully open rose was/is so erotic that it came back to me, when I myself saw such a fully blossoming rose. Its deep redness was the offspring of its surrender to the light of the sun, sunlight made manifest as shape and color. This moment was an epiphany because it allowed me to glimpse their affinity for each other, a spiritual kinship rooted in the passion of light for form and matter, and matter for the wild freedom and excesses of light. It was an epiphany that changed my vision.

For a moment, I lost sight of either the sun or the rose in their separateness;

I saw the sun through the rose and the rose through the sun. I lost single vision, the look that hardens the world into its literal facts and identifies things by virtue of their fixed identities. For a moment, I beheld this erotic display with the double vision of metaphoric eyes, which, seeing one thing through the other, is sym-pathetic to differences that establish mutual fields of attraction and desire.

The Spanish philosopher, Ortega y Gasset, situates our capacity for metaphor in this wild field of difference and desire. He writes, "how unimportant a thing would be if it were only what it is in isolation." Continuing, he says that "there is in each thing a certain latent potentiality to be many other things, which is set free and expands when other things come into contact with it." Amplifying his meditation, he adds that "one might say that each thing is fertilized by the others; that they desire each other as male and female; that they love each other and aspire to unite, to collect in communities, [to gather] in worlds."[14] I read Ortega out loud and I am made certain again that the term Spanish philosopher is and must be a contradiction in terms. Philosophy belongs north of the Alps!

Be that as it may, this epiphany of my own rose was a moment that felt quite sacred, and as I write these words I am looking at a picture of this rose, which sits on my desk. As I look at it, I recall that I also felt overwhelmed with sadness in this moment. For a moment, but only for a moment, I glimpsed the secret, sym-pathetic bonds of love, which hold creation together. It felt as if I was remembering something that I once knew, but had forgotten. Metaphoric vision opened the quiet pools of melancholy that lie in the depths of the pathetic heart.

This remark about melancholy at the heart of pathetic vision returns me to Rilke. When he returned in the late evening to the Italian garden where earlier he delighted in the exuberant abandon of the rose, he saw that it had not closed in on itself, folded itself into sleep. It had drunk too much of the sun's light, and filled to overflowing with this passion it would too quickly fade. Before its time it would die. Rilke mourned.

This image of the blossomed rose dying in the dark night also makes me mournful. It is a small thing, and, perhaps, unworthy of so much attention. So many larger tragedies surround us that it seems extravagant to be concerned with a rose that dies from an excess of loving. But I believe that these small things have gone so unattended that they have born our bitter harvests. Mindful of the big things, our politics have become a-pathetic, leaving our hearts adrift in our collective version of bread and circuses, a nightmare world where pathos for a dying rose is perverted into commercial sentimentality. In this regard, Sardello is absolutely right to place the sentimental heart as the contra to the pumping heart. The former, he says, is a metaphor without substance, while the latter is substance without metaphor. The former, I would add, amounts to soul murder, while the latter is substance abuse.

We do need witnesses for these small matters, for these useless occasions, witnesses who take the risk of being fools. We need to be useless in order to be attentive to these epiphanies. So, I am content to waste my days to wonder if the rose overreached itself in some excess of desire for its invisible "Angel." Did it glimpse its heavenly form, and delirious with this vision drink too much the sun? I think that we are not so different from this rose in those moments when, remembering something of that invisible order of being, which, being no-where is now-here, everywhere around us, like a perfume, we hurt with longing. On these occasions of remembrance, the pathetic heart taps that pool of melancholy that lies deep within its veins. This melancholy is the aftertaste and the foretaste of our Angelic existence.[15] It is the bittersweet taste on the tongue deposited in moments of personal grief. It is the honey-ash residue left by our personal losses, which deepens them into the shared, universal grief of being an orphan on a journey home. Melancholy is the mood of a pathetic heart, which remembers and feels quite at home within these words of the poet Wordsworth : "Our birth is but a sleep and a forgetting. / The soul that rises with us, our life's star, / Hath had elsewhere its setting, / and cometh from afar: / Not in entire forgetfulness, / And not in utter nakedness, / But trailing clouds of glory do we come / From God, who is our home: / heaven lies about is in our infancy!"[16]

The Praying Lotus

Recall the earlier mention of Proclus. Of the heliotrope he says that, "if we could hear the sound of the air buffeted by its movements, we should be aware that it is a hymn to its king, such as it is within the power of a plant to sing."[17] This is a wondrous vision, which is so unlike our habitual modes of perception that it deserves a specific example.

Speaking of the lotus, Proclus says that it "manifests its affinity and sympathy with the sun. Before the appearance of the sun's rays, its blossom is closed; it opens slowly at sunrise, unfolds as the sun rises to the zenith, and folds again and closes as the sun descends. What difference is there between the human manner of praising the sun by moving the mouth and lips, and that of the lotus which unfolds its petals? They are its lips and this is its natural hymn."[18]

What difference, indeed, in these two forms of praise? When we move our mouth and lips to praise the beauty of nature, perhaps in a poem, is this poetic praise a kind of heliotrope, as if poetry is a natural inclination of the pathetic heart, that heart impregnated with the passions of nature? For the pathetic heart there is no doubt that the lotus' heliotrope and human poetry are forms of prayer, that heliotrope and poetry are songs of praise. The pathetic heart knows that the universe and all its beings are a form of prayer, and, in fact, for Proclus the heliotropic hymn is the flower's way of praying.

The pathetic heart is a responsive presence to things, a response-able presence, a presence that is able-to-respond because it has listened. In this respect, the pathetic heart is an ethical way of knowing the world and being in it, a way of knowing and being, which in being response-able is rooted in obedience to its ties to nature, unlike mind, which has broken that connection. This kind of presence, however, is so unfamiliar in our age of science and technology that it would draw to itself the derisive judgment of being a fine example of the pathethic fallacy. Dismissed in this fashion, the ego mind can protect itself from being touched and moved by the beauty of the world that calls to us. For the disincarnate mind, the world cannot be alive in this fashion. The mind, in its splendid isolation will not allow it. A pathetic presence is neither useful nor productive. Leave it, therefore, to the artists, poets, madmen and fools. It is only a clown's way of pretending.

But the pathetic heart in us insists. This heart does have its reasons which mind does not know.

Sunrise

I woke early. It was still dark, but in the east the first rays of the morning sun were beginning to crack the shell of night. The camp was perhaps fifty yards from the river, and I made my way slowly down the unfamiliar path, stupidly oblivious to the danger of the animals in the African bush. The water was cold, but it sharpened my senses. Across the river, on the opposite bank, a range of hills framed the valley. As the sun gained in strength, the ridge of these hills was outlined in a thin, delicate purple line, as if someone had ribboned their craggy edges. The contrast between the dark hills still shadowed in night and their purple crown was beautiful, and as I stared at this artful display of nature I saw what appeared to be stone statues carved into the hilltop. From the distance, I could not quite make out their form. But I was certain that they were made of stone, because of their total stillness.

In one single moment, the sun broke the last vestige of night. Rising above the peak of the hills, it flooded the valley with light. And at the exact same moment of this epiphany, the stone statues came to life and filled the valley with sound. The stone carvings that I had seen just before the dawn were transformed into a troop of baboons, who were now screeching and moving in a kind of wild, ecstatic dance. I knew in an instant that in their previous frozen stillness they had been waiting for the morning sun, gathered like monks in prayer before the dawn.[19]

This example, like that of the lotus and the rose, betray a mode of presence which allows the invisible "Angel" of the moment to shine through, a mode of being in the world that is responsive to the luminosity in each moment, the shining radiance of the invisible that subtends the visible. This cardiognosis is not about facts or ideas, and one cannot access these moments through either an empirical or rational sensibility. It requires a poetic sensibility, as Corbin says of Proclus.

In a fine piece of understatement, Corbin says that "it is safe to say that not everyone perceives this silent prayer offered up by the plant-we must also speak of the poetic function of sympathy in a man like Proclus. This poetic sensibility opens up a new dimension in beings, the dimension of their invisible selves." Thus, Corbin adds, "we may speak of a pathos experienced by Proclus in common with the flower, a pathos necessary to his perception of the sympathy which aroused it and which, when he perceived it, invested the flower with a theophanic function."[20]

The poetic sensibility of the pathetic heart is a knowing in the moment of the experience, not a knowing about. It is a gnosis that arouses one, knowing as awakening. It is Plato's an-amnesis, a remembering of what we have already seen. It is also a way of knowing, which, as Proclus' words about the praying flower claim, is an epiphany of the numinous, the sacred in the ordinary, a knowing that reveals the face of the divine.

The Invisible World: Cardiognosis and Phenomenology

The examples of the rose, the lotus, and the baboons are examples of the pathetic heart as a mode of being openly attuned to, attracted by, and converted toward the pathos of all things. In this regard the pathetic heart belongs to a hieratic science practiced by Proclus. According to Proclus, those who practice this science "take as their starting point the things of appearance and the sympathies they manifest among themselves and with their invisble powers."[21]

In our own day, phenomenology partakes of this same attitude. It too is a hieratic science, not an empirical one. Ortega Y Gasset is one of these southern

Alpine phenomenologists, more poet than philosopher, who practices this science. Beginning with things as they appear, the pathetic heart at the core of a hieratic gnosis is sensitive to the non-causal connections among things. Gaston Bachelard, another phenomenologist whose heart is in the right place, provides a fine example. It is a poem by Jean Follain:

> When there falls from the hands of the serving girl
> the pale round plate
> the color of the clouds
> the pieces must be picked up
> while the chandelier trembles
> in the masters' dining room. [22]

Commenting on these few lines, Bachelard rightly situates phenomenology within a poetic sensibility, which penetrates the secret "solidarity" among things, and awakens us "from the sleep of indifference." The trembling chandelier reflects the ordinary accident of a dropped plate as a death. This poetic perception, which begins in an attitude that keeps a pathetic phenomenologist close to things as they appear, is attuned to the sym-pathetic correspondence that exists among things and between us and things.

Bachelard's commentary also situates phenomenology as a modern day hieratic science within the Platonic tradition of knowing as an-amnesis. Phenomenology's injunction of "back to the things themselves" is its way of saying remember what we once knew but have forgotten. To awaken from the sleep of indifference is to be a witness for that invisible order of being, which haloes the visible. This invisible order, as Merleau-Ponty shows,[23] is not just the absence of the visible. Rather, the invisible is the armature of the visible, the coiled energy, if you will, which generates the visible. The invisible is, we might say, the pregnant void of the visible.

Merleau-Ponty generally illustrates the invisible through the phenomenon of light. Light is not what we see; it is the means by which we see. The invisible shines through the visible, and pours itself out as the visible. Thus, the blossoming rose is the light of the sun nakedly and playfully displaying itself as a rich, ripe, sensuous redness.

We have traveled a long way on the road toward abandoning the dimension of the invisible. As I have shown elsewhere,[24] Newton's prismatic reduction of the rainbow to the spectrum was a decisive step on this path. In his darkened room, light itself became an object of vision. Perhaps only a poet like William

Blake could have appreciated the profound loss in this translation. Thus he prayed, "May God us keep / From Single Vision and Newton's Sleep."[25]

The world has become bright and noisy. We live at the speed of light in our digital world. We become beings of light and light beings. A hieratic science awakens us to our place within the web of creation by transforming our vision. In this science, the low is seen through the high, and the high through the low; or as Proclus says, "in heaven, terrestrial things according both to a causal and to a celestial mode and on earth heavenly things in a terrestrial state."[26] So, for example, one might see through a stone a weighted star, or through a spider's web framed in moonlight a galaxy of stars. An essential element in this transformation is that backward glance of remembrance, that moment when, with some sorrow, we un-forget our birthright, and begin the journey home. In this moment and through this gesture grief awakens the pathetic heart, and heart-work becomes home-work.

To see in this way is to grasp the invisible kinship and hidden solidarity among things, to see that matter is haunted by spirit and that spirit longs to matter. Thus, for Proclus plants and stones and animals have a double life. They are axes or hinges or pivots where spirit matters and matter is in-spired, subtle, imaginal bodies perceived not with the eyes of anatomy, but through visionary eyes that are sensitive to the interplay among things.

In his book *The Voyage and the Messenger*, Henry Corbin ties the experience of subtle bodies to a visionary knowledge whose essence belongs to a science of mirrors, a "mystical catoptrics."[27] Mirror play sets up a field of reflections in which the invisible domain of secret symmetries and correspondences, like the wraith of death that appears between the dropped plate and the trembling chandelier, shines through. The invisible order, which arises in this mirror play among things, is as diaphanous as a ghost, as insubstantial as an apparition, as subtle as the wind, which disturbs the trees whose radiant reflections responsively shimmer in the lake. The spirit that haunts the visible world that matters is as subtle as the image, which haunts the person reflected in the mirror.

A hieratic science practiced by a pathetic heart requires a radical change of mind. The poetic sensibility of the pathetic heart requires a metaphoric mind, a mind that is able to regard the shimmering image of the trees in the lake as a reality that is neither the tree itself nor the water, that is capable of regarding the mirror image as a reality that is neither a fact nor an idea. In the cardiognosis of a hieratic science, these themes of mirror play, metaphoric sensibility, and the subtle realities of the imaginal world coalesce to produce that change of mind.

The Pathetic Heart and the Metaphoric Mind

Perhaps now it is clearer why the Cartesian mind defends itself against the pathetic heart. To fall into the genuine sense of the pathetic fallacy as an attunement and not an attribution is to lose that mind that exists in isolation, a mind that has taken leave of its senses, that mind un-hinged from nature and set adrift in the empty void of space to wander, like a ghost with an erection, in the wonderful phrase of Walker Percy.[28] And it is to fall into that other mind, which finds itself already a participant in the cosmos, a mind that is rooted in the feeling heart. Over the years I have called this other mind metaphoric to distinguish it from the literalism of the factual mind and the rationality of the logical one.

The capacity for metaphor is rooted in the pathetic heart's sensitivity to the sym-pathetic correspondences among things, and to its com-passionate ability to resonate, dwell with, and be part of their secret kinships. This metaphoric mind, which grows from the pathetic heart, is a mind that is touched and moved by appearances before there is any factual or rational understanding of them. It is a mind that betrays in its speaking of things something of its already prior seduction by them, a mind, then, that reverses the familiar understanding of language as something that we do. The metaphoric mind is witness to the surprise that in speech we give voice to the silent tongues of nature.

The literary critic, Howard Nemerov, gives a fine example of the metaphoric mind. He tells the story of seeing a bird in his garden and not being sure if it is a purple finch. Reading the field guide, the factual description leaves him uncertain. The final line of that account—*a purple finch is a sparrow dipped in raspberry juice*— however, does persuade him. Through the metaphor he sees the purple finch. Through a sparrow dipped in raspberry juice, a reality that is not empirically real and which from a factual point of view is really pathetic, the purple finch appears. Recognize, however, that that juice-drenched sparrow is no-where! And yet, because it is a no-where that is now-here, the finch is there in the world and not just in Nemerov's mind as an idea that he projects onto the world. The sparrow dipped in raspberry juice is an invisible which allows the visible. The metaphor is like Merleau-Ponty's description of light. It is not what we see; it is the means by which we see.

Nemerov's example suggests that the metaphoric mind of an hieratic science works in an alchemical fashion, loosening the factual condition of things and dissolving our fixed ideas about them. This alchemy of the metaphoric mind is really an act of play that is a prelude to the serious business of getting to the bottom of things, a kind of foreplay. Like all genuine play, moreover, a metaphor does loosen and dissolve the fixed, certain, and rigid categories of a mind in charge of the world. The metaphoric mind plays on the border and boundaries of the real and loses itself in that other world, that invisible, subtle world of the imaginal, which is neither about things nor thoughts, that world where baboons before dawn are monks in silent prayer, and ripe red roses are the light of the sun made visible as color, texture, and aroma. This imaginal domain is the true realm of the pathetic heart as Corbin asserts, the realm where the Angel of the occasion always dwells.

Once, long ago, Marshall McLuhan, who knew how to have fun with language, approached me at a party and said that he had heard that I had written a book on the metaphorical character of psychological life. I confessed, and, without skipping a beat, he congratulated me and said, "a man's reach should exceed his grasp, or what's a metaphor." How brilliant, and how apt the insight! A metaphor extends our reach beyond our grasp, stretches us beyond the veil of the material world toward that heavenly imaginal domain, that other invisible world that solicits our pathetic hearts. Metaphoric capability is a gift of the Gods, which allows us a momentary remembrance that there is more to this world than meets the eye. And just as Ortega y Gasset refers to literalism as a form of "satanism," I would say that our metaphoric capability is the seed of the Angel deposited in our consciousness so that we would not completely forget the seductive play of the invisible with the visible. Metaphors are small miracles in the heart of the ordinary, which keep the pathetic heart aware that heaven does lie about us in our infancy, and that all the world is holy.

The Angel of Language

In the hieratic science of Proclus, the connection between the invisible and the visible worlds is mediated by the Angel. Each thing, each occasion, as it were, inspires an angel, and the function of this angel is to lead us from the visible back to the invisible. More specifically, in Sufi mysticism, this journey is described as the ta'wil, a "carrying back" of a thing to its origins, an alchemical process, which transforms the visible into its symbolic character, which liberates, we might say, the spirit that is trapped in matter. Metaphoric language is this journey of return. This journey begins when we are seduced into language because we have stopped speaking. It begins when we shut up long enough to hear the

Angel in the moment. It begins when we start with the silence of listening. The first act of this seduction occurs when we lend the "ear of the heart"[29] to the occasion.

In Rilke's poetry, this listening is the function of the heart. The heart speaks when the work of the inquisitive eye is done. This heart-work is the transubstantiation of world into word. So, Rilke asks, "Earth, isn't this what you want: an invisible / re-arising in us?"[30] His question is characteristic of a pivotal moment in the birth of the metaphoric mind. To ask this kind of question requires that one has already surrendered the tongue in favor of the ear. It also requires that proximity to things, which is the way of the sym-pathetic heart, in order to hear the world's reply, the voice of the Angel singing in the moment. With the question, we pledge ourselves to linger in the gap between in-spiration, when we breathe in the world and are nourished by its pathos, and ex-piration, when on a subtle waft of air we die for the sake of the world, surrender ourselves to speak its visions and dreams, like the dying rose ex-pired to give voice to the dreams of the sun to become color and form.

For the neo-Platonist philosopher, Sufi mystic, and poet, language is a listening that is an awakening. We are in language; it is not in us. In this regard, language is all around us, the world abuzz in song, for those who have ears to hear. The silence that precedes our speaking is the condition for responding to what addresses us. Beginning in the ear, language is responsive to a call. Language is our vocation. As such, having listened, we are called to speak, duty bound to do so, and it would be as much a sin against the cosmos were we to remain in silence, as it would be to speak before being penetrated by that silence. But then, how does one ever know when to speak, or if one's words are in service to the silence? How does one ever know if one's words are imposed upon the visible by the ego mind, or arise from the pathetic heart in response to the seduction by the invisible within the visible?

I have here only a single clue. It is the difference between language as power and as love. Does one speak from the heart in an act of love, and in such fashion that the words themselves feel delicious on the tongue, and drip blue honey on the world? If so, one's words then feel like they are in service to something other than oneself, and one senses that those words contribute to a dialectic of love, which spirals throughout all creation.

Something of this dialectic of love beats within the sym-pathetic heart of the neo-platonist philosopher, the Sufi mystic, and the poet. For Proclus, all things of creation aspire toward the next level of being above them in an act of loving desire. For the Sufi mystics, this desire is matched by God's original desire for us, a desire that springs from a deep loneliness. Corbin, in fact, suggests that the root for the divine name, Al-lah, means sadness, and he speaks of a "pathetic god," who in a sigh of sorrow releases all the names of creation hidden within himself that then manifest as the visible world.[31] Rilke's vision of poetry is a reversal of that sigh, an act of love, which leads things back to their holy names. The clue then? Language as a form of lovemaking; poetry as erotic prayer!

Of Love and Loss

Where there is love, however, there is also loss, and if the cardiognosis of a hieratic science is about awakening to what we once knew and had, then there is at the heart of this work a sense of grief. I felt this grief when I read Rilke's image of the rose that could not close. A yearning so deep for home, its death must have been for a love whose loss was too grievous to bear. Rilke's poetry, moreover, continuously links love and grief, as his poem, "Orpheus. Euridyce. Hermes." so eloquently demonstrates. So, I wonder if Proclus was sad when he saw through the heliotrope all creation as a journey of return. And, I wonder if this sadness echoes the original sadness of the pathetic god. Do these moments of hieratic vision leave that bittersweet taste of melancholy as their trace? A hieratic science requires that we be fully in the world without being of it. It is a way of being that asks that we hold onto the world in love by letting go of it.

Throughout this essay I have been playing with the pathos of the pathetic heart, and now we are at the place of grief. But that is as it should be. Etymology is a science of affinities, and in the roots of words we find their sym-pathies for each other. The pathos of the pathetic heart is kin to *penthos*, which is the root for our word grief. The pathetic heart, then, is the grieving heart. Our sym-pathies and com-passions grow from the soil of our losses and sorrows. If a hieratic science is heart-work that is home-work, then this home-work is grief-work.

Personal grief can awaken the pathetic heart to the deeper pools of melancholy where our shared grief is watered. Personal grief can be a tap-root into this melancholy. In this shared, collective sorrow all of us are orphans in time, lost in the visible. Particularly today in a time when the world seems to be increasingly filled with the visible, too noisy and too bright, too empty of the holy, too oblivious to the sacred sense of the ordinary, too fast and quick to let us linger for a while to hear the secret, silent name of the angel in the moment, we are orphans. Melancholy is an oasis in this world, an odd occasion of hieratic epiphany, when we do recall how much we have lost, and we grieve.

Heart-work as Home-work

The connection between the pathetic heart and grief was made by John Ruskin in 1856. When he coined the term pathetic fallacy and described it as a false impression of external things in which human feelings are attributed to nature, inanimate objects, and animals, he also ascribed this attribution to a state of mind in which reason is unhinged by grief.[32] In addition, Ruskin found its use, which, as a form of personification is as old as poetry itself, to be the mark of a poor poet.

In the mid-nineteenth century, this negative attitude about an animate world, in which, for example, flowers dance and waves roar, is to be expected, because the world had already become in-animate, without soul, under the distant gaze of the spectator's eye. In a world in which mind had taken flight from the body, and the heart had become a pump, the animation of the world could only be a quality attributed to it by us.[33] The quantified world had no room or time for such qualities. Under these conditions, it is easy to imagine how Pascal's earlier anxiety of a heart adrift in the vast abyss of space could easily become the heart's grief over its loss of a sense of home within nature. About grief as the occasion that undoes the anxious mind of reason, therefore, Ruskin was surely correct.

Ruskin's idea of the pathetic fallacy as an act of attribution could only exacerbate the grief of the heart. Freud, who was born in 1856, eventually extended the reach and depth of this grief, when the notion of attribution becomes the defense mechanism known as projection. With this change the anxious, isolated mind is not just defended. It is unaware that it is defended, and even unaware of its need for a defense. The shadow of grief that haunts the mind of reason grows longer and darker, and grief itself is buried deeper in the heart.

The journey home through the pathetic heart awakened by grief is a journey of remembrance. In its pathetic condition, the heart awakens to its imprisonment within a world that has lost its vision of the visible order of things as a dehiscence, a flowering, of the invisible. Because the heart cannot bear this absence of the invisible world, because it cannot bear what the mind in its isolation has done, its journey becomes one of grieving the broken connections between itself and nature, a grieving which in its remembrance of those connections begins the process of restoring them.

Long ago, Plato imagined the journey out of this imprisonment through his allegory of the cave. Reading Plato through the pathetic heart, rather than the philosophic mind, an-amnesis, this un-forgetting at the core of his theory of knowledge, becomes the pathetic heart's melancholic longing for home. Knowledge is a journey of unforgetting that begins in sorrow over loss. The world, in Keats fine phrase, becomes "the vale of soul making,"[34] the arena within which we are lost, awaken, and return. I would add here that Jung's notion of the individuation process situates his psychology within these dynamics of the pathetic heart, an-amneis, grief, and the journey home. To place his psychology within a personalistic developmental frame, and to situate his notions of psychotherapy within a context that focuses on the "cure" of neurosis, misses the radical depths of his work. The development issue is about the soul's life in its passage from forgetting to remembrance, and within this context psychotherapy is fundamentally grief work.[35]

In addition, I would suggest that Plato's cave is an image of the vertical time of the heart. Plato was writing when a radical shift in cultural history, which incarnates the history of the soul, was taking place. It was a moment when the Homeric world of orality was being supplanted by the culture of the written word, when the sonorous depths of the oral mind were being overtaken by the linear and literal cast of the alphabetic mind.[36] This change threatened to install a historical kind of memory in place of the emotional, passionate memory of the heart. In this context, the image of the cave, which carries a strong suggestion of darkness and descent, preserves the vertical dimension of the heart's way of remembering. Its memory gathers and deepens events in time by virtue of their emotional kinship, their feeling value, compared with the reasonable mind, which aligns and stretches events in time by virtue of their linear sequence.

Furthermore, Plato's image of the cave postures the awakening of the heart as that backward glance, which I described earlier in this essay.[37] In this backward glance, the orphan who is lost in the world turns away from the play of shadows on the wall and turns toward the sun as their source. It is a turning, which initiates a re-turning, a moment in the life of the heart when we become pilgrims in search of home.

The Pilgrim's Tale

To conclude this essay, I offer the image in Figure I. The illustration is a woodcut taken from Jung's essay on "Flying Saucers."[38] In his commentary, Jung places it in the 17th century. It depicts a pilgrim who is on a "pelerinage de l'ame," a journey of the soul.

This journey has taken the pilgrim to an edge where two worlds intersect,

Figure I. "The Spiritual Pilgrim Discovering Another World"
Woodcut, 19th (?) century

separated by what appears to be a veil. On the right is the familiar, earthly, material world. On the left is another, more unfamiliar world, the heavenly world, which seems less dense than the first, more subtle, more light. The earthly world is historical. It is time bound. There are houses and trees and the quotidian round of sun and moon. The other, we could say, is eternal, but that is not evident in the image. What is, however, evident in the image are the two wheels of Ezekiel, the wheels where the time-bound and the timeless intersect.

It is a striking image, but what makes it even more striking is the posture of the pilgrim. His right hand is reaching upward, indicating that he or she is being drawn upward, that he or she is on a journey of ascent out of the cave of the material world. In addition, this right hand is reaching across the veil between the worlds, toward a jagged line. What is that jagged line?

To answer my question, I must tell a story. Once, while I was teaching a workshop with my wife on the relation between Jung's psychology and quantum physics, she showed this slide. In the audience was a physician-friend of mine. After the lecture, he rushed up to me and said that the jagged line was a cardiogram. To satisfy his curiosity and mine, he did a small study in which he showed this line, without the surrounding material, to seventeen physicians. All were board certified in their specialties: ten in emergency medicine, five in cardiology, and two in critical care. Each physician independently diagnosed the jagged line as ventricular tachycardia. This is a form of arrhythmia where the heart beats faster than normal. While the rhythm is still somewhat regular in this condition, the quickened pace, if not corrected, often leads to ventricular fibrillation. Interestingly, four physicians saw the end part of the jagged line as a few moments of this ventricular fibrillation, the most disorganized rhythm, which is equivalent to death unless reversed by countershock.

In addition, five physicians felt that the lines represented a variant of ventricular tachydardia called *torsades de pointes*. This is a pre-terminal form of ventricular tachydardia, which has been associated with sudden death. In 1997, the antihistamine, Seldane, was withdrawn from the market because of the association of this medication with the appearance of Torsades.

Here is a woodcut from the 17th century, which, to the eyes of modern medicine, is the image of a dying pump. How can this be? In the 17th century, the age of Pascal's defense of the heart that has its own reasons, we had not yet created the empirical eyes with which to see the electrical activity of the pumping heart. Indeed, the earliest EKG tracings date from the first part of the 20th century. I can only conclude that the jagged line was referring to a different heart, to the heart as an imaginal reality, the heart that has its reasons that reason does not know, the pathetic heart that had been awakened to life as a journey of homecoming.

In a letter to me which accompanied these results, my physician-friend raised this poignant question: why is this heart reaching out from the past for our attention? Can it be that this old image of the imaginal heart is asking us to recognize that heart-work as home-work is not about a literal change of place, but about a radical change of heart? Is the epiphany of the invisble an attack to the heart, a different kind of heart attack than the literal ones we suffer today in such great numbers, because of the absence of the invisible? Are we being addressed by this image, called to remember that the heart is more than a pump? On the day of the lecture, my wife had accidentally placed the slide in the tray backwards. This caused my physician friend to see the jagged line initially as the EKG image of a heart that was being resuscitated. Who made the mistake? Are we not in desperate need of recovering the heart of the soul in order to resuscitate the soul of the heart?

I gaze at this image and I see an appeal that fills me with grief for what we have lost. The dark, cold, empty, black, void of space once resonated with the songs of the choirs of Angels, and our heart, before it too, on its way to becoming only a pump, was emptied of its blood, belief, and passions, belonged to that chorus. We are this pilgrim in the wasteland of the modern world. At the close of this essay, I wonder if it is possible for us to hear some faint echo of that sweet music of the spheres, a melody whose words sing that the journey home is a change of heart, an awakening of the pathetic heart from its slumber in the heart as a pump.

We have become apt in hearing the faint echo of the big bang. Why not this? Can we, must we in fact, awaken, even if only for a moment, to shed at least one tear, enough, however, to cleanse the veil between worlds and give to us a hint of the invisible that shines through the visible, a brief glance of the Angel in the moment, a glimpse of the glimmering, holy face of the divine in the ordinary. "For everything that lives is Holy" William Blake said in "A Song of Liberty."[39] The awakened heart as a journey of homecoming is a journey of liberation that transforms the lament of the grieving heart into melancholic songs of praise.

A Final Glance

At the close of this essay, the reader is invited to take another look at the image of the pilgrim on the journey home. Specifically, the reader might take note of the pilgrim's hat. It looks like the face of a clown, who is a kind of officially sanctioned fool. In addition, this fool is facing backward. We should wonder if the artist who made this illustration not only knew that home-work requires a radical change of heart, but also that this change occurs with the gesture of the backward glance made by the fool, the clown, who escorts us on our journey home to the imaginal world. Perhaps it is in those moments when we are most foolish that the journey begins.

Notes

Chapter One

1. Richard Kearney, *The Wake of Imagination* (Minneapolis: U of Minnesota P, 1988) 27.

2. Neil Postman, *Amusing Ourselves to Death* (New York: Penguin, 1986).

3. See Eric Havelock, *Preface to Plato* (Cambridge: Harvard UP, 1963).

4. For a detailed discussion of this psychological approach to culture, see Robert Romanyshyn, *Mirror and Metaphor: Images and Stories of Psychological Life* (Pittsburgh: Trivium, 2001) and *Technology as Symptom and Dream* (London, New York: Routledge, Chapman & Hall, 1989).

5. Robert Romanyshyn, "Complex Knowing: Toward a Psychological Hermeneutics," *The Humanistic Psychologist* 19.1 (1991) 10-29.

6. Quoted in Kearney, 27.

7. Romanyshyn, 28.

8. Rene Descartes, *Meditations on First Philosophy*, trans. Laurence J. LaFleur (Indianapolis, New York: Bobbs-Merrill, 1969) 11.

9. Susan Bordo, *The Flight to Objectivity* (Albany: SUNY P, 1987).

10. Descartes, 11.

11. See note 4.

12. Postman, 111.

13. For a detailed account of Alberti's procedures, their meanings and cultural-historical implications, see Romanyshyn, *Technology as Symptom and Dream*.

14. See Marshall McLuhan, *The Guttenberg Galaxy* (New York: New American Library, 1969).

15. Descartes, 85.

16. Havelock, *Preface to Plato*, 190. For a discussion of the views of Julian Jaynes, see Jaynes, *The Origin of Consciousness in the Breakdown of the Bicameral Mind* (Boston: Houghton Mifflin, 1976).

17. Descartes, 85.

18. Donald M. Lowe, *History of Bourgeois Perception* (Chicago: U of Chicago P, 1982) 9.

19. Nathan Schwartz-Salant, "The Dead Self in Borderline Personality Disorders," *Pathologies of the Modern Self*, ed. David Michael Levin (New York: New York UP, 1987) 118.

20. Schwartz-Salant, 118.

21. For a discussion of the metaphorical character of psychological consciousness, see my book, *Mirror and Metaphor: Images and Stories of Psychological Life* (Pittsburgh: Trivium, 2001). In that work the hidden metaphoric character of modern scientific consciousness is indicated, suggesting that ego, literate consciousness already harbored within itself the seed of its own symptomatic undoing.

22. Havelock, 202.

Chapter Two

Suggestions for further reading:

Bukatman, Scott. (1993). *Terminal Identity*. Durham & London: Duke University Press.

Edgerton Jr., Samuel, Y. (1976). *The Renaissance Rediscovery of Linear Perspective*. New York: Harper & Row.

Gibson, William. (1984). *Neuromancer*. New York: Ace Books.

Heim, Michael. (1992). "The Erotic Outology of Cyberspace." In M. Benedikt (Ed.), *Cyberspace: First Steps*. Cambridge, MA: The MIT Press.

_____. (1993). *The Metaphysics of Virtual Reality*. New York: Oxford University Press.

Merleau-Ponty, Maurice. (1962). *Phenomenology of Perception*. London: Routledge & Kegan Paul.

Romanyshyn, Robert, D. (1989). *Technology as Symptom and Dream*. London and New York: Routledge.

_____. (1993). "The Despotic Eye and Its Shadow: Media Image in the Age of Literacy." In D.M. Levin (Ed.), *Modernity and the Hegemony of Vision.* Berkeley & Los Angeles: University of California Press.

Sobchack, Vivian. (April, 1991). "New Age Mutant Ninja Hackers." *Art-forum International, 29(8),* 24-26.

Walker, John. (1990). "Through the Looking Glass." In B. Laurel (Ed.), *The Art of Human-Computer Interface Design.* Cupertino, CA: Apple Computer.

Chapter Three

Suggestions for further reading:

Brueggemann, Walter. (1978). *The Prophetic Imagination.* Philadelphia: Fortress Press.

Edinger, Edward. (1972). *Ego and Archetype.* New York: Putnam.

Rilke, Rainer Maria. (1939). *Duino Elegies.* J.B. LLleishman & Stephen Spender (Trans.). New York: W.W. Norton & Co.

Romanyshyn, Robert D. (1989). *Technology as Symptom and Dream.* London and New York: Routledge.

Chapter Four

1.Candace DuPuy, *Exploring Dream Image Through Acting Technique,* unpublished doctoral dissertation, Pacifica Graduate Institute, 1994. I should also acknowledge here how convergent my views regarding dream enactment are with the work of Eugene Gendlin. See, for example, his splendid books, *Focusing,* (New York: Bantam Books, 1981), and *Let Your Body Interpret Your Dreams* (Willmette, Illinois:Chiron Publications, 1986). Indeed, though I developed this approach before having read Gendlin's works, I am indebted to them and to him for having so carefully and systematically presented his material. Moreover, I am not surprised at the convergence, because he himself has noted two phenomenologists do not disagree. They do not because phenomenology is the practice of fidelity to experience.

2. For a detailed account of the mirror see my first book, *Psychological Life: From Science to Metaphor* (Boston:University of Texas Press, 1982). Since the publication of this essay, this book has been re-published under the title *Mirror and Metaphor: Images and Stories of Psychological Life.* (Pittsburgh: Trivium Publications, 2001). See also the work of Maurice Merleau-Ponty, especially *The Visible and the Invisible*

(Evanston:Northwestern University Press, 1968) and "Eye and Mind" in *The Primacy of Perception* (Evanston, Northwestern University Press, 1964).

3. This last point is, I think, important in regard to physical ailments. My oldest son, who is now thirty, has been living with Parkinson's disease for approximately 6 years. He has told me that on multiple occasions his dream body never suffers the illness, and I also and quite recently have on occasion dreamed of him as hale, hearty, and whole. I wonder, then, about the potential therapeutic impact of enacting the dream in this situation. What are the limits of this paradoxical relation of identity and difference between the dream body and the body of the dreamer? How far can this gift of being given one's body by the other with whom I am in a field extend? The actor, after all, leaves the stage; Michael steps out of character and his nausea returns. Moreover, we are, after all, also a "mechanism," that syncretic structure of behavior about which Merleau-Ponty writes in *The Structure of Behavior*, (Boston: Beacon Press, 1963), and western medicine and physiology are not incorrect but only one-sided in their recognition of this level. If, as Merleau-Ponty notes, the human body, the gestural body, is a symbolic level which preserves *and* transforms the "lower" levels, then there are real limits in our possibilities but also real possibilities within these limits.

4. This manuscript is completed but as yet unpublished. It runs counter to our culture's obsession with meaning and addiction to information by refusing to prescribe either the steps or the formulae by which one overcomes one's grief. It is not a how-to book. On the contrary, as a poetics of the grieving process it offers reveries of mourning which invite the reader into the experience. We are so far from experience because we are dis-embodied that such invitations are understandably, but sadly, too often ignored or refused. Indeed, our addiction to overcoming experience is so engrained that we often seek the proverbial twelve steps before we even have had the experience to which the information is to be applied. So much of psychotherapy, I believe, still falls into this place with its emphasis on knowledge systems and theories and practices that have a positivistic and literal cast. All too often do are theories and techniques not only get in the way of experience, they also prevent those disclosures of grace, of love, and of the sacred between patient and therapist, between me and you, which is the only source of healing. It is not because the therapist knows the patient that healing takes place. Rather, healing occurs because the therapist can witness a shared experience and thereby give it a vital place in the other's life. Such witnessing requires of the therapist more than a knowledge of techniques. It

requires character. Being a therapist is much more about who you are, than it
is about what you know. Being a therapist is about having and being a
character. Since the publication of this essay, this book on grief has been
published under the title *The Soul in Grief: Love, Death, and Transformation*
(Berkeley: North Atlantic Press, 1999).

    5. See "For the Moment, That's Enough: Meditations on Therapy
and the Poetry of Language," in *Phenomenology and Narrative Psychology,*
(Pittsburgh: The Simon Silverman Phenomenology Center, Duquesne
University, 1997). See also chapter 6.

Chapter Five

    1. The title of this paper is an affirmation of the vision of the poet
John Keats. In a lettter to the George Keatses dated April 21, 1819, he says
"Call the world if you please 'The Vale of Soul-Making,'" and then adds that
" Then you will find out the use of the world " (1988, p. 549). This paper
affirms that vision because it argues that the task of an archetypal activism is
to open the aesthetic depths of the world, not by becoming politically active
but by being a witness, as is the poet, for what is otherwise marginalized by
the collective follies of the age. These aesthetic depths are the occasions
where the timely and the timeless meet. Evoking these depths, we find the
true use of the world, which is to be distinguished, I believe, from the mind's
preoccupation with how the world—and ourselves—is, or might be, useful.
The true use of the world is its purpose, and our task as depth psychologists
is to be attentive to how the world addresses us, attentive to what it wants of
us. I find this same appeal in a poet like Rilke, a theme which is developed in
the body of this paper. I find it too in artists like Cezanne and Van Gogh.
They open these aesthetic depths of the world, the ways in which the world
wants to see itself, become itself, continue its creation. In this regard, would
we dare ask if Van Gogh's "Starry Night," for example, is useful? It would be
an absurd question which would not only miss the point of the task of the
artists, but would also imprison this work within categories which destroy its
soul. Depth psychology is particularly prone to this temptation when it seeks
to become useful.

    The original paper was accompanied by a video presentation with
music and voice over narration. To arrange for a showing of this production
piece the author can be contacted at Romany@Pacifica.edu

2. The quote is the last line of Milton's sonnet "On His Blindness." (1998, p.84, l. 14). Although I had initially misremembered the source, my inquiries about it have proven quite fruitful. The quote, which arose from some unconscious layers of the psyche, is a fitting one for this article for three reasons. First, blindness is a kind of abyss, and the major theme of this paper is what is asked of us at the abyss. Second, Milton's response is entirely in keeping with the reply to this question offered in this article. At the abyss, we are asked to be a witness, and it is this posture which defines for me the character of an archetypal activism. Archetypal activism is not about doing. It is about a way of being, a style of presence, the presence of the witness. The witness is one who also serves by standing and waiting. For additional comments on the witness see "On Angels and other Anomalies of the Imaginal Life"(chapter 8). Third, after his blindness, Milton dictated to his (reluctant?) daughters "Paradise Lost." It seems most fitting to me that it is this epic work which arose from the depths of his blindness. Another theme of this paper is that loss is the spur of the soul's awakening, the moment when, beyond the concerns of ego, one is called to be a witness for what has been lost, marginalized, or otherwise neglected individually and collectively. For a more detailed treatment of this issue, the reader is referred to *The Soul in Grief: Love, Death and Transformation* (Romanyshyn, 1999). I want to thank Prof. Glenn Arbery of The Dallas Institute for Humanities and Culture for his help with this citation, and for the historical background which he provided concerning this sonnet.

3. This notion of a pathetic God, a god of compassion who out of deep loneliness empties himself into creation, is movingly described in *Alone with the Alone: Creative Imagination in the Sufism of Ibn' Arabi* (Corbin,1969). I cite this work because it is a pathetic God whom we meet at the abyss, and not the almighty God of power. Indeed, this latter God is, I believe, the one who authors the abyss, who is responsible for our abysmal moments. It is this God image, working itself out in the psyche, which is responsible for the "slaughter of the innocents" portrayed in the video portion of this paper. At the abyss we are called to be compassionate. "To become a Compassionate One is to become the likeness of the Compassionate God experiencing infinite sadness over undisclosed virtualities. . ."(p.118). One of these undisclosed virtualities is our participation in the divine, a remembrance of our spiritual heritage. In the face of suffering we find the compassion which can move us to tears, and in the tears of ourselves and the other we find a mutual mirroring of the

Compassionate One who dwells between, around, and amongst us. But why must such moments depend so often on being at the abyss.

Chapter Six

1. A.Carotenuto, *Kant's Dove: The History of Transference in Psychoanalysis* (Wilmette, Ill.: Chiron, 1991) 110.

2. C.G. Jung, "Psychotherapy and the Philosophy of Life," *The Practice of Psychotherapy,* Collected Works, vol.16 (Princeton: Princeton UP,1966) 80.

3. Gaston Bachelard, *The Poetics of Reverie.* (New York: Orion,1969) 104.

4. Rene Descartes, *Meditations on First Philosophy*, trans.L. J. La Fleur (New York: Library of Liberal Arts, 1960) 15.

5. Robert Romanyshyn, "Complex Knowing: Toward a Psychological Hermeneutics," *The Humanistic Psychologist* 19.1 (1991): 23, n.3.

6. Romanyshyn, 23, n.3.

7. Marie-Louise von Franz, *Alchemy* (Toronto: Inner City Books, 1980) 22.

8. Charles Segal, *Orpheus: The Myth of the Poet* (Baltimore: Johns Hopkins UP, 1989) 17.

9. Greg Mogenson, *Greeting the Angels: An Imaginal View of the Mourning Process* (Amityville: Baywood, 1992) 11.

10. T.S. Eliot, *Four Quartets* (New York: Harcourt Brace,1943/ 1971) 30-31.

11. Rainer Maria Rilke. *Duino Elegies*, trans. J.B. Leishman and Stephen Spender (New York: W.W. Norton and Company, 1939) 21.

12. Rilke, 73-75.

13. John Keats, *John Keats: Selected Poetry*, ed. Paul de Man (New York: New American Library,1966) 249-251.

14. Segal, 130-131.

15. William Shakespeare, *The Tempest, Shakespeare: The Complete Works*, ed. G. B. Harrison (New York: Harcourt Brace,1952) 1501.

16. von Franz, 137.

17. Shakespeare, 1501.

18. Eliot, 19.

Chapter Seven

1. W. Morris, ed. , *The American Heritage Dictionary of the English Language* (Boston: Houghton Mifflin, 1981) 89.

2. C. G. Jung, *Memories, Dreams, Reflections* (New York: Vintage, 1965) 183.

3. C. G. Jung, *The Structure and Dynamics of the Psyche, Collected Works,* vol. 8, par. 390 (Princeton: Princeton UP, 1960) 193.

4. A. Kreinheder, "Alchemy and the Subtle Body," *Psychological Perspectives* 6.2 (1975) 135-136.

5. My first two books are explorations of these relationships among psychology, science, technology, politics, and economics, especially in terms of the origins of these relations. See *Psychological Life: From Science to Metaphor* (1982), and *Technology as Symptom and Dream* (1989).

6. Andrew Samuels, *The Political Psyche* (New York: Routledge, 1993) 3.

7. Robert Romanyshyn, "The Despotic Eye and Its Shadow: Media Image in The Age of Literacy," *Modernity and the Hegemony of Vision*, ed. David Michael Levin (Berkeley: U of California P, 1993) 339.

8. Robert Romanyshyn, "For the Moment, That's Enough: Meditations on Therapy and the Poetry of Language," in *Phenomenology and Narrative Psychology*, Pittsburgh: Duquesne UP, 1997a) 69.

9. Romanyshyn, "For the Moment" 70.

10. Robert Romanyshyn, *Technology as Symptom and Dream* (New York: Routledge, 1989).

11. Roger Brooke, "Jung's Recollection of the Life World," *Harvest* 41.1 (1995) 33-34.

12. C. G. Jung, *The Archetypes of the Collective Unconscious, Collected Works*, vol. 9, pt.1, par.121 (Princeton: Princeton UP, 1959) 60.

13. The true depth of depth psychology is the world, a lateral depth which surrounds us and whose mysteries can be plumbed in a state of reverie, which is neither an empirical, fact minded, information seeking consciousness, nor a rational, detached consciousness addicted to a dogma of fixed meanings or principles. Thus to recover the imaginal is to recover the world as the depth of soul. In this regard, projection not only eclipses the imaginal, it also de-animates the world, an ironic twist on the way this doctrine is usually understood. More precisely, projection withdraws soul from world, mis-places it in us as an interior experience, and then dis-places it back onto the

world. But then, the full anima-tion of the world is reduced to the terms of the individual human psyche, or, even with Jung, the collective human psyche. The psyche of the world is lost. Psyche in its cosmological reaches is lost. For a more detailed discussion of this notion of lateral depth see, "Unconsciousness as a Lateral Depth," (Romanyshyn: 1983).

14. Maria-Louise von Franz, *Alchemy* (Toronto: Inner City Books, 1980) 94.

15. Mary Watkins, *Invisible Guests* (New Jersey: Analytic P, 1986).

16. Gaston Bachelard, *The Poetics of Reverie* (New York: Orion P, 1969) 12.

17. Robert Romanyshyn, "Complex Knowing: Toward a Psychological Hermeneutics," *Humanist Psychologist* 19.1 (1991) 23.

18. For a more detailed discussion of this notion of the ghost who haunts our symptoms see "For the Moment, That's Enough: Meditations on Therapy and the Poetry of Language" (Romanyshyn: 1997a), That article offers a defense of psychotherapy as grief work. Its original version has been amplified and has been reprinted in *Chiron* , edited by Murry Stein, in an honorary volume to Maria-Louise von Franz.

19. Nathan Schwartz-Salant, *The Borderline Personality: Vision and Healing* (Wilmette, Illinois: Chiron, 1989) 133.

20. Romanyshyn, *Psychological Life:From Science to Metaphor* (Austin: U of Texas P,1982) 150-151.

21. David Fideler, "The Alchemy of Attachment: An Epistemology of Transformation," paper presented at the Symposium of the Palladian Academy, Vicenza, Italy, 1997, 8.

22. Bachelard, 23.

23. Emily Dickinson, *Final Harvest, Emily Dickinson's Poems*, ed. T.H. Johnson (Boston: Little, 1961) 248.

24. Von Frantz, *Alchemy*, 37.

25. In this regard, alchemy is an authentic depth psychology and Jung's move into it a stroke of genius. Jung, however, vitiates the radical character of alchemy by placing it within a Cartesian frame, within a psychology of projection. Alchemy is not a *forerunner* of Jung's psychology; it is a *corrective* of it·

26. C. G. Jung, *Psychology and Alchemy, Collected Works*, vol.12, par. 394 (Princeton: Princeton UP, 1953) 278.

27. Jung, *Psychology and Alchemy*, 278.

28. Von Franz, *Alchemy*, 123.

29. Von Franz, *Alchemy*, 136-137.

30. If projection is older than the Cartesian dream of reason; if it is a possibility of consciousness itself as von Franz suggests, still the Cartesian dream of reason which separates psyche and matter has a singular significance. As an epistemological foundation for our modern, scientific-technological culture, it made a psychology of projection into a method. Or said in another way, with Descartes there is a reversal between being and knowing, where knowing and its claims now assert themselves not in response to the call of being, but over and against these calls. Much of Martin Heidegger's work is to be situated here.

31. Von Franz, *Alchemy*, 156-157.

32. The work of J. H. van den Berg has been a continuing source of inspiration for my own work, and I can not let pass this opportunity to acknowledge again my indebtedness to him.   For some specific references see 1972, 1974, 1975.

33. *The Orphan and the Angel: Grief and the Reveries of Love* is an unpublished manuscript. Earlier versions of several of its chapters, however, appear in various journals. (Romanyshyn : 1997b, 1996,1995).

34. Jung, *Psychology and Alchemy*, 279.

35. Jung, *Psychology and Alchemy*, 245.

36 Von Franz, *Psyche and Matter* (Boston: Shambhala, 1992) 162.

37. Von Franz, *Psyche*, 183.

38. My good friend and colleague, Lionel Corbett, deals with this important question in his remarkable book *The Religious Function of the Psyche* (1996). I find our conversations fruitful in exploring this difficult question of how one safeguards ontological differences from the claims of our epistemological assertions. In Corbett's book, this issue is focused on the question of the numinous, and his work is especially helpful in sighting those relevant passages in Jung where the numinous seems to possess its own radical alterity. And yet, I always feel that Jung (and Corbett?) does not go quite far enough in drawing this distinction between epistemology and ontology, and, I believe, Philemon, as an eruption of the numinous, insists upon it.

39. Robert Romanyshyn, "The Orphan and the Angel," *Psychological Perspectives*, 32 (1995). See also chapter three of this book.

40. Ranier Maria Rilke, *Duino Elegies*, trans. J.B. Leishman and Stephen Spender (New York: Norton, 1939) 75-77.

41. For a detailed account of the structure of metaphor as an allusion to the elusive, of metaphor as a field of play see *Psychological Life:*

From Science to Metaphor (Romanyshyn: 1982), especially chapter five.

42. In the essay "For the Moment, That's Enough: Meditations on Therapy and the Poetry of Language" (1997a), I consider in detail how the language of therapy is a claiming by letting go. Philemon, like the ghosts who haunt our symptoms, requires this kind of speaking. The imaginal requires the poetic.

43. M. Fox and R. Sheldrake, *The Physics of Angels* (San Francisco: Harper,1996) 105.

44. I want to acknowledge here the contributions of my wife, Veronica Goodchild to this essay, especially the postscript. Before the experience recounted there happened, it was she who questioned the description of Philemon as an imaginal being. Those conversations sent me back to my earlier work on Angels.

Chapter Nine

1. John Keats, *The Complete Poems*, ed. John Barnard (New York: Penguin, 1973) 539.

2. See chapter 8.

3. Sigmund Freud, *The Moses of Michelangelo*, trans. James Strachey (London: Hogarth P, 1914/1955).

4. James Hillman, *Healing Fiction* (Barrytown, New York: Station Hill Press, 1983).

5. Gaston Bachelard, *The Poetics of Reverie*, trans. Daniel Russell (Boston: Beacon Press, 1971) 173.

6. Bachelard, 112.

7. Bachelard, 8.

8. See chapter 8.

9. Bachelard, 187-188.

10. William Shakespeare, *The Tempest, The New Folger Library Shakespeare* (New York: Washington Square Press, 1974).

11. Antonio Machado, *I Never Wanted Fame*, trans, Robert Bly (St Paul, Minnesota: Ally P, 1979) I.

12. Robert Romanyshyn, *Technology as Symptom and Dream* (New York: Routledge, 1989).

13. CG Jung, *Memories, Dreams, Reflections*, ed. Aniela Jaffe (New York: Vintage, 1965).

14. Jung, *Memories*, 185-187.

15. See chapter seven.

16. C. G. Jung, *Letters 1951-1961,* ed. Gerhard Adler, (Princeton: Princeton UP, 1975) 189.

17. E. E. Cummings, *100 Selected Poems* (New York: Grove Press, 1978) 35.

18. Sigmund Freud, *Three Essays on the Theory of Sexuality, The Standard Edition of the Complete Psychological Works of Sigmund Freud,* trans. James Strachey (London: Hogarth P, 1905/1953) 150.

19. Keats, 346-348.

20. See chapter five.

21. See chapter six.

22. Rainer Maria Rilke, *Duino Elegies.* Trans. J.B. Leishman and Stephen Spender (New York: Norton, 1939) 77.

23. Rainer Maria Rilke, *Sonnets to Orpheus,* trans. M.D. Herter Norton (New York: Norton, 1962) 25.

24. Rilke, *Sonnets,* 37.

25. Henri Corbin, Alone With the Alone: Creative Imagination in the Sufism of Ibn' Arabi (Princeton: Princeton UP,1969) xvi.

26. Corbin, *Alone,* 4.

27. Corbin, *Alone,* 4, his italics.

28. C. G. Jung, *Alchemical Studies,* trans. R.F.C. Hull, *The Collected Works of C.G. Jung* vol.13 (Princeton: Princeton UP, 1967); *Psychology and Alchemy,* trans. R.F.C. Hull, *The Collected Works of C.G. Jung* vol. 12 (Princeton: Princeton UP, 1968).

29. Jung, *Psychology and Alchemy,* 278).

30. Robert Romanyshyn, *Psychological Life: From Science to Metaphor* (Austin: U of Texas P, 1982); Henri Corbin, *The Voyage and the Messenger* (Berkeley: North Atlantic Books, 1998). In his book *The Voyage and the Messenger,* Henry Corbin ties the experience of subtle bodies to a visionary knowledge whose essence belongs to a science of mirrors, a "mystical catoptrics"(134). In *Psychological Life: From Science to Metaphor,* I explored the nature of Soul via a phenomenology of the mirror experience. At that time I had no knowledge of the Sufi mystic tradition. I offer this acknowledgement as an example of a key point in this essay. As an autonomous reality, Soul is deeper than mind, wiser than it, with its own logic of the heart. We are led into our work. It chooses us!

I also wish to add that this notion of being chosen by one's work is the foundation for my approach to research at Pacifica Graduate Institute.

Research as re-search is a vocation, a return to what has already claimed you. And the task of doing research with soul is a working out of the transference between researcher and topic. From that innocent and naive exploration of the mirror experience in 1982 to this essay, I have been drawn into landscapes of experience where my companions have been alchemists and mystics, poets and quantum physicists, hysterics and dreamers, angels and aliens.

31. Romanyshyn, *Technology.*

32. Blaise Pascal, *Pensees and Other Writings,* trans. Honor Levi (New York: Oxford UP, 1995) 158.

33. Harold Bloom, introduction, *Alone with the alone: creative imagination in the Sufism of Ibn' Arabi,* by Henri Corbin (Princeton: Princeton UP, 1969) xix.

34. Keats, 549.

35. See chapter five.

Chapter Eleven

1. See chapter ten.

2. See chapter nine.

3. Robert Romanyshyn, *The Soul in Grief: Love, Death and Transformation* (Berkeley: North Atlantic Books, 1999) 151-55.

4. Blaise Pascal, *Pensees and Other Writings,* trans. H. Levi (New York: Oxford UP, 1995) 158.

5. Henri Corbin, *Alone With the Alone: Creative Imagination in the Sufism of Ibn' Arabi* (Princeton: Princeton UP, 1969).

6. C.G. Jung, *Memories, Dreams, Reflections* (New York: Vintage, 1989) page 237.

7. Rainer Maria Rilke, "Turning Point," *The Selected Poetry of Rainer Maria Rilke,* ed. and trans. Stephen Mitchell (New York: Vintage, 1989) 135.

8. Gaston Bachelard, *Poetics of Reverie,* trans. D. Russell (Boston: Beacon P, 1969) 181.

9. Rainer Maria Rilke, *Duino Elegies,* trans. J. B. Leishman and S. Spender (New York: Norton, 1939) 77.

10. Rilke, *Duino,* 75.

11. Rilke, *Duino,* 71.

12. Rilke, *Duino,* 129.

13. Rilke, *Duino,* 69.

14. Rilke, *Duino,* 6.

15. Rilke, *Duino,* 67.

16. Rilke, *Duino,* 122-23.

17. Rainer Maria Rilke, "Requiem for a Friend," *The Selected Poetry of Rainer Maria Rilke,* ed. and trans. Stephen Mitchell (New York: Vintage, 1989) 73.

18. Rilke, "Requiem," 75.

19. Rilke, "Requiem," 73.

20. Rilke, "Requiem," 77.

21. Rilke, "Requiem," 81.

22. Rilke, "Requiem," 83.

23. Rilke, "Requiem," 75.

24.Rainer Maria Rilke, *Sonnets to Orpheus,* trans. M. D. Herter (New York: Norton, 1970) 127.

25. Rilke, Sonnets, 25.

26. Rainer Maria Rilke, "Orpheus. Eurydice. Hermes." *The Selected Poetry of Rainer Maria Rilke,* ed. and trans. Stephen Mitchell (New York: Vintage, 1989).

27. Rilke, "Requiem," 85.

28. Rilke, "Orpheus. Eurydice. Hermes." 53.

29. Rilke, "Orpheus. Eurydice. Hermes." 53.

30. Rilke, *Sonnets,* 67.

31. Rilke, *Sonnets,* 67.

32. J. F. Hendry, *The Sacred Threshold* (Manchester, England: Carcanet P, 1983) 122.

Chapter Twelve

1. Blaise Pascal, *Pensees and Other Writings,* trans. H. Levi (New York: Oxford UP, 1995) 158.

2. Robert Romanyshyn, *Psychological Life: From Science to Metaphor* (Austin: U of Texas P, 1982). This book has been re-published under a new title: *Mirror and Metaphor: Images and Stories of Psychological Life* (Pittsburgh: Trivium, 2001).

3. Veronica Goodchild, *Eros and Chaos.* (York Beach, Maine: Nicolas-Hays, 2001).

4. For a discussion of this issue see the essay in this volume, "On Angels and Other Anomalies of the Imaginal Life." See also Robert

Romanyshyn, *Technology as Symptom and Dream.* (London: Routledge, 1989).

    5. Robert Romanyshyn, *The Soul in Grief: Love, Death and Transformation.* (Berkeley: North Atlantic, 1999).

    6. A. Schimmel, *Deciphering the Signs of God: A Phenomenological Approach to Islam.* (New York; SUNY P, 1994) xvii.

    7. For a discussion of this point and related issues see Henri Corbin, *Alone with the Alone: Creative Imagination in the Sufism of Ibn' Arabi.* (Princeton: Princeton UP, 1969). See also Henri Corbin, *The Voyage and the Messenger.* (Berkely: North Atlantic, 1998).

    8. Romanyshyn, *Soul in Grief.*

    9. Robert Sardello, *Facing the World with Soul.* (New York: Harper-Collins, 1994).

    10. Romanyshyn, *Soul in Grief,* 97-98.

    11. Corbin, *Alone with the Alone,*107.

    12. Rumi, *Say I Am You,* trans. John Moyne and Coleman Barks, (Athens, GA: Maypop P, 1994) 40.

    13. See chapter nine.

    14. Jose Ortega Y Gasset as quoted in Romanyshyn, *Psychological Life,* 58.

    15. For a discussion of this point, see Romanyshyn, *Soul in Grief.*

    16. William Wordsworth, "Ode: Intimations of Immortality From Recollections of Early Childhood," *William Wordsworth Selected Poems,* ed. John O. Hayden (New York: Penguin, 1994).

    17. Corbin, *Alone with the Alone,*106.

    18. Corbin, *Alone with the Alone,* 287-288.

    19. Romanyshyn, *Soul in Grief,* 96-97.

    20. Corbin, *Alone with the Alone,* 107.

    21. Corbin, *Alone with the Alone,* 105.

    22. Gaston Bachelard, *The Poetics of Reverie,* trans. Daniel Russell (New York, Orion P, 1969) 164.

    23. Maurice Merleau-Ponty, *The Visible and the Invisible,* trans. Alphonso Lingis, (Evanston: Northwestern UP, 1968).

    24. Robert Romanyshyn, "Looking at the Light: Reflections of the Mutable Body," *Dragonflies: Studies in Imaginal Psychology,* 2.1, (1980) 3-7.

    25. William Blake, *The Poetry and Prose of William Blake,* ed. David V. Erdman (Berkeley: University of California Press, 1981) 693.

26. Corbin, *Alone with the Alone*, 105.

27. Corbin, *Voyage*, 134.

28. Walker Percy, *Lost in the Cosmos* (New York: Washington Square Press, 1983) 47.

29. Corbin, *Voyage*, 235.

30. Rainer Maria Rilke, *Duino Elegies*, trans. J.B. Leishman and S. Spender (New York: Norton, 1939) 77.

31. Corbin, *Alone with the Alone*, 112-120.

32. Ruskin's idea of the pathetic fallacy was presented in *Modern Painters*, a five volume work originally published between 1846-1860. His discussion of the pathetic fallacy appears in volume three of that work.

33. For a discussion of these points see Romanyshyn, *Technology as Symptom and Dream*, especially chapter three.

34. John Keats, *John Keats: The Complete Poems*, ed. John Barnard (New York: Penguin, 1988) 549.

35. See chapter four. See also Greg Mogensen, *Greeting the Angels*. (Amityville, New York: Baywood, 1992).

36. For a discussion of this point see Erik A. Havelock, *Preface to Plato*. (Cambridge: Harvard UP, 1963).

37. See chapter eleven.

38. C. G. Jung, "Flying Saucers: A Modern Myth of Things Seen in the Skies," *Civilization in Transition*, trans. R.F.C. Hull, *The Collected Works of C.G. Jung*, vol.10 (Princeton: Princeton UP, 1970).

39. William Blake, "A Song of Liberty"

References

Abram, D. *The Spell of the Sensuous*. New York: Pantheon, 1996.

Bachelard, G. *The Poetics of Reverie*. Trans. Daniel Russell. New York, Orion P, 1969.

Blake, W. *The Poetry and Prose of William Blake*. Ed. D. V. Erdman. Berkeley: University of California Press, 1981.

Bordo, S. *The Flight to Objectivity*. Albany: SUNY Press, 1987.

Brooke, R. "Jung's Recollection of the Life World." *Harvest* 41.1 (1995): 26-37.

Brueggemann, W. *The Prophetic Imagination*. Philadelphia: Fortress Press, 1978.

Bukatman, S. *Terminal Identity*. Durham and London: Duke University Press, 1993.

Carotenuto, A. *Kant's Dove: The History of Transference in Psychoanalysis*. Wilmette, IL.: Chiron, 1991.

Corbett, L. *The Religious Function of the Psyche*. New York: Routledge, 1996.

Corbin, H. *Alone with the Alone: Creative Imagination in the Sufism of Ibn' Arabi*. Princeton: Princeton UP, Bollingen Series XCI, 1997.

—. *The Voyage and the Messenger*. Berkeley: North Atlantic, 1998.

Cummings, E.E. *100 Selected Poems*. New York: Grove P, 1926.

Descartes, R. *Meditations on First Philosophy*. Trans. L.J. La Fleur. New York: Library of Liberal Arts, 1960.

Dickinson, E. *Final Harvest, Emily Dickinson's Poems*. Ed. T.H. Johnson. Boston: Little, 1961.

Eliot, T.S. *Four Quartets*. New York: Harcourt Brace, 1943/1971.

Edgerton, S.Y. *The Renaissance Rediscovery of Linear Perspective*. New York: Harper and Row, 1976.

Edinger, E. *Ego and Archetype*. New York: Putnam, 1972.

Fideler, D. "The Alchemy of Attachment:An Epistemology of Transformation." Paper presented at the Symposium of the Palladian Academy, Vicenza, Italy, 1997.

Fox, M. and R. Sheldrake. *The Physics of Angels*. San Francisco:Harper, 1996.

Freud, S. *Three essays on the Theory of Sexuality. The Standard Edition of the Complete Psychological Works of Sigmund Freud*. Trans. James Strachey. London: Hogarth P, 1953.

—. *The Moses of Michelangelo*. (James Strachey, Trans.). London: The Hogarth P, 1955.

Goodchild, V. *Eros and Chaos: The Sacred Mysteries and Dark Shadows of Love*. York Beach, MA: Nicolas-Hays, 2001.

Gibson, W. *Neuromancer*. New York: Ace Books, 1984.

Haveloch, E. *Preface to Plato*. Cambridge: Harvard University Press, 1963.

Heidegger, M. *Poetry, Language, Thought*. Trans. Albert Hofstadter. New York: Harper, 1971.

Heim, M. "The Erotic Outology of Cyberspace." *Cyberspace: First Steps*. Ed. M. Benedikt. Cambridge: The M.I.T. Press, 1992.

—, M. *The Metaphysics of Virtual Reality*. New York: Oxford University Press, 1993.

Hillman, J. *Healing Fiction*. Barrytown, New York: Station Hill P, 1983.

Jung, C.G. (1967). *Alchemical Studies*. Trans. R.F.C. Hull. *The Collected Works of C.G. Jung* vol.13. Princeton: Princeton UP, 1967.

—. *Letters 1951-1961*. Ed. Gerhard Adler. Princeton; Princeton UP, 1975.

—. *Flying Saucers: A Modern Myth of Things Seen in the Skies. Collected Works*, vol. 10. Princeton: Princeton UP, 1970.

—. *Psychtherapy and the Philosophy of Life. Collected Works*, vol. 16. Princeton: Princeton UP, 1966.

—. *Memories, Dreams, Reflections*. New York: Vintage, 1965.

—. *The Structure and Dynamics of the Psyche. Collected Works* vol.8. par. 390. Princeton: Princeton UP, 1960.

—. *The Archetypes of the Collective Unconscious. Collected Works* vol. 9, pt.I, par.121. Princeton: Princeton UP, 1959.

—. *Psychology and Alchemy. Collected Works* vol.12, par. 394. Princeton: Princeton UP, 1953.

Kearney, R. *The Wake of Imagination*. Minneapolis: University of Minnesota Press, 1988.

Keats, J. *John Keats: The Complete Poems*. Ed. John Barnard. New York: Penguin, 1988.

—. *John Keats: Selected Poetry*. Ed. Paul de Man. New York: New American Library, 1966.

Kreinheder, A. "Alchemy and the Subtle Body." *Psychological Perspectives* 6.2 (1975).

Lowe, D.M. *History of Bourgeois Perception*. Chicago: University of Chicago Press, 1982.

Machado, A. *I Never Wanted Fame*. Trans. Robert Bly. St Paul, Minnesota: Ally P, 1979.

McLuhan, M. *The Guttenberg Galaxy*. New York: New American Library, 1969.

Merleau-Ponty, M. *The Visible and the Invisible*. Trans. Alphonso Lingis, Evanston: Northwestern UP, 1968.

—. "The Philosopher and His Shadow." *Signs*. Trans. Richard C. McCleary, Evanston: Northwestern UP, 1964.

—. "Eye and Mind." *The Primacy of Perception*. Ed. James M. Edie. Evanston: Northwestern UP, 1964.

—. *The Structure of Behavior*. Boston: Beacon Press, 1963.

—. *Phenomenology of Perception*. Trans. Colin Smith. London: Routledge and Kegan Paul, 1962.

Milton, J. "Sonnet XVI." *John Milton: The Complete Poems*. Ed. John Leonard. New York: Penguin, 1998.

Mogenson, G. *Greeting the Angels: An Imaginal View of the Mourning Process*. Amityville, NY: Baywood, 1992.

Morris, W , ed. *The American Heritage Dictionary of the English Language*. Boston: Houghton, 1981.

Pascal, B. *Pensees and Other Writings*. Trans.Honor Levi. New York: Oxford UP, 1995.

Percy, W. *Lost in the Cosmos: The Last Self-Help Book in America*. New York: Washington Square Press, 1983.

Postman, N. *Amusing Ourselves to Death*. New York: Penguin, 1986.

Plato. *The Republic. Plato: The Collected Dialogues*. Ed. Edith Hamilton and Huntington Cairns. Princeton: Princeton UP, Bollingen Series LXXI, 1989.

Raine, K. "The Use of the Beautiful." *Defending Ancient Springs*. West Stockbridge, MA: Lindisfarne P, 1985.

Rilke, R.M. *The Selected Poetry of Rainer Maria Rilke*. Ed. and Trans.

Stephen Mitchell. New York: Vantage, 1989.

—. *Sonnets to Orpheus.* Trans. M.D. Herter Norton. New York: Norton, 1942.

—. *Duino Elegies.* Trans. J. B. Leishman and Stephen Spender. New York: Norton, 1939.

Romanyshyn, R. D. "Alchemy and the Subtle Body of Metaphor." *Pathways into the Jungian World.* Ed. Roger Brooke. New York: Routledge, 2000.

—. "Yes, Indeed! Do Call the World the Vale of Soul Making: Reveries Toward an Archetypal Presence. *Depth Psychology: Meditations in the Field.* Ed. Dennis Slattery and Lionel Corbet. Einsiedelan, Switzerland: Daimon Verlag, 2000.

—. "On Angels and other Anomalies of the Imaginal Life." *The Temenos Academy Review.* Ed. Kathleen Raine. Ipswich: Golgonooza P, 2000.

—. *The Soul in Grief: Love, Death and Transformation.* Berkeley: North Atlantic, 1999.

—. "For the Moment, That's Enough: Meditations on Therapy and the Poetry of Language," *Phenomenology and Narrative Psychology.* Pittsburgh: Duquesne UP, 1997.

—. "Egos, Angels and the Colors of Nature." *Alexandria-4: The Order and Beauty of Nature.* Ed. David Fideler. Michigan: Phanes P, 1997.

—. "Starry Nights, Sexual Love and the Rhythms of the Soul." *Sphinx-7: A Journal for Archetypal Psychology and the Arts.* Ed. N. Cobb. London: The London Convivium, 1996.

—. "The Orphan and the Angel." *Psychological Perspectives,* Vol.32 (1995).

—. "The Despotic Eye and Its Shadow: Media Image in the Age of Literacy." *Modernity and the Hegemony of Vision.* Ed. David Michael Levin. Berkeley: U of California P, 1993.

—. "Complex Knowing: Toward a Psychological Hermeneutics." Ed. C. Aanstous *The Humanistic Psychologist.* 19,1 (1991).

—. *Technology as Symptom and Dream.* New York: Routledge, 1989.

—. "Unconscious as a Lateral Depth: Perception and the Two Moments of Reflection." *Continental Philosophy in America.* Ed. Hugh J. Silverman, John Sallis, Thomas M. Seebohm. Pittsburgh: Duquesne UP, 1983.

—. *Psychological Life: From Science to Metaphor,* Austin: U of Texas P, 1982.

—. "Looking at the Light: Reflections of the Mutable Body." *Dragonflies: Studies in Imaginal Psychology,* 2, 1, 1980.

Rumi. *Say I Am You.* Trans. John Moyne and Coleman Barks. Athens, Ga.:

Maypop, 1994.

Samuels, A. *The Political Psyche.* New York: Routledge, 1993.

Sardello, R. *Facing the World with Soul.* New York: Harper-Collins, 1994.

Schimmel, A. *Deciphering the Signs of God: A Phenomenological Approch to Islam.* New York: SUNY Press, 1994.

Schwartz-Salant, N. *The Borderline Personality: Vision and Healing.* Wilmette, Illinois: Chiron, 1989.

—. "The Dead Self in Borderline Personality Disorders." *Pathologies of the Modern Self.* Ed. D. M. Levin. New York: New York UP, 1987.

Segal, C. *Orpheus: The Myth of the Poet.* Baltimore: John Holpkins UP, 1989.

Shakespeare, W. *The Tempest. The New Folger Library Shakespeare.* New York: Washington Square P, 1974.

Sobchack, V. "New Age Mutant Ninja Hackers." *Artforum International,* 29 (8), 1991.

Strand, Mark. "The Night, The Porch." *Blizzard of One .* New York: Alfred A. Knopf, 2000.

Van den Berg, J.H. *The Changing Nature of Man: Introduction to a Historical Psychology.* New York: Dell, 1975.

—. *Divided Existence and Complex Society: An Historical Approach,* Pittsburgh: Duquesne UP, 1974.

—. *A Different Existence: Principles of Phenomenological Psychopathology.* Pittsburgh: Duquesne UP, 1972.

Von Franz, M-L. *Psyche and Matter.* Boston: Shambhala Publications, 1992.

—. *Alchemy.* Toronto: Inner City Books, 1980.

—. *Projection and Recollection in Jungian Psychology.* London: Open Court, 1980.

Walker, J. "Through the Looking Glass." *The Art of Human-Computer Interface Design.* Ed. B. Laurel. Cupertino, CA: Apple Computer, 1990.

Watkins, M. *Invisible Guests.* New Jersey: Analytic P, 1986.

Wordsworth, W. "Ode: Intimations of Immortality from Recollections of Early Childhood." *William Wordsworth Selected Poems.* Ed. John O. Hayden. New York: Penguin, 1994.

Sources

The following essays in this volume are reprinted with kind permission:

The Despotic Eye and Its Shadow: Media Image in the Age of Literacy. *Modernity and The Hegemony of Vision* (1993), David Michael Levin (Ed.), Berkeley: University of California Press.

The Dream Body in Cyberspace. *Psychological Perspectives*, Ernest Lawrence Rossi (Ed.), Number 29, Spring-Summer 1994.

The Orphan and the Angel: In Defense of Melancholy. *Psychological Perspectives*, Ernest Lawrence Rossi (Ed.), Number 32, Fall-Winter 1995.

Psychotherapy as Grief Work: Ghosts and the Gestures of Compassion. *The Body in Psychotherapy* (1998), D. Johnson and I. Grand (Eds), Berkeley: North Atlantic Books.

Yes, Indeed! Do Call the World the Vale of Soul-Making: Reveries Toward an Archtypal Presence. *Depth Psychology: Meditations in the Field* (2000), D. Slattery and L. Corbett (Eds.), Einsiedelan, Switzerland: Daimon Verlag.

For the Moment, That's Enough: Reveries on Therapy and the Poetry of Language. *The San Francisco Jung Institute Library Journal*, John Beebe (Ed.), Volume 18, Issue 1, 1999.

Alchemy and the Subtle Body of Metaphor. *Pathways into the Jungian World*, (2000), R. Brooke (Ed.), London: Routledge.

On Angels and Other Anomalies of the Imaginal Life. *Temenos Academy Review*, Kathleen Raine (Ed.), London: Temenos Academy, Issue 3, Spring 2000.

Psychology is Useless; Or, It Should Be. *Janus Head*, Victor Barbetti, Brent Dean Robbins, and Claire Cowan-Barbetti (Eds.), Pittsburgh: Trivium Publications, Volume 3, Number 2, Fall 2000.

On Not Being Useful: The Pleasures of Reverie. *The Salt Journal*, David Barton (Ed.), Volume 2, Number I, Fall 2000.

The Backward Glance: Rilke and the Ways of the Heart. *The International Journal of Transpersonal Studies* Vol. 20, 2001, Honolulu, HI: Panigada Press.